What
Would

Jackie

Do?

An Inspired Guide
to Distinctive Living

What
Would
Do?

SHELLY BRANCH and
SUE CALLAWAY

GOTHAM
BOOKS

GOTHAM BOOKS
Published by Penguin Group (USA) Inc.
375 Hudson Street, New York, New York 10014, U.S.A.
Penguin Group (Canada), 90 Eglinton Avenue East, Suite 700, Toronto,
Ontario M4P 2Y3, Canada (a division of Pearson Penguin Canada Inc.); Pen-
guin Books Ltd, 80 Strand, London WC2R 0RL, England; Penguin Ireland,
25 St Stephen's Green, Dublin 2, Ireland (a division of Penguin Books Ltd);
Penguin Group (Australia), 250 Camberwell Road, Camberwell, Victoria
3124, Australia (a division of Pearson Australia Group Pty Ltd); Penguin
Books India Pvt Ltd, 11 Community Centre, Panchsheel Park, New Delhi –
110 017, India; Penguin Group (NZ), cnr Airborne and Rosedale Roads,
Albany, Auckland 1310, New Zealand (a division of Pearson New Zealand
Ltd); Penguin Books (South Africa) (Pty) Ltd, 24 Sturdee Avenue, Rosebank,
Johannesburg 2196, South Africa

Penguin Books Ltd, Registered Offices: 80 Strand, London WC2R 0RL, England

Published by Gotham Books, a division of Penguin Group (USA) Inc.

First printing, January 2006
10 9 8 7 6 5 4 3 2

Gotham Books and the skyscraper logo are trademarks of Penguin Group
(USA) Inc.

LIBRARY OF CONGRESS CATALOGING-IN-PUBLICATION DATA
Branch, Shelly.
    What would Jackie do? : an inspired guide to distinctive living / Shelly
Branch and Sue Callaway.
        p.   cm.
    ISBN 1-59240-190-2 (hardcover : alk. paper)
1. Onassis, Jacqueline Kennedy, 1929–1994   2. Women—Life skills guides.
3. Women—Conduct of life.   4. Etiquette.   5. Home economics.   6. Fashion.   7. Interpersonal relations.   I. Callaway, Sue.   II. Title.
    HQ1221.B785 2006
    646.7'0082—dc22   2005020892

Printed in the United States of America
Set in Electra with Torino Modern and Fenice
Designed by Sabrina Bowers
All illustrations by Monika Roe

◆ ◆ ◆

For Barbara, Louise, and Liliora,

inspirations in grace,

wit, and beauty.

◆ ◆ ◆

Contents

What
Would
Jackie
Do?

"I've asked myself 'what would Jackie do, what would Jackie think' on a number of occasions. One time I was sitting in a restaurant next to a woman who'd been fooling with my man and I got terrible butterflies. I thought 'Oh my God' and asked myself what Jackie would do. Immediately, my spine straightened. I assumed a position of great dignity. And I just sort of became my posture. It was very much a whistle-a-happy-tune thing. Once I was Jackie in my mind, I was above it all."

—CARLY SIMON, SINGER/SONGWRITER AND

A CLOSE FRIEND OF JACKIE'S

◆　◆　◆

Introduction

What was it about her, dammit?

Almost from the moment she made her debutante turn at Hammersmith Farm in 1947, it was obvious that the elegant sylph known simply as "Jackie" possessed something enviable, intangible.

A true "American Idol," she represented a standard that many women have tried to copy, from her clothes to her gestures. But it was her cloak of unusual dignity that earns her the greatest admiration. You can't help but want to be like her. Who can resist such effortless, multilingual poise? People the world over have long marveled at how she handled the jagged, painful turns of the Kennedy legacy and the Onassis years. And how, beneath those iconic pillboxes, she never seemed to sweat.

Which brings us to the point of this book. Dozens of works have sought to portray the "real" Jackie, and fix her mark on events historic. Yet no book has applied Jackie's day-to-day philosophies to your life, or extrapolated her timeless coping skills for the twenty-first-century woman. With the public's interest in all things Kennedy hardly abated, it seems appropriate—even necessary—to now view Jackie through a more modern prism. To connect the dots of her richly textured life and distill them into a practical, instructive guide.

Over the last four decades, Jacqueline Bouvier Kennedy Onassis has attracted almost as many writers as fans. Her public life as a young mother in the White House, followed by more Garbo-like periods in Greece and New York, continue to fascinate people who knew only her photograph. Her allure, and her example, go well beyond the printed page: When New York's Metropolitan Museum of Art displayed her White House finery in a 2001 costume exhibit, it attracted an international sell-out crowd. And two Sotheby's auctions featuring items from her estate and her homes yielded dizzying bids.

Still, the somber words and the artifacts are not enough. We are ever fascinated by this private woman—our royal equivalent—who will always be the pinnacle of beauty and wisdom. *What Would Jackie Do?* explores the alchemy of Jackie's timeless living arts to show what it takes to be a creature of true substance today. The first book of its kind, it aims her famous gaze in the readers' direction through advice, insight, and humor (Jackie did, after all, possess quite the wicked wit).

At a time when classic smarts have gone missing in our fractured popular culture, this book is meant to serve as the print equivalent of having Jackie herself analyze—indeed, make over—your life. *What Would Jackie Do?* will show you how to be steely yet soignée—a tonic that the Jennifer Anistons and J.Los (starlets with only fleeting fame)—crave. With the Elegant One as your personal advisor, you can acquire some of that Jackie O magic, be it of the heart, the mind, or the home.

You'll know, for example, when a designer is worth his couture costs, and when you are better off with a good knockoff. You'll learn to deftly approach everything from mating rituals to office politics with as much savoir faire as Jackie did in her time. If she could make guests both plain and privileged feel at ease in the White House, how can you do the same in your own home? As for her famously strict and successful child-rearing ways, how might you translate and apply similar methods? And how can you interpret for your own purposes her complex ability to handle powerful men?

By definition, this is a work that must straddle the lines of history and myth, observation and advice, reverence and irreverence. We also suggest what Jackie might do today in a world where the rules of social conduct are ever more fluid. Would she e-mail thank-you notes? Use a BlackBerry to deliver bad news? Consign old clothes? Try Pilates? Withhold sex until the second date or fifth? Fly the kids first class or coach?

What Would Jackie Do? takes its cues from dozens of original interviews, as well as biographies, historical references and documents, articles, oral histories, photographs, and other previously published works. As a reality check, let us underscore two key points. First, Jackie, for all her gemlike facets, was hardly without flaws. To that end, this book will help you understand what she knew all too well: How best to transform your weaknesses into strengths. Second, most women lack the financial resources and/or social connections to lead the life that she did. With that in mind, we reveal how even Jackie cut corners and pinched a few pennies.

In summary, this book is designed to give you a solid yet whimsical foundation from which to draw inspiration and advice. To compel you to ask, when confronted with matters sartorial, ethical, practical: *What Would Jackie Do?*

Chapter 1

Daily Bred:

Exude Grace in Everything You Do

"A beautiful gesture is really a very rare thing . . ."
—JBKO

S hall we dare to be . . . like her?

It's an alluring—and terrifying—idea. After all, Jackie O was the model for how to do practically everything right. There was the indestructible coif, chic whether windswept or tethered by a silk scarf. A whispery voice that could alternately charm, devastate, captivate. Even her physical carriage had an easy grace that seemed lit from within. Then, of course, there were the outfits—beaded bodices and A-line coats. They dazzled in the absence of colossal gems. The very image is enough to make us straighten our backs, pat our hair in place, and pull our beau a little bit closer.

And no wonder. Much that we've seen and read about her is so reverent, distant, unattainable. But at a time when everything in our world is so brilliantly recherché—from clothes and entertaining to manners and even language—what better opportunity to intrigue as if *"Jack-leen"*?

Perfection isn't the goal, of course. To transcend the ordinariness that Jackie so feared in youth means feasting on a diet of discipline and restraint—whether you're into dungarees or Dior. As Jackie knew, fabulousness is a state of mind, something you harness day in and day out to neutralize the "dreary" things and people that threaten to drag you down.

OBSCURE YOUR EGO
TO REVEAL YOUR TRUE QUALITIES

It won't, it can't, it mustn't always be about you. And even if you don't agree, you'd do well to at least pretend so some of the time. A substantive woman—and Jackie was nothing if not that—can check her hubris as easily as she does her evening wrap. It's always there, of course, but sometimes it's better left in the background.

Shift the spotlight. Self-promoters, Jackie once said, "really get my back up." But because people tend to crave the limelight so much themselves, they'll be thrown (and delighted) when you transfer some of the attention you command. Out for aperitifs with girlfriends? Insist that the cute guy in the opposite banquette is ogling one of them, not you. Tell your hairdresser that his splendid updo—not your fine form—drew gasps at the charity ball.

A master at shifting the spotlight, Jackie would playfully say to friends that the press "must know you're here!" when helicopters buzzed overhead. Even when the pressure was on, she knew to turn the focus away from herself. Once, when one of Jackie's Doubleday authors—Tiffany design director John Loring—asked the editor to do a rare interview on his behalf for *The New Yorker,* Jackie at first agreed, but ultimately reneged by using a clever deflection technique. She told him, "You don't really want me in that profile, because people will only remember me, and you'll just be forgotten completely."

Overlook faux pas. You mustn't let the minor transgressions of others interrupt your daily flow—or block your precious *chi*. When people stumble with their words, their manners, or their wit, there's just no need to take an emotional tumble. Jackie wouldn't give a damn if you said, "I love your Gucci!" (if in fact she was wearing Pucci) or "How was the bear hunt?" (when foxes were her thing).

To show how deftly Jackie handled such potentially embarrassing moments, a Doubleday colleague recalls how she stopped by his office to bum a book of matches. "As I was handing it to her, I noticed it had a JFK memorial stamp on it," he says. "It was a fleeting moment, not more than a second." Jackie didn't acknowledge any awkwardness. Ditto when interior decorator Mario Buatta came to dinner at her Fifth Avenue apartment and promptly split his pants on a chair. Without missing a beat, Jackie covered his back at the buffet.

Invoke others' names. Need a favor? Need to curry favor? Put a brake on the number of times you say "me" and "I." You'll seem like less of an egomaniac—and more of a conciliator—if you pin your request on someone else. Jackie was known to use such harmless substitutions to get what she wanted, saying things like, "Jack wants . . ." or "My sister advises against," or "So-and-so won't allow . . ." The less-than-overt method had its charms. "She could impose that will upon people without their ever knowing it," observed White House usher J. B. West.

Be a master flatterer. The point of advanced flattery is to remind someone how special he or she is, while also hinting at your utter dependency on them. This technique comes in handy when you are trying to salvage professional relationships or have something very specific to gain.

To snare a "magnificent" portrait of Benjamin Franklin for the White House, for example, Jackie rang up publishing magnate Walter H. Annenberg. She was ready to grovel, all right, but with an air of decorum and purpose: "You, Mr. Annenberg, are the first citizen of Philadelphia," she purred. "And in his day, Benjamin Franklin was the first citizen of Philadelphia. And that's why, Mr. Annenberg, I thought of you. . . ." She went on to remind him that the White House—and America—desperately needed his tasteful acquisition. Are we at all surprised that he handed over the $250,000 painting by David Martin?

Dare to diss yourself. How to boost the comfort level when you're mingling outside your own social set? Knock yourself down by a precious peg or two. Jackie had a talent for making herself seem less rich, less smart, less beautiful when the situation warranted it. She was known, for instance, to refer to her Fifth Avenue manse as "this old dump." Even among those who sought to impress her (folly indeed), she held back. If someone prattled on about an obscure book, for example, "Jackie would be well mannered enough to say 'I've never heard of that' when she'd read the whole thing," says her friend Carly Simon.

◆ ◆ ◆

"If you want the world to adore you, you must take a deep interest in other people. Jackie was full of wonder and enthusiasm—with her, you felt you were the most important person." —DR. DEEPAK CHOPRA

◆ ◆ ◆

NOBLESSE OBLIGE FOR BEGINNERS:
How to Be a Goodwill Ambassador to Strangers, Colleagues, Malcontents

Jackie preferred hailing taxis to get about in New York City. And in those yellow chariots, she would sometimes lean forward and do what so few ever bother to do: ask how the driver's day was going. In one case, she beseeched the cabbie to quit his shift in order to get home safely in soggy weather. What good is it, after all, to be a cut above if you don't let your own splendid qualities trickle down to others?

Coddle bit players. It's terribly wicked not to give props to all of the people who make your path smoother in life. These include the door-man, the mailman—and if you're so lucky—the cook and pilot. In Jackie's case, the list also extended to all sorts of minor politicos. Go beyond tips and nods. As a campaign wife, Jackie was able to recall the names, unprompted, of umpteen mayors and convention delegates. And in the White House, she stunned her new staff by properly ad-dressing members upon their first face-to-face meeting.

Don't (publicly) criticize your enemies or opponents. Leave such base behavior to modern-day politicians and reality show contestants. Par-ticularly resist the temptation to bad-mouth people by e-mail: There's nothing worse than electronic slurs, which can be endlessly forwarded. Though surrounded by enemies (political) and jealous types (frumpy women), Jackie refused to get nasty. During the 1960 campaign, she declined to take potshots at Hubert Humphrey. And two decades later, when Nancy Reagan got swamped with negative publicity, Jackie waxed empathetic, going so far as to call her to offer advice on handling the press.

Tap higher powers to help the helpless. After you've maxed out your immediate resources, look to your left and right, above and below to harness those six degrees of separation between you and the solution to the problem at hand. Don't be too proud to ask an influential friend to step in on behalf of someone you know—even if the two have never met. That's what connections are really for.

In 1980 Jackie summoned medical philanthropist Mary Lasker to help an impoverished sick boy, the son of a manicurist, gain access to proper treatment. As a follow-up to the favor, Jackie wrote her friend Mary a heartfelt note: "Now they don't feel that they are just a cipher because they are poor," she scrawled on her Doubleday stationery. "Whatever happens, they know that someone with a noble heart made it possible for them to get the best care they could."

Turn the other silken cheek. Sometimes you must show people what you are made of by staying elevated when you'd least like to—say, when someone zips into your primo parking space, or snatches the last pair of Loro Piana gloves on sale at Bergdorf's. Like Jackie, you'd do well to let mild acts of ugliness pass without much fuss.

Traveling with Thomas Hoving, then-director of the Metropolitan Museum of Art, Jackie was stunned—and frightened—by the French paparazzi who swarmed her at a low-key Left Bank restaurant. An infuriated Hoving returned to their hotel, the Plaza Athénée, and demanded that the doorman who disclosed their whereabouts be fired. Informing Jackie of the fait accompli, Hoving recalls, "She got mad at me." She said: "You suffered a man's livelihood because of that?"

Mute the call of mammon. The classiest cash is also the quietest. So if you're fortunate enough to have an endless supply of crisp bills, just don't crumple them under the noses of those with less. This doesn't mean you should deprive yourself of fine things. Certainly our lady did not. But wealth does require you to be somewhat stealth about what you've got.

Don't gab on about money either—yours, your parents', your boyfriend's—or your over-the-top plans for it. When Jackie received a $26 million settlement from Aristotle Onassis's estate, society types needled the widow about how she intended to spend the windfall. "You don't talk about things like that," was her stunned reply.

To be a cut above, don't cut. Even if your social status or connections somehow permit it, resist any temptation to leapfrog over more common folks. This means no line-jumping at Disney World, no flashing that Burberry plaid to snare the next cab. In New York, Jackie waited in crowds like everybody else—or avoided them altogether—rather than nudge her way to the front of movie-house and museum queues.

FIRST LADY-LIKE IMPRESSIONS:
How Not to Be an Interchangeable Woman

◆ ◆ ◆

"You can polish, arrange, fix, but you cannot fool people.
Jackie was a total woman, not like anybody else you know.
It wasn't sex appeal, it was magnetism."
—MANOLO BLAHNIK, SHOE DESIGNER

◆ ◆ ◆

It's important to be more than witty, pretty, and splendidly turned out. And who cares if you make a swell crowd-pleaser, or man teaser? If you are content to be a like-kind, same-this-or-that chick, ready and willing to swap lipsticks, secrets, jobs—men!—with the next gal, then you risk being an Interchangeable Woman.

An Interchangeable Woman is neither memorable nor original. She talks a lot and may even have an MBA—yet manages to say precious little. Her gym membership is active, and it shows, but her sense of self is altogether weak. She is quick to please, slow to question, and often overstays her welcome (especially where men are concerned). She uses the word "me" too much, and hasn't a clue that others find her redundant.

This shall not be you.

If you take away but a single pearl from Jackie's life, let it be this: Never be mistaken for an IW. Jackie had many enviable qualities, and she was certainly a master practitioner of feminine ways. Yet she disdained "empty-headed women" who gabbed about manicures, and even in youth dreaded the company of those who "just giggle and are snippy and mean and sort of dumb." As for women who fling themselves at the other sex? Ugh. The world is overpopulated by such creatures, so she—and you—wouldn't want to be one.

Never hasten to the side of those who haven't earned the pleasure of your company. Don't be too anxious to lend your charms and talents to folks who don't appreciate them. Always keep people guessing, carefully rationing your clever bits. Deviate from the mean, putting your special spin on everything from Kafka to Catholicism. And if you do decide to be a joiner—to a club, a cause, a relationship—ad-lib your own rules.

During her courtship with JFK, Jackie showed the Kennedy clan just how determined she was to not be an IW—even under seemingly benign circumstances. It was 1953, and the young Ms. Bouvier was still taking her first bows with the family. Ethel Kennedy had decided to have a St. Patrick's Day party and gave the guests a single directive: Wear black. Suspecting trouble—and whiffing, no doubt, the danger of being perceived as an IW—Jackie arrived, in black garb, yes, but with more colorful tricks up her sleeve.

Ethel, sure enough, made her entrance in a brilliant emerald gown, reducing the other women to IWs. Canny Jackie triumphed, though, when she showed up last in a chauffeur-driven Rolls-Royce and kept it purring by the curb for all to see. (The message: "I've got other places to go. . . .") So as not to be confused with the IWs, she did little mingling and instead held court before the fireplace. She also made sure to depart early, apologizing for a "dreadful headache," before stealing au revoirs with each dazzled guest. Sliding into the Rolls as they all watched, a mysterious Jackie lowered her window to wave good-bye—blowing away any notions that she was an Interchangeable Woman.

A few ways to avoid the IW moniker:

Be riveted, not just riveting. When you turn your attention to others, especially new acquaintances, be more than polite. Be truly (if briefly) engaged and grant everyone, even buffoons, a gracious nod or two. Jackie "never in public let people know she did not like them," recalled art critic John Russell. "People always went away thinking, 'She quite liked me, yes, she was impressed by me.' It was a very endearing quality."

Strut on an invisible red carpet. Just look around you, at all the slumping bodies! The "society slouch" (i.e., a bored, insouciant hunch) may from time to time find trendy reprisal, but remember, the concave look doesn't become most of us, even the most richly adorned. To stand taller, pretend there is a red carpet before you at all times, and that people are watching. If you look at some old pictures of Jackie, you can almost imagine her doing precisely this.

Do a reflexive roll call. Some IWs have a neat trick of failing to remember names—especially those of other women. This is not only rude, but it robs them of the chance to maneuver around a cocktail party or a conference. Jackie learned the value of the personal greeting well before her White House days. This salutatory skill shows that you are a worldly sort—that indeed you know everyone!—even if you've only recently met.

Pump up small talk. You've been in situations where the conversation was way below base. What did you do to lift it? The herd mentality often causes IWs to go mute, or nod in unison. When this happens, you might nonchalantly ask who's been to Afghanistan lately.

Celebrate selectively. Don't be a fixture at trendy clubs, bars, and other IW hangouts, no matter how popular or "exclusive" they are. This is simply another version of being too available—something Jackie's father warned her against at a very early age. It also distinctly contradicts her rule to be unpredictable, mysterious.

Be a go-to girl. When it comes to the rules of social engagement, you're better off in many cases by letting others supplicate. Never beg for an invitation to a swank dinner, for instance, or plead to be on a certain man's arm. A mere whiff of desperation is unbecoming.

GIFTING AND GETTING
Take Stock of How You Exchange

Think "personal gift registry." A list of preferred items can help loved ones, colleagues, and anyone who wants an invite to your country home know what's expected of them—if they aim to stay on your good side. Jackie made note of things she wanted, often books, so that her White House staff and others could shop accordingly. Sort of like her own personal registry (an idea, that, handily, is taking off in retail circles today).

As Jackie's authorized biographer, Mary Van Rensselaer Thayer, wrote: "Jacqueline feels guilty at suggesting [art books] since these volumes are very costly. But to guide relatives and close friends at holiday time, she has left a list of books she'd like to own at a bookstore near her former house in Georgetown."

With Onassis, she had another gift game—one you'd do well to suggest to any man you date who travels for business or pleasure. The rule: Whenever Onassis left Greece, he was to bring her back a trifle. Being one of the wealthiest men of the era, he often (but not always) returned with lavish spoils. If your sweetie can't meet such standards, just make sure to encourage his imagination—something small but fabulous will always do.

Delete "Oh, you shouldn't have!" from your vocabulary. Jackie didn't mean it, and neither should you. Instead, show gift-givers how much you love their thoughtfulness.

Jackie accepted all manner of bounty from admirers, diplomats, family members, and minor acquaintances. Flattering words and letters of thanks are the way to encourage more ruby bracelets and Thoroughbreds—the kind of sparkling and hooved presents she amassed over the years.

Fib to avoid hurting innocents. When the loot's a letdown, spare the giver's feelings. Don't ask for the receipt; do say, "How sweet," even as you pack it up for Goodwill. Plenty of people sent gifts to the White House (including frightening portraits of the First Couple rendered in Rice Krispies). Many of them ended up at charities; others were whisked away for security or other practical reasons. But Jackie would never let the giver know. When a family sent a cake to the Kennedys in the White House, Jackie's staff dispatched a letter saying how very much they'd enjoyed the confection. A separate internal memo was attached in the correspondence files, however, revealing the real fate of the cake: "Destroyed by Secret Service."

Re-gift, with feeling. In special cases, you may want to boomerang gifts you've received back to the original giver. This applies if the item has sentimental value, and your giveback gesture can somehow be construed as charming rather than cheap. Jackie once got as a gift from presidential advisor Ted Sorensen some drawings JFK had done during the Cuban Missile Crisis. Later, as a Christmas gift, a clever Jackie repackaged the sketches (framing them first, of course) and enclosed an understated note that required no further explanations: "for all you were to him."

Spare yourself the horror of holiday queues. As strange as it may seem to shop for Christmas gifts in summer months, you'll

continues . . .

love yourself for avoiding the triple aggravation of crowds, low inventory, and the inevitable shortage of tissue paper at department stores. Jackie was known to get her holiday shopping started as early as July, which, given sales patterns, is also a good way to pick up a few bargains (from home furnishings sales in July and white sales in August). Instead, savor holiday strolls through Bergdorf's to enjoy the windows and pick up a few minor gifts, like Jackie did with her grandchildren. (It's the perfect place, by the way, to get snapped with a snappy Santa—he's ensconced on the seventh floor, and the store gives you two Polaroids for free.)

PLEASE DO COME:
A Smashing Hostess Makes the Most Sought-After Guest

Staging memorable soirees is a balancing act likely to throw sloppy sorts off their satin sling-backs. You want your guests to feel welcome and relaxed, but stimulated by the riveting crowd and chatter. You want them to step into your lair and appreciate the details—votives in the powder room, rosemary sprigs in the martinis—and hopefully exchange mobile phone numbers or at least winsome looks. Perhaps most important, it should all seem like much ado about nothing. As if dishing out pleasure is your calling, no matter how frightful the task really is.

Jackie, clever dear, remastered the art of the party as First Lady. She brought back the Jeffersonian custom of dining at intimate round tables, eschewing the stuffy "E" shape of more recent tradition. French-themed food and wine reigned. Much to the delight of cultural figures and heads of state, she even slipped pre-dinner cocktails into the mix. So how shall you raise your entertainment value?

◆ Entrance Cues ◆

From front-door aesthetics (glow-in-the dark ding-dong button or taste-ful knocker?) to your first words of welcome (try a breathy "How good of you to come . . ."), the preamble sets the tone for your evening. Next, use your flair for flattery, flecking little personal references into each introduction you make. As Letitia Baldrige recalls, Jackie excelled here. "You don't say, 'This is my old roommate from California, Mary Smith,' " Baldrige cautions. "You say, 'This is my fabulous former roommate from California, Mary Smith, who was the prom queen, always got straight As—and we were all terribly jealous of her.' Everyone knows it's an exaggeration, but she's pleased and the people sitting next to her at dinner know what to ask her about."

At more formal gatherings, where the dreaded receiving line, or some incarnation thereof, is in order, be sure to keep things moving by doing as Jackie would: Say "Thank you! How lovely to see you! Bye!" to each guest, then quickly turn and repeat the drill. Jackie's head maneuver is key here, as it serves to let all comers know that he or she must move on. Scat! If a person lingers, freeze-frame your smile and cast a haze of silence. The pregnant pause should do the trick.

◆ The Alchemy of the Guest List ◆

What to do with all the business cards you collect—the really good ones that end up dog-eared in the bottom of your purse? You might adapt Jackie's cataloguing instincts and mark them "A" for artsy, "H" for hot, and "I" for intellectual. From there, think Paris in the 1920s. Think rousing get-togethers. Think *salon*. Jackie summed up the allure in a 1981 interview: "The French know this; anybody knows this—if you put busy men in an attractive atmosphere where the surroundings are comfortable, the food is good, you relax, you unwind, there's some stimulating conversation. You know, sometimes quite a lot can happen."

HAND GESTURES:
Scoring Big with Courtly Correspondence

A woman with an erudite aura writes *à main*. She knows that words that flicker on a screen may land her a job interview, even a few good dates. But she also gets that words flowing directly from a pen are apt to deliver more—if less immediately tangible—riches.

Jackie was a model correspondent. She used her trademark stationery (light blue sheets with embossed white lettering) and loopy script to curry favors, charm lovers, maneuver out of tight spots, and evoke her famous wrath—usually in effusive fashion.

Most people reserve a good handwriting job for more formal affairs these days. That is a mistake. An ambidextrous Jackie would dash off an eight-page letter of sympathy (like the one she wrote to publisher Phil Graham's widow after his suicide), then shift to more intellectual prose with lofty-minded dear hearts such as a former Deputy of Defense Secretary Roswell Gilpatric.

A note about her notes: They usually emphasized something personal up front. Rather than open with a generic "thank-you," Jackie's first words "would be something like 'what a spectacular soufflé!' " says longtime Kennedy family aide Melody Miller. "After her opening lines, she'd return to thanking you for a memorable evening."

Today, Jackie would surely be inclined to reach out electronically, but without giving short shrift to her longhand. "She'd write little things by e-mail, important things on good stationery," says

Letitia Baldrige, Jackie's White House social secretary. "If she knew someone very well, she'd e-mail a thank you. But to anyone else, or older people, she'd definitely write." Be sure to scribble off any missives in good time. After receiving a gift, for instance, Jackie would send out a thank-you note within twenty-four hours.

Mind your sheets, and get a sexy hand. Choose cards and paper that are appropriate for the message you wish to transmit. Though embossed stationery—Jackie preferred Smythson's, among other brands—makes a fine, formal impression, you need not always scrawl on the fancy stuff. To mix it up (and save money in the process) Jackie used postcards from museums, as well as letterhead from high-end hotels (Jamaica's Half Moon Hotel was once a favorite source of sheets). These helped to project a "you-are-there," in-the-moment tone—the perfect vibe for earnest scribes.

Of course, your penmanship will need to be up to scratch, a tough task for many whose grade-school skills have lapsed due to tapping out everything from e-mails to babysitting instructions. Focus on developing a distinctive style, rather than Hallmark neatness. Jackie's cursive was seductively askew; she wrote people's names in large letters, began lots of sentences with "you," and made use of every inch of the tiny, 3.5" x 4.5" notecards she favored, often writing on the back and up the sides.

Express in-the-moment regrets. If you can't accept an invite, consider expressing regrets twice—once to clear up the head count, and then again to let the hosts know they're on your mind. Once, when Jackie couldn't attend a dinner party, she made polite apologies to the hosts in advance of the event. Later, at the appointed hour, an infirm Jackie took up pen and paper to tell her

continues . . .

friends she was thinking about them, and missed being in their company. Even if you must skip a wedding, you can still manage to catch the etiquette bouquet.

Offer a no-fault apology. It's often possible to write a courteous note that acknowledges your foible without making an outright apology. Jackie was very good at this: After sending a typed thank-you letter for a book of short stories to literary critic Lionel Trilling in May of 1962, she soon realized—oops—that her minions had confused his gift with another. Jackie glossed over the blunder with a quasi-apologetic, albeit handwritten, note, admonishing: ". . . why didn't you write inside it!"

Master the PBO. Rudeness is never really acceptable. However, if you need to say "no" or discourage nuisance acquaintances, do what Jackie did: Fire off a neutral-tone letter, making your ambivalence toward the subject clear. Jackie used such letters on occasion, and she even had a term for this type of correspondence: the "PBO," or polite brush-off.

An example: For Christmas in 1977, Thomas Guinzburg, Jackie's former publishing boss at Viking (with whom she had a major falling out) sent her a heartfelt letter and a magnum of Perrier-Jouët champagne. Jackie did thank him, but curtly and after the holiday had come and gone: "Dear Tom—Thank you so much for your thoughtful gift, and a Happy New Year to you."

Write to ensure happy returns. Nod to your hosts even if they are absent. Secondhand invitations—those from friends and family who have access to property belonging to others—are definitely worth protecting. To show your appreciation and keep A-list status on South Beach or the South of France, send a note to the owner of the house who has tacitly granted you entrée. Jackie got the hang of this in 1951, when she wrote to Rose Kennedy, her mother-in-law to be, thanking her for a stay at her Palm Beach home.

So nix your usual guest rotation and stir up intriguing people from different walks of life. Cover basics such as gender, age, and profession (one cellist, one billionaire, one designer, etc.) but blend disparate political views at your own risk.

Jackie loved to flesh out a dinner with an aspiring writer or artist. And she relished being part of such haute luck gatherings, too: In the early 1990s, she and longtime beau Maurice Templesman attended a dinner party for eighteen at former New York City mayor Ed Koch's Fifth Avenue home. Koch held to a little tradition of having all the guests state their name and what they did. When it was Jackie's turn, she followed suit, identifying herself as a book editor. "She responded like every other guest, which was nice," recalls Koch. "Nobody distinguished her presence from the presence of anybody else."

• PEARL •

As hostess, you can't check egos, but you can make sure all butts are in their proper places. If one guest is more important, be it your boss, mate, or publicist, do aim to give that person prime seating. That means close proximity to you, the food, and booze, as well as the sauciest guests. Says Baldrige: "[Jackie] knew to put the most powerful man present on her right, the second-most-powerful man on her left—and to seat the crusty old man between two beautiful women."

Keep it clubby. For an informal dinner, you might want to hold off on an invitation list, and make your calls just beforehand—no more than a day or two in advance. Not only does this raise the commodity of your invites among friends, but it will also decrease the odds that anyone will blow you off.

Jackie and JFK adored hosting small, impromptu dinners for six to eight friends in the White House. These were always last-minute affairs, since Jackie waited until the end of the day to gauge her husband's emotional state. Jackie finely tuned the guest list accordingly, favoring those who would keep the conversation buoyant and never inviting people she knew wouldn't get along. For Jackie, the magic was all in the intimacy. "All the big receptions, the cocktail parties— or the big embassy dinners even. I'm not sure that anything of substance is really accomplished there," she once said.

Put on your party beard. Sometimes the best fun is to stage an OTT (over-the-top) party such as a costume ball replete with powdered wig-sporting guests. But doing so without an obvious cause to celebrate can feel awkward. The solution: Make one up.

Although Jackie's favorite events were the private black-tie dinner dances they'd host at the White House, she and JFK were reluctant, according to journalist Ben Bradlee, to throw them without a good cause. And so they'd showcase family members or friends as the evening's raison d'être. One such event was a grand affair where Jackie billed her sister, Lee, and her second husband, Prince Stanislas Radziwill, as the main attractions.

A pair of newlyweds, say, or a birthday-month chum, can be your guest(s) of honor and raison d'etre all at once. And if you're as wily as Jackie, you'll look for a tax write-off while you're at it. Jackie wasn't above getting the government to foot the bill for a soiree if she had enough dignitaries on the guest list. Perhaps a Christmas affair that includes your boss and a few coworkers can qualify as a business expense? Nothing ventured, nothing gained.

It's in to be out. If you're asked to a late-starting evening—a post-performance celebration or a nightclub bash—take it upon yourself to pull together a pre-party party. Chances are your gathering will be a lot more fun than the larger, impersonal event—and you'll get the credit for kick-starting the evening's fun.

The Kennedys were occasionally in the position of having to throw enormous affairs—and they sometimes didn't have enough room to invite close friends to the pre-dance sit-down dinner. And so members of their inner circle were happy to host clubby get-togethers before joining the dance part of the Kennedy fete. Attendee and journalist Ben Bradlee couldn't resist joking about the First Couple's lack of seats. In *Conversations with Kennedy*, he wrote: "We were so out that we were in. . . . The Kennedys couldn't afford to snub anyone . . . except their really good friends."

◆ ◆ ◆

"Jackie had a sense of tastefulness, discretion.
But I think she'd agree that anyone who misbehaves
in your presence, you throw them out."
—LETITIA BALDRIGE,
FORMER WHITE HOUSE SOCIAL SECRETARY

◆ ◆ ◆

The Clever Conversationalist:
◆ Fine China and Cliffs Notes ◆

It's an old geisha technique: Plan your "ad-lib" discussions in advance to match the mood you want to set. Jackie made it seem spontaneous, but she cleverly steered conversations by discouraging

Your Right to Uninvite

It's the dark secret of every good hostess: There are times when you simply need to uninvite would-be guests or even bow out yourself. Jackie was super-smooth at all facets of reneging:

1. *The Forces-Bigger-Than-You Scenario.* If life pitches you a curveball that shatters your dinner party plans, let your guests know as quickly as possible. On the eve of the Cuban Missile Crisis, Jackie called J. B. West into the White House on a Sunday—his one day off. "There's something brewing that might turn out to be a big catastrophe—which means we may have to cancel the dinner and dance for [the maharajah and maharani of Jaipur] Tuesday night. Could you please handle the cancellation for me? This is all very secret." (Ah, yes, it also doesn't hurt to have someone to delegate this to.)

2. *The Something-Better Scenario.* You've got a big corporate awards banquet scheduled—when suddenly along comes the chance for a dreamy date instead. Jackie wasn't above playing sick when an event didn't hold her fancy; the First Lady once blew off a luncheon for congressional wives and went to the ballet in New York instead. Just exercise extreme caution when you turn tail. News of Jackie's cultural excursion hit the papers, causing much ill will among the stood-up spouses.

3. *The One-Bad-Turn-Deserves-Another Scenario.* If someone does you a social disservice, it's within your rights to return the favor. Jackie hosted a Christmas bash at 1040 Fifth in 1978—and was appalled when Andy Warhol had the temerity to bring along a crasher, writer Bob Colacello. Although she didn't flinch at the time, she later made sure that Warhol was not invited to friends' fetes.

heavy political talk and choosing more esoteric topics so that JFK could unwind and enjoy himself. She even asked power-friends to recommend other potential invitees based on their ability to keep the evening appropriately stimulating. Oleg Cassini—Jackie's official couturier in the White House and a good friend of the Kennedys—for example, always had a bevy of international types at his fingertips.

If this seems contrived, just remember that it can be a good way to actually keep any stalled conversations going. Canned banter can also rescue you if guests turn contentious: Have your verbal ammunition at the ready to put an end to any friendly fire.

❖ Get Down in Your Updo ❖

Some of the most successful soirees run on a dash of secret sauce: A pinch of naughtiness, a touch of the wild. It's a particularly heady brew when it comes directly from the hostess, whether she's gently flirting, fixing up two singles, or being the first on the dance floor. Kick up your Louboutin spikes and set a rollicking example for your guests.

Jackie often did: At one party, she and Lee taught guests to do the twist. During another private shindig, the First Lady tossed off her heels and busted a few moves in the White House's grand marble entrance hall. Jackie also noted who wasn't letting loose—and intervened. "Once she shoved me into the arms of Ken Galbraith and said, 'Now you'll have a good time!' " says longtime friend Solange Herter.

Just don't take it too far. Leave the most extreme behavior to others—like Oleg Cassini, who sported a silk lampshade at one White House party.

❖ The Goddess Is in the Details ❖

You conjure the guests of your dreams—and realize too late that there's no place for them to park. People rave about your selection of wine—just as it runs out. The scintillating conversation across the table is blocked by . . . your exquisitely tall floral arrangement. Some mistakes need never be made, if you sweat the small stuff.

Detail-oriented Jackie knew that friends enjoyed her intimate lunches for two—served on trays in her living room. Never trusting all the flourishes to house help, she mastered little things, like how long to leave the Brie at room temperature. She added zest to her menus by using proper French—très elegant. Your next get-together may be your best yet if you perform a post-party mortem, as Jackie did. According to J. B. West, Jackie wrote her staff a memo outlining the flaws of a state dinner: "There was a ten to fifteen minute wait for the first course, and a consequent lull in the spirit of the party; the wine wasn't served until people had finished their fish . . . finally, the name of the dessert was misspelled on the menu." Does this surprise you, coming from a woman who had her silk stockings pressed?

Cocktails vs. Dinner

You think you'll sidestep having to dish up dinner by hosting a cocktails-only affair. But in truth, after a few daiquiris (a Jackie favorite; see box, p. 28), you won't get rid of the guests until bedtime anyway. So serve a meal, make plenty of it—and always serve yourself seconds, as Jackie did. That way your guests will know it's okay to help themselves, too. Never one to skimp on food (always seasonal and always with dessert), Jackie piled her buffet table high.

Location, Location, Location

No matter how swell your digs, spice up your next fete by making it a movable feast. Parks, courtyards, and the beach can all be a refreshing change. For a truly special occasion you may want to go to greater logistical lengths—plunking a platform atop your swimming pool, for instance, or erecting a series of tents on the lawn.

Despite the considerable headaches involved, Jackie decided to hold a party for the president of Pakistan, Ayub Khan, on the lawn at

Mount Vernon in July 1961. A convoy of Army trucks hauled all the accoutrements needed for such a production, including a staff of 150. The guests fared better, traveling down the Potomac River in boats while being serenaded by small Marine bands. The menu: Poulet Chasseur avec Couronne de Riz Clamart (that's haute French for chicken and rice, a dish that could withstand the trip from the White House kitchen). A marquee arched above the diners, elaborately decorated with floral garlands and matching linens. The grounds were sprayed—twice—against a particularly insidious bloom of mosquitoes. Everyone who attended declared it a raging success.

◆ Think Theater, Think Round ◆

To make your guests, your food—and you—look as good as possible, you'll need to do a bit of staging. Candles are key, as are the right soft incandescent lights (which inexplicably reduce speaking volume to whispers). "In the White House, lighting was always kept low, and we never used any bright overhead illumination—ever. It kills skin and makes food look bad," says Baldrige. Indeed, you can almost never have too many dimmer switches. Jackie made sure to fit chandeliers with them.

Another foolproof part of the production: round tables for seated dinners. If you limit each to six to ten people, you'll inspire full-circle conversations. Jackie was a big believer in the power of the round— and she tailored her centerpieces (flowers or fresh fruit in the summer) to be low enough to never block the view across the chintz.

A Proper Jackie Daiquiri

Every woman worth her margarita salt has at least one cocktail—pleasing to both men and women—that she can whip up in a blink. Jackie's was the daiquiri, which was her favorite way to unwind after a long day. She was so particular about its balance, however, that she made the staff at the White House tape her recipe to the wall by the bar. Her final admonishment to its maker: When in doubt, less is more on the sweetener.

> 2 parts Bacardi rum
> 2 parts frozen limeade
> 1 part fresh lime juice
> A few drops of Falernum as sweetener (a sugar cane–based
>   liqueur)

Mix these as you please—and always pour from a pitcher, never a blender.

◆ Get Personal ◆

We all love a good goody bag. But nothing charms guests more than a truly personal token lavished upon them. If your talents are verbal, craft a little wordplay to amuse your charges—and warm any honorees. Assuming your skills lean toward the visual (and are up to snuff), present invitees with a sketch or photo album of the event. If you do resort to the more standard stuffed bag, be sure to customize each, and spend uniformly—guests will notice.

Jackie was deft on all fronts. When Baldrige left her White House post, Jackie and the entire staff commemorated the event by crafting a

> ### • PEARL •
>
> One of Jackie's smartest hostessing moves was to repeat herself. If you make killer pigs in blankets (a JFK favorite), let them become your signature hors d'oeuvres. If people love your flan (and ask for the recipe), don't hesitate to serve it again. Jackie and her longtime nanny/cook, Marta Sgubin, kept updated records of guests' preferred dishes.

unique keepsake for her: a small table, made on site and topped with parchment, which they had all autographed. To thank Kitty and Kenneth Galbraith for all their kindnesses during her trip to India, Jackie threw a party for the ambassador and his wife at a New York restaurant. She summoned her artistic skills for the evening, creating a life-size cutout of Kenneth to greet guests and a painting featuring him astride a pachyderm.

AT THEIR LEISURE?
Having Houseguests

The *grand jeté* of entertaining is to choreograph a homeful of guests. Your skills must stretch well beyond one great evening and inspire your friends to want more, more, more. This means well-appointed quarters (like Jackie's heated towel racks), fancy and fetch-it-yourself food and drink (Jackie loaded up on caviar and champagne in the Onassis era), as well as light diversions (mandatory poker rounds) that don't require too much hand-holding.

A common, if nettlesome, stay-over scenario is the weekend visitation, with folks landing Friday night for dinner and staying through Sunday. By mastering but a few of Jackie's hyper-hostessing habits, you'll end up with well-trained and well-sated guests and even retain a sense of sanity. But beware: Provide too good a time, and they'll be back, begging for an encore—perhaps sooner than you'd like.

◆ Weekending: A Host's Survival Guide ◆

Keep it on your terms. You marry a gazillionaire and all your relatives ache to see the new "family" beach house (or ski chalet or mountain retreat or Manhattan brownstone). And yet you don't want to open your nest too soon, or worse, send a signal that it is a free-for-any-and-all compound. Discourage impromptu visits and drop-ins, and instead outline a few weekends when it will be convenient for you to host. And prioritize. Jackie did just that, leaving a trail of wannabe visitors from Washington to Greece to Martha's Vineyard. In the Onassis era, the list from Ari's star-struck camp was daunting.

Leave little to chance. When friends descend for three days, all sorts of unpredictables are bound to occur. So to nix cottage chaos, nail down as much as you can in advance—menus, tee times, multiple copies of the Sunday paper to avoid fistfights over the crossword puzzle. Also be prepared to accommodate special catering requests (for your famous daiquiris, perhaps) and any dietary quirks—those raw-food vegan diets, for instance, that are shudderingly in vogue. (Jackie had the benefit of staff, but she still oversaw menus and made sure the fridge and bar were well stocked.) Also assign rooms in advance to avoid brawls over the best digs. And bribe your housekeeper (or hire a temporary one) to come on Friday. Your place will be spotless and you'll have an extra pair of hands to acquire last-minute local provisions such as fresh corn (Jackie often served it as a first course), lobster—and mint sprigs for pitchers of iced tea.

Fawn—and fade. No matter how dazzling you are, every houseguest needs and wants a break occasionally. Try a preemptive strike and suggest some downtime before folks wear out their welcome. You'll look like a sympathetic friend—and you'll get a moment of peace in the bargain. Set up a buffet breakfast, and point the way to the local museum, historic site, or shopping center. Also write down the names of good restaurants; this may save you a midday lunch panic in the kitchen. And place a few good books or a well-stocked iPod by their bed—in the event of rain, words and tunes can save the day.

When Jackie had orchestra leader Peter Duchin and his wife, Cheray, as guests aboard Ari's 325-foot yacht, the *Christina*, she left a note on their bureau: "Promise that you will do what you feel like doing today," she wrote. "All that matters is that you are happy."

Give them a taste of your life. When friends do a mini live-in, it's a chance for them to learn what makes you really tick. If you're a hiker, set up a morning outing to your favorite trail. Love animals? Organize a field trip to your local marine preserve—and use it as an excuse to pack a picnic lunch (a Jackie favorite). Whenever she was on Martha's Vineyard, Jackie swam daily in the ocean—and when she had guests, she took them to the water to join her.

Make it memorable. Assuming all's well that ends well, package the weekend's highlights for posterity. On Skorpios, Jackie often assembled photo albums for guests, complete with amusing captions (she made one for Rose Kennedy after her first visit). And after photographer Peter Beard, who spent a whole summer there in 1971, won a big-bucks bet with Ari that he could hold his breath underwater for four minutes, Jackie presented him with a watercolor of his submersed moment of glory. If you're no Pissarro, a clever assembly of digital snaps will do.

◆ . . . And Be a Have-Back Houseguest ◆

Jackie often felt safer tucked away on a friend's estate than she did risking the public exposure of hotels. Though she was naturally something of a trophy guest, she knew better than to act entitled. So when it's your turn to don the guest slippers, allow yourself to relax and feel "at home"—what every good host encourages. At the same time, don't do anything to plunge your pool privileges.

Easy on the orders, princess. Only one brand of headache reliever works for you? Then pack it, rather than relying on your host's pharmaceutical arsenal. Don't care for hazelnut coffee in the morning? Quietly sip tea instead of serving up a fuss. Jackie's one modest request to hunt-country friends: a closet rod on which to hang her clothes.

Casual: caution. Weekend hosts are notorious for tossing about dress directives. Beware—you don't want to end up at the cookout in a sweatshirt when everyone else is in Bergdorf's finest. Even worse: twirling around in a frilly frock when the other guests are in jeans. Aim for the middle ground and if casual is the cry, be sure to bring jewelry and wraps to sharpen your look just in case. Jackie once struck the right chord when she showed up to a party in Hawaii (while she was staying in a friend's guesthouse) dressed appropriately in a summery skirt and sandals. Everyone else wore cocktail dresses and suits—and they were all horrified at their over-dressed faux pas.

Know when to fold. The best houseguest is a sensitive creature, so use your antennae to pick up any clues that you're wearing out your welcome. When visiting the wealthy Mellons in Virginia horse country, for example, Jackie knew to bolt if others were expected. "She'd call and say 'they're having important guests and I have to find a place for the weekend,' " recalls Dana Reuter, a riding partner of Jackie's who also runs a bed and breakfast, the Red Fox Inn (see "Jackie Here and Now," p. 265). The generous Reuters would sometimes vacate their own home and make room for Mrs. O—a gracious offer that she accepted on several occasions.

Give good thanks. Although your note-writing skills will later be called into action, your gift-giving skills had better be teed up when you arrive. Booty such as flowers, champagne (enough for all guests, please), and fresh-baked cookies are a few natural choices. A twist, says home-décor impresario Harry Slatkin: "Candles are the new wine." If you wait until after your stay to lay on the swag, then up goes the ante: Presents have to be more personal and more thoughtful. And hurry—Jackie always did—before fond memories of your hosts and their home fade.

CLAN DESTINY:
Friends and Family Maintenance

They delight us, surprise us, and seriously test our illusions of normalcy. Family and friends (F&F) require the best of us—and often a few well-drawn boundaries, too. Mom insists on a daily phone call, but you barely have time to sleep, let alone chat. Your bachelor-girlfriends pine for Cocktail Thursdays, just like the old days, and wince when you mention diapers.

Your job, like Jackie's: Help mom and all other F&F to recalibrate their expectations as life (theirs and yours) chugs ahead. When you do come together—and all those less-than-lovely patterns jump out in a nanosecond—harness your sense of restraint and humor to turn things around. And as the years tick by, take every opportunity to assess your place on the extended family tree: Are you climbing, or merely clinging, to it?

◆ Pick a Pecking Order ◆

We all have a mental flow chart that dictates how we tend and manage our F&F. Some of them—along with their calls and problems—get top priority; others may dangle close to the bottom, meaning those ties are in peril. We carve out our time and attentions accordingly—even if those decisions are subconscious, or by whim.

Jackie wasn't one to leave much to chance. She squeezed the reins in this arena, going so far as to prioritize her F&F (husband and kids first; snooty, social-climbing classmates last) during all sorts of occasions. As a newly minted First Lady, for instance, Jackie was so inundated with demands that she instructed the switchboard about which calls to put through. Much to their dismay, not all relatives made the cut.

Such a pecking (or mirth) order can actually be more kind than cruel: It will force you to assess who is truly nearest and dearest to you—and prevent you from making empty promises, a firm Jackie no-no.

◆ Damp Competitive Chords ◆

You know the warning signs: The friend who copies all your clothing purchases. A coworker who serves your date a bosom cocktail at the Christmas fete. A stepsister who sulks over your good looks, your swell job. There is no room for petty jousting among true friends or relatives. And yet, such ugliness abounds. Jackie got her fair share of nail scratches, including from Lee, who had once been featured in *Life* magazine as a "debutante of the year," yet felt that her older sister encroached on her fame. Jackie's behavior in return wasn't always perfect, mind you, but she knew enough to take a few steps back from the relationship when things got particularly combustive.

Distance, meted out carefully, can be a useful way to deal with your on-again off-again fans. Jackie would give bile-spewing family and close friends time to fret, lick their wounds, and mull reconciliation. But lethal doses of poison have to be dealt with accordingly. Those who truly can't handle your lot in life will make both of you miserable, and may eventually warrant one of two harsher maneuvers.

Maneuver No. 1: Trump envious "allies" once and well, and you may end any further debate about who is the show-grade alpha dog. Say you and your college friend are both writers—and yet she chooses to brag about her own assignments rather than trade sisterly notes. This pattern will end abruptly when you invite her to the Pulitzer Prize ceremony. The recipient? You. Jackie twice flipped just such a high-voltage switch: She married JFK and then Onassis, poster boys for power and money.

When all else fails, move to **Maneuver No. 2:** the heave-ho — a tactic Jackie could have patented (see "Snip! Cutting People Off," p. 39). Just be very sure of your feelings and the repercussions when you decide to sever. Jackie usually never looked back at such times: She cut off her cousin John Davis for writing books about her and the Kennedys, and shunned his mother, Maude, as well.

❖ Help Them Sidestep Ruin ❖

Your father announces a plan to "invest" his retirement savings in real estate hawked on channel 999. A friend quits his sober advertising job to pursue an online gig selling trendy "green" drinks. Is it your place to step in and show them the possible folly of their ways? Unsolicited opinions are tricky business between F&F, but it's likely you can count on one finger or fewer those who are honest with you. In turn, assume that no one else is being straight with them, and bite the truth bullet — time will tell if you're correct, and they'll eventually come to appreciate your candor.

If you suspect your advice won't go over well, try an indirect approach. When Jackie learned that people were actually encouraging Lee's desire to act, she took her sister's supporters to task. "Kitty, what the hell are you doing!" she demanded of actress Kitty Carlisle Hart, believing that Lee's thespian ambitions were born more of vanity than passion and talent.

Snapping the director's "cut!" sign is trickier with parents, but sometimes just as necessary. Jackie sucked it up and confronted her mother about her pending third marriage, to J. Bingham "Booch" Morris. Janet dismissed her daughter's advice, only to admit misery after returning early from her month-long honeymoon.

◆ Know When to Cede the Stage ◆

You and your brother have children of the same age—yours is an academic and sports star, while his is shy and an average student. Do you invite your sibling to see your son star in the school play, knowing yet another accolade will bother him, or do you keep mum and risk making him feel forgotten? When you find yourself in such a no-win situation, opt to take the quieter path. There's never a need to rub accomplishment in another's face—and you can explain away the oversight by describing the performance as a "small school event."

Jackie learned the hard way that you can't please all F&F all the time—so don't kill yourself trying. In 1966, she caused nothing less than a paparazzi sensation when she showed up in Newport, R.I., for her half sister Janet's wedding; the overlooked bride wept openly amidst the chaos. The lesson apparently soaked in: A year later, when Lee starred in *The Philadelphia Story* in Chicago, Jackie— surprise, surprise—was on a different continent for the play's duration.

◆ Yours, Mine Doesn't Equal "Ours" ◆

You don't have to be like Jackie—a woman blessed with beautiful homes, Pulitzer-caliber men, and speed-dial access to potentates—to suffer an insidious family problem: relatives who believe they are entitled by blood to share all that you have.

It's a lovely conceit, just not that practical. Perhaps your sister is a bit too enamored of the jewels from your loved one? Jackie had to contend with just that issue when Lee ogled the premarital bounty from Ari (who, after all, had been her amour first). You'll have to sail above the jealousy fray at such times—Jackie simply ignored such whinings—and decide whether borrowing or lending is part of your repertoire. In the meantime, drop hints in your path. Fearful that reckless Kennedy kids would trash her place in Hyannis Port, Jackie was known to remove the good furniture when she wasn't on the grounds.

Of course, such riches, should you be lucky enough to possess them, are also yours for the giving. What's the point of having five bedrooms if you can't invite an ailing friend to convalesce *chez toi*? Jackie, despite a lifelong love affair with privacy and boundaries, was generous to a fault with F&F where it mattered. When her mother was faced with the death of her husband, and later was diagnosed with Alzheimer's, Jackie set up a million-dollar trust for Janet's care, ensuring her financial security.

◆ Preserve Thyself ◆

He loves you for who you are, right? So don't change. Ignore how he purrs in your ear—or how his relatives press thumbs into your back. Doing back-flips to fit into another family is unnecessary and unflattering, no matter how fabulous or larger-than-life his clan may be. Just because they're born-again, for instance, doesn't mean you want to wake up to find yourself speaking in tongues.

At first, Jackie tried to keep up with overbearing, insanely sportif Kennedys. But after she broke her ankle taking part in their "touch" football games ("They'll kill me before I ever get to marry him—I swear they will," she sighed), Jackie opted out of the Hyannis Port Olympiads, preferring instead to go off and do her own thing. As she summed up her visits with the clan: "Once a week is great. Not every night."

One disclaimer: Preserving your identity is key—but not in every situation; know when to fold your hand. If you marry into a vegetarian family, you don't have to give up meat—just don't serve them filet mignon. Jackie, not exactly a political activist, quietly switched her party affiliation to Democrat when she married JFK.

◆ Cast a Silent Ballot in Family Politics ◆

You've got more relatives than you can fit in a shoe: uncles, aunts, step-this and that, cousins, in-laws, and folks once removed (not to mention those you might wish to permanently remove). They bring you great joy, of course—when they're not dragging scandals, in-fights, and other messy problems to your welcome mat.

Jackie was no stranger to tangled family webs. Her own parents divorced when she was young, and her mother (with whom she lived) remarried and procreated some more. The tension over "losing" her father never lifted, and she cherished her moments with the handsome ne'er-do-well. But she made sure that her mother was far, far away and not apprised of the details of their times together.

How to handle today's Technicolor family dynamics? When you all must congregate—weddings, funerals, graduations—keep everyone on their best behavior by cajoling in advance and then take lots of pictures at the event. As Jackie well knew, people hate to look evil on film. At other times, you may need to divide—separate dinners, separate outings—to keep things peaceable and conquer any ugliness.

Trying times offer an opportunity to bring families together, too. Show loyalty to your loved ones in their lesser moments by offering at least your tacit support. You don't need to take sides—and probably shouldn't—and you won't want to get dragged into the quicksand yourself. Just be there to lend a shoulder—and remember how much you'd appreciate the same if roles were reversed. Jackie quietly went to Hyannis Port immediately after the Chappaquiddick disaster. Although she dodged the press, she was there for Ted in his hour of need. And in 1991, she took her children to the annual Kennedy Labor Day touch football game to show support for Jean Smith, mother of accused rapist William Kennedy Smith.

❖ In-law Intelligence ❖

All's fair in war and families. So no matter how many siblings and attendant spouses your mate has, go for the number-one spot in his parents' hearts. This may cause some intra-family jealousy short-term. Pay no attention: Your focus must be on wooing his folks—they are the ones with access to the purse strings, and probably your man's ear as well.

Jackie quickly wrapped JFK's father, Joe Kennedy, around her nail-bitten pinkie. She talked straight to him—everyone else was too afraid to—and homed in on his high tastes. Joining a Kennedy family outing early in her relationship with JFK, she one-upped Eunice's peasant-like lunch fare of peanut-butter-and-jelly sandwiches. Ever the epicurean, Jackie had packed a gourmet spread for herself, including pate and wine. When she offered some of her feast to others, Joe Kennedy—who would later turn a deaf ear to Jack's complaints about her haute couture bills—eagerly accepted.

Over the years, you'll need to reassess who wields the family power, and go to lengths to cater to them. Jackie won over Onassis's older sister, Artemis, by taking a serious interest in Greek history and culture, as well as by bestowing lavish gifts. Their close bond helped after Onassis's death, when Jackie struggled with his daughter, Christina, over his will.

◈ Snip! Cutting People Off ◈

When all other measures fail, you may need to sever ties to those who are dispensable or unworthy. It's never a move to make lightly. Here are Jackie's top reasons:

Lack of loyalty. Who can you count on—in perpetuity? Ben Bradlee and second wife, Tony, had an all-access pass to the White House and were especially close to the Kennedys. But, after Bradlee published *Conversations with Kennedy*, Jackie dumped him again, feeling that his book was a breach of their relationship. Even if they were within inches of each other, she wouldn't acknowledge him. Her ire deepened when Bradlee and his third wife, Sally Quinn, bought a property, Grey Gardens in East Hampton, that had belonged to the Bouvier family for decades.

Telling secrets out of school. Sometimes family business should remain just that. Jackie air-brushed half brother Jamie Auchincloss out of her life after he revealed the whereabouts of her wedding dress (to JFK) and blood-stained Dallas suit. He spilled the beans when speaking to Kitty Kelley for her 1979 best-selling biography, *Jackie Oh!* "Kitty's fame was my infamy," says Auchincloss.

Moral grounds. You've had it with your friends' racist slurs. Don't waste time trying to change them—estrange them. Jackie, too, stood up for maligned sorts—even showing solidarity at one point for JFK's most famous paramour, Marilyn Monroe. When the American National Theatre sought Jackie's support, she flatly refused, citing the company's staging of an Arthur Miller play as the reason. Why? Because in *After the Fall* (which opened in 1964), Miller characterized Monroe—his ex—as a suicidal floozy, which Jackie viewed as a serious betrayal. "I won't have anything to do with that theater because of the way he treated Marilyn Monroe," she said.

For exhibiting stupidity. Who needs flagrantly foolish followers? Jackie didn't. Famous Washington hostess Perle Mesta had the audacity to criticize both Kennedys for their attire at her black-tie champagne party for campaign wives in 1956. Mesta disdained JFK's brown shoes and Jackie's bare legs (she was seven months pregnant at the time). Such sartorial slander bit Mesta back: She never stepped foot in the White House during the Kennedys' reign.

If you look back, you might trip. Cutting people off may also have to do with lightening your baggage. Jackie didn't turn up for reunions at Miss Porter's or Vassar, never relishing the idea of reliving the past.

PILLAR OF STRENGTH:
Enduring Tragedy and Indiscretion

It's a coping mechanism that no one should ever have to study. But when you suffer life's inevitable losses and indiscretions, you'll need far more than the usual toolkit of restraint, good manners, and a stiff upper lip.

Jackie was forced to master adversity, having lost two husbands, three babies, a brother-in-law, and several other relatives—all by the age of 45. Through it all she kept going, saying, "One must not let oneself be overwhelmed by sadness." Her techniques? She adhered to protocol (JFK's artful funeral mirrored Abraham Lincoln's, something Jackie researched in the days after the assassination). She gained solace through spirituality (she met frequently with her priest in the wake of misfortune). She stayed busy. And she found ways to look past the moment—through her children, her friends, her causes, and her intellectual curiosity.

Your rites. Is there any way to be "appropriate" in the face of tragedy or wrongdoing? Jackie believed so. The urge to break down—at a memorial mass, a dying friend's bedside—may be strong, but it's a reaction that Jackie didn't often allow herself. During JFK's memorial services, she stoically kept it together behind a European-style veil she had carefully chosen for the occasion, and didn't shed any visible tears. She held her own between a weeping Christina and a sobbing Artemis Onassis at Ari's services. Even as her own illness had her firmly in its grip, she insisted to friends that she was doing just fine, and made forward-looking plans.

Of course, there's no one way to govern our emotions in such times. But there are some distinct Jackie take-aways here: When the weight of tragedy falls upon you, console yourself by consoling others. Jackie expressed her sympathies and concerns to a stunned White House staff on the night of the assassination, and later found solace in replying to some of the thousands of cards and letters sent to her in the aftermath. Remarkably, she even threw a joint birthday party for Caroline and John Jr. on their last day in the White House.

Another balm for the grief-stricken, as Jackie so famously taught: Work to ensure loved ones will be remembered in the most favorable, permanent, light. In her case, of course, that meant almost immediately shaping her husband's legacy with the "Camelot" theme she dictated to *Life* magazine writer Theodore White. Setting up a college fund in a loved one's name or producing a video memorializing their life may be smaller gestures, but they have the same air of commitment and historical purpose that Jackie prized.

When it comes to healing from a tragedy, don't listen to others' musings about when you should be "back to normal" or "snap out of it." The world was impatient to see Jackie come out of mourning—yet she just let it wait.

Shrinks, medications, and other pain plans. Some tough stuff is too much to handle without professional assistance. Even if shrinks and pills aren't your style, Jackie (who often received amphetamine shots at times of stress) would most likely implore you to at least consider therapeutic, as well as pharmaceutical, aid. This is especially important if you feel any urge to do harm to yourself, as Jackie considered in the months following the assassination, according to *Grace and Power* author Sally Bedell Smith. Such attention—whether it's from a religious advisor, a social worker, a doctor, or an Eastern healer—at least provides another way for you to channel your grief.

Give gossip the slip. If you suffer misfortune, chances are that scrutiny—from near and afar—is around the corner. Do your damnedest to ignore it. Wallowing in what-might-have-beens and what-could-have-happeneds will only keep your emotional wounds festering. Jackie put up an invisible curtain to skirt the endless whispers around her. Whenever anyone had the audacity to raise the topic of conspiracy theories relating to JFK's death, for example, she would simply stare at them quizzically, and then change the subject.

Don't freak out if the world seems to disapprove of your next moves. When Jackie married Ari, one Italian headline screamed, "Jack Kennedy Dies Today for a Second Time." The criticism was sharp indeed. Jackie eased up on her "none of your business" rule, however, and carried on to Greece with her mother, stepfather, and a few Kennedys at her side to show that she was confident and supported. She even reversed her decision to disallow press at the nuptials. You, too, can counteract bitter pills by trying a little spin: If a new beau is reviled, trot him out early and often, so that your friends get used to seeing you together. Once the novelty abates, hopefully the gossip will, too.

Do a "devil may care." If you've been dealt a bad—indecent!—hand, extricate yourself from the situation quickly, and don't look back or point fingers. Jackie promptly quit her Viking job upon publication of a controversial novel about the assassination of a fictional President Ted Kennedy. Her departure made it clear that her loyalties were with the Kennedys, and the swiftness of her action left little room for recriminations on either side.

On the other hand, certain, um, compromising positions call for a light touch, if you can swallow your pride. When *Hustler* publisher Larry Flynt ran some nudie spy shots of Jackie, she defused the potentially heated moment with devil-may-care comments. "It doesn't touch my real life," she said. "I suppose I should be flattered."

◆ Bedside Manners ◆

Whether you like it or not, at some point you're going to get some experience in dealing with illness—a friend, a mate, a relative. And though not everyone has the temperament for endless sickbed hand-holding—the way Jackie did during JFK's three back surgeries—the key is to let the afflicted know how much you care. A kind gesture or two, coupled with phone check-ins, will go a long way toward making an under-the-weather loved one feel less alone.

A steely Jackie softened considerably when it came to tending to the sick. After Joe Kennedy's stroke in 1961, doctors wondered if he'd ever walk again. To play to his determination, Jackie bought him a beautiful walking stick—and engraved it with "To Grandpa, with love, Jackie." When, six months later, he took his first steps, he did so using Jackie's gift for support.

Don't let illness frighten you. Despite her mother's Alzheimer's disease and attendant erratic behavior, Jackie insisted on including Janet in public functions, such as the dedication of the Kennedy School of Government at Harvard. Jackie also visited her friend Solange Herter frequently during her two cancer scares, always bringing cheer and little gifts.

Would Jackie . . .

◆ **Give cash or cash equivalents as a gift?** Ye$. Despite her fa-
mous shopping sprees—and the highs she got from finding
just the right book or trinket for F&F—Jackie didn't have time
to do it all. (Sound familiar?) Even at Christmas, she sometimes tucked money into notes: "Not much time for shopping
this X-mas, so use this to get something you want," she wrote to
maid Provi Paredes. To mark her half brother Jamie's birthday,
she would send him a check equal to his age, plus one. Today,
yes, Jackie would love the convenience of gift cards.

◆ **Beg to gain admission to a social club?** Never. Stung once in
college—Vassar's prestigious Daisy Chain clique spurned
her—Jackie learned that rejection can actually be a potent
motivator. Eventually (ha!) she showed up all of those Interchangeable Women. Marrying a hot, wealthy senator surely
helped.

◆ **Defy family members to preserve her sanity?** Yes, and can't we
all relate? Try as you might to please everyone, sometimes you
need to tend to you—even if it means ruffling some feathers.
Jackie liked to hide out in her bedroom for an entire day—
reemerging refreshed and delighted. During one such spell in
Florida, she even tuned out her mother-in-law Rose Kennedy
by refusing to alight for a luncheon. Such moves may not do
much for your popularity, but can do wonders for your psyche.

◆ **Interfere with her kids' wedding plans?** Definitely not—no
matter who is paying. It's the couple's day, after all, not a parent's. Jackie went through a tough time planning her wedding
to JFK (endless Kennedys, bickering divorced parents, a dress
she abhorred). As a result, she'd insist her children have exactly what they wanted. Caroline went all out, with 450 guests

and a Carolina Herrera gown that Mom didn't select. The chosen few who attended John Jr.'s radically different ceremony thought Jackie would also have approved of the simple, private affair.

Be a donor for a sick relative or friend? Not everyone would step in to give a kidney or other body part. Such procedures can be scary and time-consuming, not to mention risky. But proving that it is the stand-up thing to do, Jackie scrubbed up. In an unsuccessful attempt to save Janet Auchincloss Rutherfurd from lung cancer, Jackie donated bone marrow to her half sister in the mid-1980s.

Chapter 2

O! That Dress:

What Your Clothes Say About You

> A woman "is well dressed if people say,
> 'She looked heavenly but I can't remember
> what she had on.' "
> —JBKO

I s it your sartorial destiny to make women covet and men swoon? To dress in a manner that is so confidently smashing that you can dismiss—with a flick of a glossy magazine page—the often tortured, cookie-cutter looks churned out by today's fashion conglomerates? If it's your wish to be a "geometrical goddess"—designer Oleg Cassini's preferred term for his famous client—then close study of Jackie's fashion alchemy is required.

Despite the thousands of photos and dozens of tomes that pay homage to her classic style, Jackie's fashion know-how has never been deconstructed for practical, postmodern use until now. This, after all, was a forward-thinking woman who scoured the pages of *Women's Wear Daily* to stay abreast of global street and runway trends; who paired T-shirts with designer slacks long before such "cross-shopping" was *branché*; who commissioned couture outfits only to retire them to secondhand shops as a way to fund new purchases. Even accessories had a covert mission: to dramatize otherwise simple, architectural clothes.

Like any respectable fashionista, she used every resource available to her, from Kennedy and Onassis money to couturiers, fashion scouts, and personal tailors. ("An inch off can make all the difference," she once said, referring to hemlines.) On one occasion, Jackie even sent the official White House photographer to snap a New York fashion show—very naughty! In fact, she rarely missed an opportunity to browse or shop, inspecting loot from the open-air bazaars of India and Morocco, as well as the opulent ateliers on Paris's Right Bank.

Indeed, it was the "Sex and the City" mix-and-match ethic, just forty years ahead of time—and with better editing. Unlike Carrie Bradshaw, who always seemed to be tangled in her pearls, Jackie never looked fussy. Whether formal or casual, heavily beaded or plain, her outfits had an easy, accessible logic. Rather than "trend-right," they were occasion-right, an important idea to recapture at a time when fashion's rules have become so fluid. She knew what it took to be correct for the various events, moods, and phases of her life.

HOW TO MASTER THE EFFORTLESS RICH LOOK

Many have observed that Jackie looked rich, and that she did so effortlessly, without the bourgeois trappings often associated with wealth. She wore few furs, favored pants, and despite her bulging jewel box, made stingy use of those mega-watt gems—including a finger-cramping 40.5-carat diamond ring from Ari Onassis.

Achieving the "Jackie look" of her day was hardly simple. Any woman who wanted to appear similarly unstudied had to juggle numerous historical and aesthetic references. These included austere European silhouettes, the military looks that influenced Coco Chanel, as well as body-conscious Greek drapings revived by Hollywood.

It also meant being an early adapter—having an outfit before it hit the prestige-sucking vortex of copycat fashion. "I want all mine to be original and no fat little women hopping around in the same dress," she said in a letter to Oleg Cassini, her official White House couturier, in December 1960.

◆ Don't Get Tripped Up by "Fast Fashion" ◆

Today's fashion cycles are getting shorter and shorter, faster and faster. Within every price range there are more choices, more fads and trends, that will come and go long before you can redeem those Membership Rewards points. Women who get carried away by the constant "newness" in stores usually resort to bingeing, with little regard for what looks good on their bodies, or what styles go with the other pieces in their closets.

Jackie wouldn't be moved by such fashion distractions. Nor would she let fussy stylists dupe her into a garment that didn't suit her taste, her figure. She was certain of what worked on her long-waisted, small-chested frame, having studied armholes, drop waists, and button placement with Washington, D.C., dressmaker Mini Rhea in 1951.

This helps to explain why her style, which evolved considerably over the years, remained hair-pullingly consistent. She knew she looked terrific in pants, both flares and straight legs. She had broad shoulders, a Thoroughbred's gams, and wore pieces that showed off those features whenever possible.

Boat necks and V-necks did more for her small bosom than plunging tops; and busy prints, which might have looked cartoonish on her 5'7" frame, were usually limited to the bodice of a dress, or to short, Pucci-like styles. By being brutally honest about what really works on your figure (remember—salespeople often work on commission), you'll reflexively reject flash-in-the-pan fashion.

◆ ◆ ◆

"Jackie understood her body and coloring very well.
Her clothes were beautifully tailored, from her trousers and
tees to suits and gowns. I think everyone should take an
honest assessment of themselves in a three-way mirror,
get a good tailor, and remember that it's quality,
not quantity, that counts when getting dressed."
—MICHAEL KORS, FASHION DESIGNER

◆ ◆ ◆

Know the Difference Between
◆ Luxury Clothing and High Fashion ◆

In Jackie's day, wealthy women could get themselves into only so much fashion trouble. They could overdress, over-jewel, clash colors. Today, women of means have a completely different set of risks at hand. One of the biggest is called high fashion, and it is not necessarily for novice babes who aspire to be on the Best Dressed List. By "high fashion," we mean pieces that not only turn heads and cost a fortune, but garments whose intent is to change the perception of the body. Think Yohji Yamamoto, As Four, and Comme des Garçons.

Wear such clothes at your own peril; any item that outshines the wearer is a potential danger. The consummate Jackie look, by contrast, is more about appearing classically beautiful and luxurious. She wore "nothing scary or intimidating," observes Simon Doonan, creative director at Barneys New York. "She wasn't trying to provoke a class debate."

◆ Never Confuse "Classic" with "Static" ◆

Being classic means much more than clinging to the same old cashmere twin set season after season. A true classicist also keeps up with the times, cycling looks in and around the basics of her wardrobe—things such as trench coats, designer denim, knee boots, and big tote bags—items that invariably return to style time and again.

Some forty years after Jackie first appeared on the International Best Dressed List, the "mod" look has returned in earnest, complete with lollipop-sized buttons, A-line dresses, low-slung hip-huggers, and miniskirts. Designers like Marc Jacobs have latched on to all things '60s, while labels from the era, such as Pucci and Courrèges, are enjoying a heady renaissance.

At any age, you'll want to acknowledge a fun or important seasonal look. Just don't immerse yourself in the trend. (If you must have an Hermès-style rubber "jelly" as a beach bag, forget about the matching sandals and wallet—you'll look like a jiggly fool.) Seeing entire rafts of young and not-so-young women falling over themselves to catch the next trend—pink everything, cargo pants, bare midriffs—would have struck Jackie as de trop.

Instead, pick one or two current pieces that make sense within the context of what you already own. "I think a young Jackie today would definitely wear jeans mixed in with tailored pieces and show off great bare legs," says designer Michael Kors. "An older Jackie would mix glamorous evening skirts and jackets with sporty pullovers and trousers, and not always wear traditional gowns."

Any faddish items you choose to own should pass a crucial price tag test. Six-hundred-dollar beaded flip-flops and two-thousand-dollar floral bags may look swell, but such indulgences are likely to stay on your credit card bill far longer than they linger in *Vogue*. Go for a cheaper non-designer rendition instead, spending the real money on items such as coats, dresses, or other pieces that can be pressed into service every day, and are less likely to turn heads as "last year's" look.

PEARL

Do ask and do tell. "Where'd you get that?" Jackie wouldn't be too shy to ask a near-stranger, and neither should you. She was also known to share some of her fashion secrets with friends, whispering one-word endorsements such as "Fogal" (stockings).

Keep a Cynical Eye on Runway Fashion

Jackie attended her fair share of fashion events in the Onassis years and beyond, hobnobbing with designers of the day such as Yves Saint Laurent, Calvin Klein, and Halston. And yet we're sure that she'd tell any girlfriend to take the runway looks with a huge grain of salt—as she did. Most designers send fanciful creations down the aisles, not always the stuff that actually ends up in stores. The point of watching is to pick up the key colors of the season, as well as silhouettes and attitudes.

Nowadays, that's easier to do than ever. Sites like style.com and firstview.com let you be your own market editor, giving you a virtual front-row seat to New York and European fashion shows shortly after they happen.

Repeat

Women who flaunt too many different looks seem more confused than erudite, more rattled by trends than committed to a distinctive look.

Jackie was known for reprising the same simple items, from coats to gowns, over and again. In Washington, she squeezed more than seven years' worth of wear out of a favorite black Chanel suit. Later, she was particularly fond of an old sheared beaver coat, which she would sport to lunch with fashion types.

You'd be wise to make repetition a key part of your acquisition strategy. Heed the urge to buy multiple items that you absolutely adore—a pair of shoes with the perfect heel height and toe cleavage, a sweater that hugs just so. Buy several, especially if they are on sale. You'll save time and energy and pat yourself on the back for such forethought. When Jackie found something she really liked, she'd astutely buy it in several colors.

An important note here is attitude. You mustn't give a damn about what prying relatives, spiteful colleagues—or even the fashion press—might have to say about repeating your greatest hits. Perhaps the best evidence of this credo? Jackie wed Onassis in an ivory lace Valentino high-collar number she'd worn to a friend's nuptials several months earlier.

◆ Don't Attempt to Match Seriously Dressed Women ◆

When it comes to fashion, never try to "one-up" mega-clad women, a conceit that is sure to fail. Instead, when you find yourself under sartorial threat, make it your business to "one-under" the babes instead.

You'll stand out in a crowd of fur-swaddled women—as Jackie did on Inauguration Day—by wearing something much more subtle, something that quietly purrs, "Over here." Adorning her simple camel coat was a collar ringed with sable. The look nodded to wealth but didn't dwell on it. So when others are channeling head-to-toe sequins, tuck yourself into a matte jersey gown and carry the most precious sparkly purse.

The same principle applies to accessories. Meeting up with a woman known to pack Harry Winston? Let her eat her carats as you go for a different, more original course (ostrich plumes and Lucite chokers come to mind). Such was Jackie's strategy with the Iranian Shah's wife at a state dinner in 1962. Not wanting to compete with the empress's tonnage of gems, she selected pendant earrings and a simple starburst diamond pin. To augment the effect, she stuck the latter not on her bosom, but in her hair.

If you happen upon a Major Woman, a well turned-out beauty

whose style you admire, don't flinch—flirt. Chat her up, ask her out for a cocktail—and then invite yourself over to have a good prowl through her closets. Such behavior is very, very Jackie. Mrs. O sought out as style confidante *Vogue* editor Diana Vreeland. She was also known to spend hours in the closets of another good friend, Bunny Mellon. Pay particular attention to how a Major Woman puts things together (gray gabardine with camel cashmere; patent shoes with a satin bag), not just the individual items that hang from her racks.

• PEARL •

If forced to choose between two beautiful dresses, always pick the one in the more scrumptious, sumptuous fabric. Luxurious (natural) threads—Jackie favored double-faced cashmere and silk satin—hold up longer, and pay another priceless dividend: They make you irresistible to the touch.

◆ Perfect Palettes ◆

Give a jolt to your wardrobe with monochromatic outfits. Some of Jackie's most ravishing looks, such as her ivory satin Inaugural gala dress, owe their "wow" factor to a simple whitewash, or other single-color scheme. Consider single-tone get-ups for their practicality (no heavy lifting on the matching front), and their magical ability to shroud bodily flaws—you'll look as sleek as an Ionic column.

An abundance of like-colored garments also cuts down on the visual clutter in your closet (Jackie's heaving clothing racks were arranged by hue and length.) If you embrace the monochromatic look, remember that it is best executed in subtle, not scary, shades. White, black, gray, and other neutral hues work best—Jackie favored "greige," a cross between gray and beige. Red and pink are also fashion neutrals—just ask Ralph Lauren or Narciso Rodriguez. Best to stay away from head-to-toe purple, unless you want to be mistaken for a certain preschool idol.

Mixing colors is another science altogether. Though the arguments to go bold are many—bright colors look swell in photos; and men, visual creatures that they are, can barely resist them. With designers latching on to an infinite number of Pantone hues and Technicolor prints, however, it's all too easy to affect a candy-pop look.

If you don't feel comfortable blending orange and pink, as Jackie gamely did, choose three or four colors that look best—not on the store mannequin, but against your own skin (Jackie refused even precious ear clips if the shade didn't flatter her face). Darker-haired (and perpetually tanned) women can pull off jewel tones, while fairer types may do better with pastels. From there, feel free to punctuate your wardrobe with occasional licks of color: a bag in pink or turquoise (the one shade a young Jackie felt she couldn't carry); a camisole the hue of sunflowers.

◆ Never Let Your Style Quotient Sag. Ever. ◆

Consistency is what helps you to earn the "well-dressed" moniker. Be appropriately smart at the office, keeping a snappy look on hand for post-work, ahem, opportunities. Do dress for the opera, even though a few box-dwellers show up in baseball caps; choose ensembles for weddings, New Year's, and other no-room-for-error events well in advance. Also, be your own wardrobe mistress, making sure your best outfits are freshly dry-cleaned and ready to go in case you are summoned to a last-minute soiree.

Jackie managed to keep her fashion priorities straight at all times. Her sartorial will held even in the darkest of moments. After Onassis's death, her first call was to a trusted family member, Ted Kennedy. Her next order of business? Making sure she'd look fantastic behind the casket. She rang up Italian couturier Valentino to arrange an appropriate funeral frock—a black lace below-the-knee number.

◆ Know When to Fold Your Fashion ◆

Jackie saw fit to retire her famous glove-and-hat look after the White House. Not just because she was no longer First Lady, but also because she recognized that the prim, mannered aesthetic—one she no doubt fueled—was over. Done. She moved onto a fabulous new era, showing everyone how to flaunt new designers, like Yves Saint Laurent and Courrèges. She even did the matching logo thing for a quick minute. It's always difficult to know when the moment is right to shed one look and chase a new one, but here are a few clues:

- If you look like everyone else everywhere you go—paying special attention at airports—it's over.
- If anyone in the British Royal family is wearing anything remotely close to what you own—it's over.
- If women stop asking, "Where'd you get *that?*" or cease to give you the icy up-and-down—it's over.
- If it reminds you of a scene in a hokey, post-Hepburn movie— *Annie Hall, Flashdance, Charlie's Angels*—it's over.
- If it's beyond gussying up with a fresh pair of Manolos or a cute bag—it's over.
- If your mother likes it too much—it's over.

IN PRAISE OF THE KNOCKOFF

While daily clothes should be workhorses, with the promise to last for years, formal garb—ball gowns, prom confections, bridesmaid outfits— have a far simpler burden. They need to look good for your date, your guests, and the cameras that admirers wield.

Appearing at a state dinner honoring President Félix Houphouët-Boigny of the Ivory Coast in 1962, Jackie descended the stairs in a

VOGUE-ING

At one point, surprise, surprise, Jackie aspired to be a Condé Nast girl, and sought a gig at *Vogue* magazine. Applying in 1951 for the publication's prestigious internship, the Prix de Paris, she wrote several essays to express her fashion views: "Harking-back clothes will make you feel quite secretly mysterious," the young Bouvier wrote.

Jackie won the prize, but—ever mercurial—she quickly bowed out of the job (see "Career Whirl," p. 196). She did, however, manage to leave something of her own *Vogue* legacy, positing that a woman could summon whimsical personalities simply by changing outfits or cheaply tweaking a plain style to effect a couture look.

To illustrate the latter point, she chose a simple item of clothing—a sleeveless sheath—with which to create myriad effects. Two highlights:

The Big Hat: Wear it in the afternoon, unadorned, with a great dip brimmed black hat that makes you look like the femme fatale one takes to hear tangos at teatime.

The Transparent Sleeve: Attach two balloons of organdy at the shoulders and you could be in the corps de ballet of *Giselle*.

shimmery white embroidered tulle column. A Cassini interpretation of a Karl Lagerfeld style, it lacked couture flourishes—such as specially embroidered panels. In such instances, observed *Vogue*'s Hamish Bowles, "all Mrs. Kennedy required . . . was a dress that was perfectly photogenic."

Though she didn't relish the idea of others aping her, Jackie relied on several designers (including Cassini), to copy European fashions from magazines, favoring such names as Lagerfeld and Hubert de Givenchy. She was clever enough to modify existing styles, even if ever so slightly. "I saw a picture of Bardot in one—in *Match* or *Elle*—in black, but mine could be red—covered up long sleeves—transparent," she wrote in a letter to Cassini in January 1962.

This knockoff strategy worked for Jackie in large part because the fashion world didn't churn out mass copies of high styles as easily as it does now. Today, department stores carry look-alikes of famous gowns literally weeks after they've appeared on Hollywood's red carpets. Those versions may be suitable in a pinch, especially if you have them nipped and tucked. Even better is to invest a few more dollars to have a tailor mock up a favored design, asking him or her to render the outfit in a different fabric, color, or length so as to seem more "original."

You remain well within bounds to hoard copies of a current designer styles—so long as they're well done. That can mean hand-stitched, private-label items from Saks Fifth Avenue or Barneys, or good mass-market facsimiles—with extra buttons, good linings, natural fibers, etc. from the likes of Zara and Mango.

When it comes to accessories, fakes—damn good ones—can also elevate a woman's wardrobe. Jackie's rendition of the three-strand faux pearl necklace, which continues to bask in its own celebrity today—went for $211,500 at auction in 1996.

She condoned knockoffs of her other precious jewels by having designers like Kenneth Jay Lane copy her (mostly Ari-gifted) pieces. One such item, a simulated diamond, emerald, and ruby necklace, gained enduring celluloid fame—a fact that amused Jackie. "Kenny, I saw our necklace again on *Dynasty*," she once whispered to the jeweler.

Note: The terms "knockoff" and "fake" exclude counterfeits, which are an entirely different matter. Peddlers of falsely labeled goods face federal criminal charges, and Jackie would never risk having a fashion source being hauled off to jail.

APPROPRIATENESS

There's more to being stylish than being nattily dressed. Beyond choosing good clothes is the challenge of wearing them in the proper contexts—for the event, for the time of day, for the season, even for the culture you're in. Such factors require some humbling thoughts as to what's truly right for the mis en scene, regardless of what some sadistic stylists and editors would have you believe.

Jackie knew enough to pick an eye-catching lavender ensemble to tour an Indian silk factory; she complemented the colorful local saris while still managing to stand out. In Europe, she donned something long, black, and high-necked (read: pious and non-threatening) when being received by the Pope. And she looked to Old Master paintings for art-historically rich hues (Veronese green, Nattier blue).

Each new venue, every event is the opportunity to envision the whole scene—and costume correctly for it. (Note to Martha Stewart: That pricey Hermès Birkin bag made exactly the wrong statement at a trial about greed.)

◆ At Ease! ◆

Jackie certainly valued comfort: She darted around the White House in bright Capri pants, a first for such a public woman, and shocked some by attending church bare-legged, in a sleeveless sheath. But don't let comfortable clothes lull you into a fashion faux pas. "I never leave my house unless I'm suitably dressed," Jackie insisted to the *Boston Globe* in 1960.

◆ ◆ ◆

*"Jackie wouldn't understand why girls [today] make
themselves ugly with gratuitous flesh exposure
and overly contrived hairdos."*

—SIMON DOONAN, AUTHOR;

CREATIVE DIRECTOR, BARNEYS NEW YORK

◆ ◆ ◆

At the time, that meant nothing a mother wouldn't approve of. Today's minefield is much broader. Let's start with velour tracksuits, yogawear, and anything that a pop singer has affixed her name to. Marketers may call this comfy stuff "athleisurewear," but the boyfriend who spots you on Saturday morning at Whole Foods will be glad to simply call you an ex.

Whether traveling afar or traipsing to a neighbor's poolside party, you'll want to carefully traverse fashion's fault lines. The talent is to make others as comfortable with your choice of garb as you are.

When Jackie visited France in 1961, for example, she momentarily shed her official (and politically correct) cloak of American clothing and wore Givenchy, a particular fave. She figured that Americans would forgive her and the French would applaud—and they did. Cries of "Shza-KEY!" echoed in the streets of Paris to the extent that JFK finally introduced himself at a public gathering as "the man who accompanied Jacqueline Kennedy to Paris."

That same year, she greeted the Canadian people in red—the uniform shade of the handsome Royal Mounties surrounding her. Once again, her hosts were flattered by her ingratiating gesture. It's really not an impossible act to follow: When in Rome, skip the oh-so-American sneakers and don some fine Italian leather footwear (believe us, the locals will notice and commend you). And in Paris, a fetchingly flung Hermès scarf will get you further than even a well-pronounced "s'il vous plaît."

Comfort, or some modicum thereof, should extend all the way down to your feet, so don't fool yourself about high heels. While Jackie was a fan of Manolo Blahnik's artful shoes, she did not, and certainly would not, teeter around in four-inch spikes every day. Pricey points, no matter how sexy, just don't cut it for women who must balance themselves in the real world.

❖ Remember That de trop = La Trollop ❖

You shall not let your designer obsessions fester to the point of cliché. This means you must resist the urge to wear head-to-toe Chanel (or any other bank-busting name). Ladling on labels doesn't evoke *The Best of Everything*—that marvelously stylish Joan Crawford flick set in the publishing world. Rather, it takes the mystery out of a woman's appearance. It's a dead giveaway that she is unoriginal. Or worse, the "B" word—bourgeois.

How to tell if you sniff of false airs? Someone asks what you're wearing and you find that one word—"Armani" or "Prada"—describes every item on your body, from watch and bag to shoes, coat, and lipgloss. Other Jackie O-nos: wearing too much perfume, having your hair look salon-perfect at all times (our girl was most fetching in the Ron Galella photo "Windblown Jackie"), and yapping about how much you paid for a particular indulgence.

❖ Sexiness and Dressing for Men ❖

Jackie deployed sexy clothing deftly and sparsely, using it as cautiously as a morphine drip. She knew that too much exposure (cleavage, leg, ass, etc.) would kill off any chance to be taken seriously—especially by men. The worst possible scenario: to be mistaken for a mistress.

• PEARL •

If you don't possess Jackie's language skills, at least learn to fake it in the dressing room. Know your numeric clothing sizes according to the French system (an 8 is a 38) and the Italian (an 8 is a 42). When trying on European shoes (38, 39, etc.) remember to drop the first digit and then go at least a half size up to get your American size.

A Guide to Your Global Size

USA:	6	8	10	12	14
UK:	8	10	12	14	16
FR:	36	38	40	42	44
IT:	40	42	44	46	48

• **Draw attention to your fine points.** Show off your back cleavage—and flaunt what all that hard work at Pilates class is accomplishing. A boat-neck dress highlights the collarbone brilliantly (try a brooch instead of a necklace to elongate your neck and broaden your shoulders). A three-quarter sleeve is an invitation for a great bracelet to dangle preciously on your wrist.

• **When in doubt, show less flesh, not more.** During the White House years, many of the alterations Jackie had performed on outfits consisted of lowering hemlines (she knew that many a photograph would be taken of her seated and never wanted to risk a Sharon Stone moment) and raising necklines. The suggestion of décolleté is far sexier than barely covered breasts flapping about in a low-cut top. Just as her sotto voce speaking style reeled men in closer, so did the mystery of what was behind the well-draped façade.

✦ **Give your man some say.** No, you needn't relinquish all purchase decisions, or hold him hostage outside the dressing room. But every man wants, at least sometimes, to realize his vision of you. Jackie occasionally asked JFK's opinion before trotting out a daring new style. When she was deliberating whether a one-shoulder number was too risqué, for instance, she sent Cassini straight to the Oval Office for her husband's vote. He approved.

✦ ✦ ✦

"Jackie would not be seen in velour drawstring pants in the daytime—no! And she certainly wouldn't have anything scrawled across her behind."

—SUSAN FALES-HILL, AUTHOR AND

INTERNATIONAL BEST DRESSED LIST HALL OF FAMER

✦ ✦ ✦

WHAT WORKS AT WORK

Jackie hit the professional scene late in life, at the age of 46, claiming a windowless office at Viking in 1975. Yet even in the publishing world, where salaries tend to be disproportionately low in relation to brainpower, Jackie seamlessly blended in—once again using clothes to smooth the process.

In order to let her intellect shine, she did what too few women in the workplace do today: She rationed the fashion.

✦ Furlough All In-Your-Face Frocks ✦

Whether you're at entry level or on top of the bonus heap, don't flaunt that you spend your time and money shopping. Even if your clutch of designer fare is Costume Institute–worthy (and you know Jackie's was), hold back on exhibiting your latest acquisitions. (Even *Vogue* editor-in-chief Anna Wintour, with her generous wardrobe allowance, tends to wear the same handful of Chanel suits.) Your coworkers may compliment you to your face, but you'll be getting more attention than you want behind your back. Commit to a simple, interchangeable range of pieces and occasionally sneak in something new. Jackie not only wore a pinstripe suit to big meetings, she often wore the *same* pinstripe suit.

Her daily diet of slacks and silk shirts may have been a calculated effort on Jackie's part to downplay her Best Dressed List status, but sticking to a uniform had two less obvious side effects. First, it made everyone around her comfortable (colleagues didn't feel like Halston have-nots). Second, it allowed her creative abilities to transcend her inescapable fame. You may not be a cause célèbre like Jackie (yet), but before you go dressing like one at the office, remember that it's better to be known for your work ideas, not your fashion id.

✦ When in Rome ✦

Know your company's culture; in fact, be its reigning ambassador — even if it means neutering your own fashion sense to some degree. Say you work in a conservative industry — investment banking — where gray and blue suits are the norm: Don't weep, just make sure your versions look really sharp. And wield a few touches of subtle color if you're itching for individuality (see "Office Color Guard," p. 65).

Assuming you are lucky enough to work in a creative environment — magazine publishing, say — where a bit more flair is welcomed, then take your cues from the top. If your boss is a woman, notice — but never outdo — her design quotient. (If she wears Armani, don't dare show up in custom Kiton.) Dressing around a stylish male boss may require you to defer just the same. Is he the outré type who sports Jean-Paul Gaultier and Paul Smith stripes? Then don't cluck about your own fashion, letting him keep the spotlight he so clearly craves.

Learn to Break Apart the Pieces
◆ from the "Career-wear" Racks ◆

It's a skill that any woman needs to master reflexively today. In many workplaces, the crisp-suit look has given way to not only suit pieces worn separately, but also to separates of a more extreme sort—items that range from stretch wool jackets to leather skirts and beaded tops.

Designers have responded in kind, with a slew of new, gently priced career lines from Calvin Klein, Michael Kors, and even Oscar de la Renta. Some women love the new flexibility; others shudder at the prospect of putting themselves together in the morning.

Jackie knew, long before her time, how to break apart the pieces of an outfit to create a more casual look with separates.

To master the talent yourself, canvass all the new career lines in your price range, paying little—yes, little—attention to how they appear on the racks. The jacket that best goes with the skirt that goes with the top won't necessarily be shown together—so this is the time for you to either bring along your best-dressed girlfriend, or use a department store's (free) personal shopping service. Just don't let either advisor rook you into buying the perforated leather jacket, if it strays too far from your professional mission.

Confused by all the camisoles and other sexy fare curiously on display on the career floor at Bloomingdale's? If you're unsure whether something is too "evening" for the office, it probably is.

◆ Be an Office Color Guard ◆

Her coworkers at Doubleday remember that Jackie often wore browns, purples, and mauves. In fact, she staked that color palette out as her territory, and if anyone else dared to copy her, she'd bristle. You needn't carry it that far. But picking a range of colors to work within helps to build an identity for you while also simplifying your wardrobe. The real brilliance of Jackie's earthy mauve as a choice is that it is muted, and yet still stands out as a feminine accent color—much softer than black. Brights can also be versatile. If Hermès orange is your pick, for example, it gives you a surprising amount of room to move in, from pale peaches to rusty burnt orange—just avoid the more shrill, Day-Glo hues.

GENERATIONAL DRESSING:
Grace at a Pace

Jackie got it right: She never dressed explicitly to look old or young, but she was extremely careful not to try to pull off an outfit that smacked of a different age zone. At a time when aging starlets like Madonna flout the rules of appropriateness, the best choice you can make is to steer clear of their style denial.

All girls need something to look forward to: Jackie, for instance, saved furs for womanhood. Although her classmates wore them back in high school, she simply refused. Even a woman with all the resources in the world must understand the importance of restraint, unleashing her fashion lusts and musts over time.

Shamelessly Seize All Style Possibilities
◆ in Your Twenties ◆

As a twenty-something, Jackie—like most women of this young age—was annoyed at what she perceived as bodily flaws. She pined for a tinier waist, smaller feet, and bigger breasts. Unlike most women, however, she didn't dwell on her physical lot—so take heed and get to working with what you've got. Jackie decided, for example, that she didn't want to be "bothered with complication"; that the three-quarter sleeve length suited her; that fabrics with more weight—heavy silks, wools—did her body good.

Your twenties are the perfect time for roaring fashion experimentation—and forgiveness. No wonder it was at this early stage that Jackie discovered fashion "rules" were for breaking. When sleeveless gowns were all the rage in Europe, she realized how smashing her athletic arms looked in the style. So much so that she ignored convention and began wearing, and later touting, sleeveless shifts for day.

◆ Firm Up Your Id in Your Thirty-something Years ◆

This is the decade to assess where you're headed fashion-wise, and to slow the pendulum swings as you go. Do you have favorite stores and know the lines that suit you best? If not, you could be headed for the Land of Misfit Forties—a decidedly sad scene where there's little hope for recovery.

Jackie knew this, and subtly communicated as much to another First Lady—one who'd been razed in the press for her dowdy, inconsistent taste. Over lunch in the early 1990s, Hillary Clinton asked Jackie if she should consider hiring stylists to help her find her groove. Jackie vetoed the idea, saying, "You have to be you." We bet she'd have given much different advice—or at least offered a few gentle tips—to a younger woman navigating her fashion voyage.

So if in your thirties you're still clinging to combo-suggesting magazines like *Lucky*, it's time to turn the page. Notice how people react to your clothes, and how you feel in them. And remember, professional advice doesn't have to mean hiring Nicole Kidman's handlers. Better department stores may have awful service, but most still have personal shoppers who will dote on you for free if you make an appointment in advance. Their help is only as good as you make it. Pay attention to how they canvass the store, and have them explain why a particular shape or fabric or designer does or doesn't work on your body. Once you find a good fashion consigliere, stick with him or her for the sake of institutional memory. Jackie had the folks at Bergdorf Goodman trained and running.

◆ Pucci and Pearls at Forty ◆

Assuming you've still got the body for it, parade in the hottest global fashion currents—up to a point. Hanging on to hip for her fortieth birthday, Jackie partied at an Athens nightclub in a thigh-grazing sleeveless Pucci shift—a bold, energetic choice that, in some ways, signaled a farewell to her pop indulgences. Of course, she added just the right note to her ensemble: a long pearl strand, a statement that helped her seem more regal than rock-star.

You too may want to tone things down a bit as you modulate from earnest fashion follower to coolly erudite clothing collector. Keep the heels, guard every last one of your sleek black dresses. But give everything else—especially expendable casual clothing—a fresh appraisal. Reconsider, for instance, super-short minis (it's tough to look sexy and elegant in a skirt length less than 16 inches) as well as deadly combos (time to say bye-bye to the catsuit-and-stilettos look, assuming you were ever Halle Berry–bad enough to pull it off).

Also rethink those itty-bitty tees and tidbits you picked up from Abercrombie & Fitch and Forever 21. (No one, from this point forward, should describe your look as "cute.") If you feel the need to go wild, indulge with accessories. A kicky Marc Jacobs bag adds instant youth to any outfit. Just ask Jackie's sister Lee Radziwell, who was shouldering various models after her 70th birthday.

If you haven't already explored some of the more tailored looks your work certainly demands by now, it's time. Think sharp Saville Row dressing, with a powerfully feminine twist. A few investment-grade labels to rev up your professional closet ethic without sagging down your style: Kiton, Agnona, Luciano Barbera, Carolina Herrera. The latter brand was especially dear to Jackie, who was fond of Herrera's dresses.

◆ Don't Fight It in Your Fifties-plus ◆

Given that fifty is the new thirty, don't resist the occasional urge to go younger—or the instinct to stay chic. Try perhaps layering a white leather fencing jacket over black (a recent Lee favorite). Take a tip from Oprah—more fashionable in her fifties than ever—and skip the caftans, too. If you've got great gams, show a little of them, as Jackie did in 1993, when at the age of 63 she stepped out in a white satin Herrera gown that billowed open above the knee.

Other than the obvious—cover up the cleavage, loosen up the cuts—age actually gives you more license to be bold, especially when it comes to accessories. In her 50s and 60s, Jackie wore dramatic pieces—such as ruby-and-diamond necklaces, and hefty Greek gold cuffs. The megawatt jewels, many of them presents from Onassis, drew attention away from any age-related imperfections. This is also a good time to try out some luxuriously smart "one-size" creations from designers such as Zoran, who cut expertly enough to flatter frames small and, well, not so. If you can't remember when you last wore a size 8, you'll appreciate the nod to democracy.

JACKIE LOOKS THAT ALWAYS CLICK

Black turtleneck. It should be form fitting, but not suggestively tight, with a neck snug enough to perfectly frame the face. Always worn out, always hitting at the hip, always in a natural fiber (with a hint of stretch today, of course). Although today we think she'd favor brands like Kors and Prada for their simplicity and durability, she actually sported a simple model from Jax, a moderately priced, albeit now defunct, line.

Jack Rogers sandals. No surprise that these hippie-cum-hipster sandals are enjoying a thorough comeback. (And we do mean thorough—Sears introduced a pretty good knockoff called "Jacquie," for $19; Michael Kors designed pricey high-heeled versions.) These versatile thongs, with a contrast whip-stitched embellishment, come in dozens of colors, and look as great on the streets of Manhattan as on a private yacht in Skorpios.

Black and white. These opposites attract attention in any season, on any frame. But please wield this combo carefully. The trick: to not look like a waiter, caterer, or widget-maker. Notice how Jackie typically favored white on the bottom, black on top. Reverse the order, especially for a casual or spring ensemble, and the effect can quickly turn servile.

Chanel jacket (or a good facsimile). Jackie was famous for her ability to combine separates. The Chanel jacket is the perfect mixer, as it lends itself to being worn with a matching skirt or jeans. While it's hard to argue with French fashion, several copies are up to scratch and worth checking out. (Yes, even Jackie wore custom knockoffs, including the pink-and-navy suit she wore in Dallas.) Make sure yours is made of natural fibers, and that the color scheme contains at least two or three hues to pair with various bottoms in your closet.

A-line skirts. Ah, the forgiving nature of an A-line, whose flattering shape looks much like the letter. Whether a dress or skirt, an A-line minimizes hips and skims over stubborn flesh rolls. In longer versions, this flare-bottom cut shelters less-than-perfect legs, slimming calves and ankles in the process.

Brooches. Whether it was the ruby-and-diamond Schlumberger berry pin that JFK gave her, or the diamond starburst that so often accented her formal attire, Jackie used a single brooch as an eye-catching device. Today, there's nothing hotter, from a Chanel gardenia to a jewel-encrusted bug, real or paste. They can highlight a neckline, sure, but are equally dazzling in your hair, on a handbag or shoes, or even gracing the back of a sexy evening dress.

WILDCARDS THAT WIN

Leopard print: Anything with animal print hits the spot—throws, coats, handbags. Jackie was perhaps the first First Lady to drape White House furniture with leopard throws.

Black leather: It's both naughty and nice, whether fashioned into a straight skirt, a trench coat, or a pillbox hat. Jackie sported all three iterations.

Men's clothes: Few things are sexier on a woman than a Brooks Brothers blue Oxford shirt tailored to fit. For structure, Jackie added shoulder pads to hers.

Fringe: On capes, ponchos, even scarves that adorn your mink (a surprisingly hip Jackie look, circa 1969). This one's easy—fringe passes muster because it flutters like a horse's mane.

Polka dots: So long as they're no larger than a pea. Jackie displayed them with élan from toddler to grande dame.

Cowboy boots: With your jodhpurs or other sleek pants tucked inside. Yep, Jackie proved that this improbable combo works.

Wild color combos: Orange and pink can hit the spot when paired just so. Jackie was loud and proud—was it the Lilly Pulitzer influence?— in her pink capris and an orange pullover.

STICKY SARTORIAL SITUATIONS

Sticky Sartorial Situation #1: You've gone on an overzealous spree, and now you have too many Jimmy Choos and one more Narciso shift than you really need or can afford. Should you risk embarrassment by returning the goods, or keep them, hoping for the simultaneous miracles of instant credit and wardrobe repair?

♦ *Bring the goods back.* Be matter-of-fact, never apologetic, about returns, so long as the tags are still on. Jackie often overindulged and later returned her excess purchases. What matters here is intent. Just don't buy an item you plan to wear once and then return. You will feel tacky when you trot it out, and even tackier when you haul it back to the store.

Sticky Sartorial Situation #2: Your fabulous new boyfriend has a big heart and a bigger bank account, and he soon utters words you've only dreamt about: "Meet me at Barneys. . . ." Should you—an independent, highly evolved woman in frantic need of a new Prada suit—take him up on his offer to dress you from head to heel?

♦ *Not so fast.* Any man who's raring to take you shopping—and pay the tab—probably has some major control issue festering (think Mickey Rourke in *Nine 1/2 Weeks*). He's also probably done this before, which means you might have to face smirking salesclerks who may—accidentally, of course—call you by the wrong name. The bottom line: You'll be obliged to get what he likes (which may not be your taste) and strut in it to boot. You may feel more like a tart than a treat.

Far better to have a man who surprises you with gifts (which you can eagerly accept and later return/consign if necessary). Jackie happily accepted bounty from men her entire life, from horses to rare sculptures and fabulous jewels. So if a man simply offers his Amex card, and urges you on to a solitary shopping spree, Jackie would have just one word of advice. "Taxi!"

Sticky Sartorial Situation #3: You're out on the town, wearing an absolutely luscious, covetous fur. Your date steers you to the coat check. Do you dare trust it to strangers, or tote it around to avoid having to file a claim with Lloyd's of London?

♦ *Check it.* Clinging to anything other than your sweetie—or bigger than a fur stole—can seem crass. Also, why spoil it for the coat-check folks, who will surely want to cop a harmless feel? About six months before marrying Onassis, Jackie turned up at a Manhattan speakeasy with date Mike Nichols, sporting a floor-length coat that "they must have killed five million sables for," recalls Joan Rivers, who performed that night. Jackie checked it, much to the glee of the cast of players. "We all went into the coat room and tried it on, even the gay guys," says Rivers. "If only she knew!"

Would Jackie . . .

Shop online? Are you kidding? Why, she'd love the chance to troll the selections at Bergdorf's and Neiman's from her desk. Not only does online shopping offer anonymity and convenience, it's a neat way to hunt for sales and bargains, even of a swish sort, at sites like ashford.com and eluxury.com.

Brave "big box" stores? Yes, at least to see what all the fuss is about, and perhaps on visits with the grandkids (even Caroline was spotted at now-defunct Caldor, for goodness sake). Though we doubt Jackie would stock her wardrobe with Target togs, her intrepid, curious nature might lead her there to pick up a few pieces—perhaps for her yoga practice.

Shop designer outlets? Not in person. There are just too many turnpike exits between them and the sale racks at Bergdorf's to make the trek worthwhile. Also, stuff there is often old news and overhandled, not the ticket for fastidious Jackie-types. But being a bargain hound, she might call up very high-end outlets (Yves Saint Laurent or Loro Piana) to inquire about the availability of specific styles.

Emulate "celebrity" fashion? No, no, a thousand times no. Most celebs suffer from a distinct inability to dress themselves, instead relying on a battalion of freelance stylists for red-carpet events. This lack of self-study tends to retard their own fashion sense rather than advance it. So watch the runways as Jackie would—but pay scant attention to the photo-op actresses in the front row who don't know A-line from A-list.

Overstuff her (A) cup? No—Jackie wouldn't be up for much fake cleavage, at least not the heavy-duty Wonderbra kind. Instead, she'd head to the famous corset and bra makers of Europe to fashion a custom underpinning—one that would provide support and a wee bit of padding, but not so much as to misrepresent what lies underneath. Remember, being minimally endowed never hindered Jackie's abilitiy to captivate men. One famous photo shows her reveling braless in a snug-fitting, nipple-highlighting T-shirt.

Sport designer logos? Yes, although initial indulgence should somewhat be determined by age. It's okay for a younger woman (under 50) to flaunt logos on clothing and accessories. As a young widow, Jackie loved her Yves Saint Laurent "maxi coat" with a giant YSL stitched on the pocket. Prowling the streets of Paris, she cinched her waist with a V (for Valentino) belt. Just don't overdo it by wearing multiple logos at once, or endorsing initials with little prestige (H should be for Hermès, not Hilfiger). And as you mature, better to keep your designer tags inside rather than out.

Don a tiara? *Non, mon dieu!* Let silly celebrities and brides poke a diamond or crystal crown in their hair. Just don't join in their Cinderella folly. Those who recalled Jackie sporting a tiara at Versailles in 1961 were mistaken: She astutely observed that tiaras and crowns are suitable only for royals (or tacky wannabes—Celine Dion and Judith Giuliani come to mind). To get the princess effect, she arranged several diamond pins—on loan from Van Cleef & Arpels—in her coif.

Do the monogram thing? To a degree. But monograms can blur the lines between class and crass—and hence are safest on stationery and tea towels. Rather than splay your initials over your wardrobe—JBKO wasn't into that—it's more patrician to brand your accessories, both large and small. Jackie, for instance, used her monogram on a belt, as well as on a cobalt-blue metal trunk she kept at her riding stable.

Chapter 3

Bliss and Makeup:

How to Affect the Jackie Glow

"I was a tomboy. I decided to learn to
dance and then I became feminine."
—JBKO

The defining "swan" 'do that inspired a million copycuts. The svelte physique on which clothes hung with artful precision. The yoga and trampoline workouts decades before the rest of America caught on to the beauteous side effects of far-out fitness. These were all part of the Jackie formula for maintaining a polished presentation—a choreography de corps that took into account every sultry inch, from acid-white teeth and hairless arms to an intoxicating scent.

Nothing has really changed: Her essentials are still essential. And yet, with a world awash in beauty aids, anti-aging creams, lunchtime cosmetic procedures, fitness trends, diets, supplements, and so much more, achieving Jackie's Brahmin-buff look may be tougher, not easier, today.

HAIRDOS–AND TABOOS

♦ ♦ ♦

"Jackie's hairstyle was iconic—it was distinct, modern, and classic at the same time. Her look wouldn't need much changing today. I'd give her a bob with maybe a little less volume and more layers so that you do not need to tease the hair—a wash-and-wear version of the Jackie O look."

—FRÉDÉRIC FEKKAI, HAIRSTYLIST,
SALON OWNER, AND HAIR PRODUCT GURU

♦ ♦ ♦

♦ Yes, Hair Paranoia Is Permissible ♦

We all have our definition of what makes a good hair day. And if you're as detail-oriented as Jackie, you'll want to tip the odds (or winds) in your favor. Before driving in an open motorcade with JFK, Jackie had a female White House staffer tool around Washington in a convertible and report back on the hair treachery. When traveling to France as First Lady, she was so concerned about her state of head that she sent a lock of hair—*en avance*—to the stylist she would use there. Later in life she insisted on regular Monday and Thursday blowouts (and manicures). For big events, you'll want to fuss almost as much, summoning a professional even if it's inconvenient. When locals simply won't do, consider importing a trusted hair pro. (Jackie often flew her first longtime New York stylist, Kenneth, to Washington.)

And when—horrors!—no one is available to redo your 'do, try to sleep sitting up to preserve the style. Though Jackie employed this technique in Greece, we admit it might seem a tad awkward today—especially if you don't retire alone. Never mind. Just tell your sweetie you nodded off while reading. Or, better still, take a page from

African-American hair care and learn "the wrap" aka "the doobie." This hair-spooling maneuver uses clockwise brushstrokes from the nape of the neck around the head to create one giant swirling beehive (secure with bobby pins as you go). Cover your conehead with a fetching silk scarf.

◆ Hair-care Conundrums Solved ◆

Hairdos are non-transferable; the style that looks glorious on Beyoncé may have tragic consequences for your face. Jackie learned at an early age that light bangs and some height on top were the best equalizers for her square head and wide-set eyes. And though she experimented with different lengths, she never entirely parted with those face-softening layers. If you're unsure of what to do, consult a professional (think Frédéric Fekkai, not Supercuts)—and then get a second opinion.

Wigs are also a handy tool when searching for the right coif: They allow you to try out different looks without committing to a cut. Jackie also used them on bad hair days, and she experimented with falls to fill out her hair or create even more volume for an upswept evening style. Invest a few extra bucks in high-quality fakes. They'll look better, last longer, and style better. Just be sure to secure your faux locks properly—a ponytail is the last thing you want to leave on your date's lap.

Don't be too timid to tell a girlfriend when her hair needs a (literal) lift. If you're feeling playful—or think the situation is truly dire—you may even want to share some do-it-yourself techniques. Once, at Camp David, Jackie took friend Solange Herter aside and demonstrated the art of the tease. "I was amazed!" recalls Herter, who observed Jackie's comb strokes in a mirror. "My hair was flat, so it was necessary."

◆ Avoid Extremes ◆

Very few people beyond Sinead and Demi can pull off a shaved head. Bottom-tickling tresses are Morticia morbid—unless you're Naomi

Campbell. Most of us should also avoid radical color changes. Like it or not, your own natural hue is apt to best match your eyes and skin tone. As a lifelong brunette, Jackie was ahead of the hair game. More women these days are asking their colorists for mocha hues: Brown hair tends to reflect light better than blond shades—a benefit Jackie played up by wearing diamond hair ornaments. And don't believe celebrity hawkers like Sarah Jessica Parker, who touts Garnier Nutrisse hair color: No boxed tint can equal a pro job. "I'd give Jackie hair color to take with her when she went away rather than chance it," says Thomas Morrissey, her longtime colorist.

You May Cheat on Your Stylist

Yes, stylists are jealous, mercurial sorts. In the event that your regular hairdresser is sick, unavailable, or throwing a tantrum, you'll want to have someone else trained to tend your tresses. (Just don't fess up—the last thing you need is some nasty peroxide payback.) A cautious First Lady recruited Kenneth to teach her maid Provi Paredes to do her hair in an emergency.

Although you may not have the benefit of hired help, you can still look your best while traveling by finding out, before you depart, which salons are top-notch. Just be sure to know how they say "blow-out," "relaxer," and "extensions" in Denmark and Dubai.

Press and Process with Care

Let's face it: Some hair simply handles better when straightened—a process Jackie often used to smooth her wavy locks (and to blunt criticism from JFK and her mother, who both felt her hair was too frizzy). Nowadays, white women can either get a Japanese "permanent" straightening, or do something that a young Jackie probably couldn't: Get the job done at a black hair salon. Ever since African-American beauty salons became fixtures in larger cities, savvy white women have flocked to them for their expertise in handling harsh lye-based straightening agents. This is another job you do not want to try at home.

The Daily Grind

When Jackie applied for *Vogue*'s Prix de Paris prize in 1951, one essay called for her to write about personal grooming. At twenty-one, her opinions were amusingly firm (even though she also smoked and bit her nails). Sure, she would later prefer wax to depilatory creams, and the number of hair-brushing strokes would go down as the complexity of her coif went up. Yet her earnest thesis on feminine upkeep proves remarkably useful even today. An upkeep summary, in her own words:

"If you buy decent materials and take care of them (no dirty powder puff, unwashed brush and comb, dried-out nail polish), eat and sleep sensibly, remember that cleanliness and neatness are what you are working for, and that they can be attained with ten minutes of washing and brushing a day and a little extra time one night a week, you should never have to scream in anguish and take an hour to get ready when told that your best beau has arrived unexpectedly and is waiting downstairs."

MAKEUP, WHAT MAKEUP?

When it comes to makeup, soignée sorts strive to look natural. Ironically, that sun-kissed glow can be much harder to master than a full-pancake face—the sort of heavy-handed job you've no doubt suffered at your local department store counter. Isn't that reason enough to hunker down and learn your own subtle tricks?

Go ahead and take lessons, studying as seriously as you would with a portrait painter. In 1993, Jackie paid close attention when she summoned New York makeup artist Pablo Manzoni to her home. Manzoni was surprised at how Jackie insisted on holding a mirror while he worked, in order to see each dab, every layer of color. She kept a pad of paper nearby and wrote down his techniques, point by point.

Match your makeup: Jackie's brilliant face test. When Jackie had Manzoni do her face for the American ballet Theatre's Spring Gala, she insisted he practice first. It wasn't that she didn't trust his abilities; she wanted the chance to experiment with various makeup and clothing combinations. Eleven days before the big event, he turned up at Jackie's apartment to find her in a red robe—the same shade she was going to wear out that evening. The night of the gala, she donned a white cover-up for their session, since her gown was also snowy. As Manzoni recalled later, he was shocked by Jackie's brilliant face test. He'd never seen anyone go to such lengths to match color.

Candy it ain't; use restraint. Overbuying at mega-beauty stores (Sephora) and on snazzy Web sites (blissworld.com) is easy: With infinite potions and little personal guidance, you can load up on many wrong shades. Instead, seek out the known stars at local cosmetics counters and get advice on a signature palette. Then stick with it— people will notice your makeup (and flaws) less. The more you try to hide an imperfection with paint, the more you end up accentuating it, especially as you age. The same goes for strong colors on the face. Jackie preferred Elizabeth Arden Flawless Finish foundation, a delicate Erno Laszlo pink cream blush, and Adrien Arpel Perfect Pink lipstick. She'd surely adore the skin-toned neutrals available today from the likes of Bobbi Brown, Trish McEvoy, and Laura Mercier.

Stock your (alligator) paintbox with the finest tools. Once you have found your favored products and understand their best application, arrange them in one place. Preferably a swanky one, like the red alligator makeup case Jackie received from an admirer. Elizabeth Arden, perhaps? For mobile touchups, carry only the minimum essentials in a neat pouch. It's unattractive to dig for a little lipstick in a big bag.

Don't scrimp on the implements. Good brushes last longer, the right sponges ensure a featherweight layer of foundation, and color-coordinated lip liner makes for a more polished look. Jackie made sure to always have on hand an ample supply of pricey powder puffs. Hers were $1.13 apiece—that's almost eight bucks in today's dollars—and well worth it for the smooth finish they gave her.

Never show your hand (mirror). Men—especially those who hold sacred the feminine mystique—don't need to know what it takes for you to look your best. Lock them out of the bathroom at makeup time or, like Jackie, simply retreat to your own bath. The one acceptably discreet exception: dabbing on a bit of lipstick post-meal (or post-kiss). It can be a terribly sexy gesture, as Jackie proved.

Heed local makeup customs. Sometimes, blending in is the best tactic, especially when exotic beauty marks are involved. When Jackie traveled to India in 1962, she donned a *bindi*—the customary red dot on the forehead—out of respect for her hosts. Disclaimer: Local makeup customs do not include permanent tattoos, which Jackie would never abide. Anywhere.

• PEARL •

Turn up the lights. Whenever you apply makeup, you need to be able to see everything clearly. Jackie particularly cared about bathroom lighting, and she requested better beams in all the old European palaces she visited during her travels. "Most of them," says Tish Baldrige, "were so dimly lit that if you had a fly on your nose, you couldn't see it." Try dimmers in the bathroom to adjust your moods, and spring for lighted vanity mirrors in your car.

JACKIE'S JUSTIFIABLE RITES

You have them, whether your list is short or Jackie-long: weekly manicures, at-home pedicures, and pre-date waxings. Following are some choice Jackie "must-dos," along with a key to the fiscal burden for each.

$ Jackie on a budget

$$ Worth saving for

$$$ Onassis bucks

Massages. Both pleasurable and defensible in that they combat stress, reduce muscle soreness from workouts, and promote the healthy glow that Jackie so valued—and that men respond to. In the White House, she got rubbed as often as daily, and kept up frequent appointments throughout her life, sometimes going to Elizabeth Arden's Red Door salon in New York. Note that 90 minutes, rather than 60, is now the standard table time. $$

Skin pick-me-ups. You go, girl: straight to the dermatologist, that is. Jackie would swoon over today's array of derma-peels, collagen injections, and other anti-wrinkle treatments—all ready to be administered in your doctor's office. She did the most she could in her day, getting regular facials and masques at Janet Sartin—probably a result of having had bouts of bad skin as an adolescent. Jackie also routinely saw a dermatologist to keep ahead of the aging curve. $$

A year-round tan. Jackie used to sunbathe for her ruddy complexion, but today a (safer) golden glow is only as far away as a bottle or spray can, preferably professionally applied. Just don't overdo it (you'll muss your satin sheets), and, for heaven's sake, don't ask the aesthetician to sculpt fake muscles or cleavage. $$

Breakfast in bed. By treating the beginning of each day as special, you'll improve the likelihood that the rest of it will be, too. And if you can manage to digest croissants along with your daily affirmations, all the better. Jackie used her bedroom as command central. She propped up in bed for her morning breakfast tray—toast with honey was a favorite—and summoned various helpers to her bedside. $

Daily naps. Think of them as virgin afternoon delights. Reorient your office couch so passersby can't catch you in a prone position. Jackie would even slip on a nice nightie for her afternoon snooze—something we don't recommend at work! In fact, Jackie—a nearly obsessive sleeper—enjoyed fresh linens after each round in bed; on nap days, that meant two changes of the pale pink silk sheets she favored. It's worth the splurge to get the full-body experience of all that *soie*, but at the very least, don't forgo using a silk pillowcase, which minimizes hair rumpling, eye puffiness, and facial lines. $$$ (full service) $ (if you merely splurge for the lavender-scented linen spritzer water that's a perfect olfactory freshener)

Therapy. There's a lot to be said for being as together mentally as you are physically. Don't ignore the benefits—and the luxury—of paying someone to help you sort through your problems. Adjusting to her post-Ari life, Jackie was said to visit a therapist several times a week. (Forget the co-pay level of therapist; this is where only the best will do.) $$

SCENTS AND SCENTS-ABILITY

When choosing a fragrance, go for what your nose loves, not just a name. Jackie never touched the perfume called "Jacqueline" that JFK's team whipped up for the 1960 election and handed out along the campaign trail. She preferred a good French bouquet. In fact, she was known to draw an analogy between the intoxicating effects of fine wine and fine perfume. "Joy" was a particular favorite of hers—expensive, feminine, not overpowering, and very exclusive. For similar reasons, she also loved Chanel No. 5.

Spritz and dab, never douse. As Jackie knew, it's far better to employ less-obvious tactics when placing a fragrance—in your hair, behind the knees, inside the elbow, deep in the décolleté. She would appreciate today's array of scented body creams—even more subtle. Either way, your skin's warmth will awaken the scent. Just avoid misting the pearls; real ones peel after exposure to perfume products.

If you've chosen wisely, you'll get compliments. But keep your scent a flirtatious secret. When sister-in-law Joan asked Jackie what fragrance she used, Jackie said playfully, "I never tell anyone what perfume I wear. I can't take the competition."

GYM DANDY:
Chic Physical Fitness

You want a sublime body, you know you have to work out to get it, and yet time is precious. How to choose? Activities that provide not only sweat appeal but also put you in proximity to healthy, wealthy males are obviously preferable. Messy team sports don't make the list—Jackie eschewed the Kennedy family's raucous touch-football games after she broke her ankle during one—but sports that allow you to look good while practicing them do:

Horseback Riding. Think fitted jackets, perfect posture, and the thrill of the hunt. Riding can be as physical and competitive as you want to make it; Jackie took the sport to its extremes, jumping and doing dressage competitively, and hunting with as many as three clubs regularly. Obviously, you'll only reap such glamorous side benefits if you ride English saddle.

Trampoline. They're fun, they're cool in a retro way, and they give you a great opportunity to spy on the neighbors. Although it was ostensibly purchased for Caroline and John Jr., the trampoline perched outside JFK's office at the White House ended up being a favorite workout for Jackie. Today you can opt for a mini-

continues . . .

tramp, which provides the same circulatory benefits and takes up no more room than a bath mat.

Pumping Iron. From increasing bone density to boosting your metabolism and muscle definition, there are myriad reasons to hoist weights. Jackie often used the weight room at the White House, having Secret Service clear it of men before she entered. Decades later she was still at it, lifting with a personal trainer (it's always preferable to have someone else help to drive your drive) at the Vertical Club in Manhattan.

Yoga. Have you ever seen a flabby yoga instructor? Exactly. Other benefits: flexibility, agility, and tranquillity. Jackie, well ahead of her time, first tried yoga on her 1962 trip to India with sister Lee. Her instructor? Nehru himself, of course. Later on, in New York, she had a yoga instructor come to her apartment twice a week. They worked out together for sixteen years. "If you want to be like Jackie," says Carly Simon, "put your leg around your neck."

Jogging/Speed Walking. All you need is a good pair of sneakers—and in Jackie's case, a "Moynihan '88" T-shirt. She preferred circling the reservoir (now named after her) in New York's Central Park—it was peaceful, and it gave her the rare chance to stargaze behind her own protective shades. Don't even think about bailing on chilly days: Precious crisp air, according to the Jackie playbook, promotes good circulation and always-enviable healthy color.

Kayaking. It's adventurous, peaceful, and a superlative core and upper-body workout. Jackie loved to hit the water in her single-seater while on Martha's Vineyard.

Swimming. Sure, it's great for the joints, but it's the weightless leg-toning that's irresistible. Jackie's predilection? Salt-water swims—with fins, which gussy up the gams while propelling you through the surf at warp speed. "If you wear flippers," she advised Joan, "it's a great way to trim your thighs." One body of water she avoided: the White House pool, where JFK often entertained other women.

Waterskiing. Tan, strengthen your whole body, and look fab all at once. Jackie suited up for hour-long acrobatic waterskiing outings around Skorpios twice daily—often in her fave seaside attire, a bikini. Just be sure not to fall and lose the wrong half.

Skiing. The beauty of skiing, like horseback riding, is that it puts you in a gorgeous place with gorgeous people; Jackie favored Aspen, Sun Valley, Gstaad, and Canada's Mont Tremblant. Even if you can't bang the bumps with the best of them, at least you can stand out on the slopes by wearing a classic Dr. Zhivago fur hat, as Jackie did.

◆ ◆ ◆

"I think Jackie would disagree with senseless exercise.
She would not like machines, because they lack creativity—
you're not arriving at any place, you cannot change
direction. She had a very natural way of keeping herself
in shape, always confronting what's outside
as if to say, 'I can do this, I can perform.' "
—RADU TEODORESCU, PERSONAL TRAINER TO THE STARS AND

A LONGTIME KENNEDY FAMILY COACH

◆ ◆ ◆

BODY ENHANCEMENTS:
The Dos and Don'ts

At a time when plastic surgery has gone truly public, it's easy to lose sight of where to draw the line on good taste and realistic expectations. Jackie herself had an eyelift in 1979 at age 50, and at least one face-lift in the ten years after that.

If you are considering any form of body enhancement:

◆ Do: ◆

- Take the least extreme measure possible. Try Botox before an eye job (Jackie would no doubt love this non-surgical option), and an eye job before a full-fledged face-lift.
- Be discreet. Even though the whole world seems to be parading their new surgerized selves these days, good taste dictates silence on the subject. When Jackie had her eyes done, for instance, she did so under a pseudonym.
- Take the time to find the best doctor for the procedure. You may wake up and suddenly decide that you need immediate liposuction, but the last place to turn is the ads in the back of a magazine. Jackie's surgeon had a three-month waiting list.

◆ Don't: ◆

- Alter your body in a way that is blatantly unnatural. Small-breasted women who are a size 4 really shouldn't be sporting a DD cup. For Jackie, such a distortion would have been déclassé. And it's a move that overtly sexualizes the body, and Jackie wasn't about doing anything so obvious.
- Change a part of you that is a trademark. You may hate your Roman nose, but if you carve it down to a little pixie snout, you may be losing the most distinctive part of your look. Jackie

would surely recoil, for example, at the cosmetic toe-shortening surgery in vogue today—despite her size 10 feet.

* Get jobbed just because a man asks you to. Men come and men go, but the effects of plastic surgery are (usually) forever. If you're comfortable with yourself the way you are, get another man—one who feels the same way.

COMPETITIVE EATING, JACKIE-STYLE

Jackie was every bit as obsessed with what she put in her mouth as the rest of us are, whether we are too big or too small (or delusional about either).

Her philosophy of staying slim—she was 5'7" and between 120 and 130 pounds her entire adult life—was based on a few principles. First, she exercised daily. Second—and not something we're recommending—she smoked. Third and most important, she was as disciplined about her eating habits as she was in her competitive riding. Says Baldrige, "If she put on a couple pounds, she wouldn't eat anything for the next day or two beyond a little broth and fruit."

But Jackie suffered from a fair amount of body-image paranoia. She skated on the edges of over-dieting at times, skipping meals, and occasionally relying on appetite-suppressing medications to stay slim. Please don't go there: Today, hopefully, we're armed with enough knowledge and self-confidence to avoid radical eating behaviors—under- and over-.

If you must indulge, nibble. A forkful of risotto or crème brulee won't burst your couture seams. When she worked at Doubleday, Jackie and Tiffany design director John Loring used to have lunch at Le Cirque. The owner would, according to Loring, "send over a sampling of desserts after lunch. Jackie would never touch them. She might stick her fork in and eat two crumbs and say, 'Isn't that wonderful,' and that was the end of that."

Arm yourself with snacks. Munching on healthy stuff during the day will prevent you from downing the entire 14-ounce filet mignon at dinner. Jackie's colleagues at Doubleday remember her snacking on packets of cut carrots and celery she'd bring from home (and the occasional Tootsie Roll, which she kept around to offer visitors). She also nibbled on raw peas.

Pick your battles. If you are unwilling to give up certain foods, limit yourself as to when you will have them. Jackie used to allow herself gourmet fare at dinner, but would eat a salad or light lunch to compensate. Instead of scarfing down a bag of potato chips, opt for a higher-end treat. Jackie's? She was crazy about Marta Sgubin's homemade fried zucchini slices.

THE ALLURE OF ALTERNATIVE CURES

Conventional Western medicinal practices have never had more competition than today: Chinese herbs are as common as multivitamins, dogs and cats get acupuncture, and Pilates and Gyrotonics studios give everyone a chance to be double-jointed. Jackie would have loved such a smorgasbord of alternative health treats, as she zealously pursued the best from the East.

Mind the Line Between
◆ Leading Edge and Bleeding Edge ◆

Eager to try the latest and greatest elixir, weight-loss potion, energy booster? Some of them—aura cleansing with music, powdered green-vegetable drinks—seem harmless enough. Others—such as the now-banned fen-phen—seemed like a good idea at the time, but are now known to be about as safe as arsenic.

Jackie did go to some extremes: She and Ari were said to have received live sheep-cell injections (thought to promote both longevity and virility). She got vitamin B shots long before they were in vogue and even experimented with Max Jacobson's (of Dr. Feelgood infamy) amphetamine-steroid pick-me-up injections—even though she hated needles. Use some common sense: If it's illegal or sounds too disgusting to ingest, stay away. And don't be a guinea pig: Let any "cure" earn a good reputation on health-food store shelves before you try it.

Be Proactive

Sure, most of us have trekked to the chiropractor for a good neck-cracking when things get bad. To be sure, spinal adjustments, acupuncture, and shiatsu are all capable of fixing some problems. But if you add such practitioners to your list of regular appointments, as Jackie did, the benefits are apt to multiply. Jackie was devoted to her shiatsu acupuncturist and her chiropractor, who also doled out some fruity alternative diet advice: She once went on a plum fast to cleanse her system at his suggestion.

Cleanse the Soul Along with the Body

Whatever brand of spirituality moves you, there are healthy reasons to embrace it, whether the goal is to experience inner healing at the highest level, belong to a community of like-minded sorts, or simply focus on faith. Just as she did with her fitness, Jackie preferred solitary spiritualism; after she read some of Deepak Chopra's works, she wrote to him. They became friends, and she asked him to come over and teach her how to meditate. "We sat on the floor, and she brought in candles and incense," remembers Chopra. "We had a big laugh because I told her we didn't need any of that stuff, but she said, 'Oh, why not?' " From then on, she meditated each evening from 7 to 7:30.

Practice the Philosophies,
◆ Eschew the Product Peddlers ◆

Yoga is undeniably worthwhile—but a $400 Marc Jacobs mat bag over-capitalizes on a good thing. Alkaline water may have its benefits, but are you really going to spend $1,000 on a machine to produce the strange-tasting stuff? Jackie—never one to embrace derivative *anything*—would surely keep clear of such marketing hype; she engaged in her healing arts in their original, pure form.

Would Jackie . . .

◆ **Get a hair weave?** You bet she would. As early as the White House and certainly later, she often sported falls to lengthen and thicken the appearance of her 'do, and she even wore the occasional wig, too—causing all sorts of speculation in the press. Such hair helpers are totally acceptable today—just don't get something that's so far from your natural hair as to arouse suspicion.

◆ **Follow a low-carb diet?** Sure—within limits. She was ahead of her time in terms of avoiding high-carb, sugary foods. Except for that toast with honey she liked on her breakfast tray. With her silver palate, she would also shun those nasty Atkins-branded food products on the market.

◆ **Practice sweaty, hot-room Bikram yoga?** Absolutely. In fact, the room at 1040 Fifth Avenue that she used for her yoga sessions with Tillie Weitzner wasn't air-conditioned and occasionally reached 100 degrees. So she'd love steamy, body-slimming Bikram for its quick-acting effects.

Get a Brazilian? Certainly not. Although she was fastidious and understood the need to tend to things down there, she didn't believe that body rituals should be subject to trends. Besides, the look is extreme — and not in any way natural beyond infancy. But she would love the twisted-thread brow-shaping technique available today. The results are precise — and there's the tie to the Eastern cultures that so intrigued her.

Go for strong nail colors? No and yes: No on her perennially bitten fingernails, and yes on her toes. Later in life, she preferred a sassy fuchsia on the feet, which she had applied every three to four weeks during her hair color touch-ups at New York's Thomas Morrissey salon. But some hues — green, for one, according to Coco Chanel — look horrible against the skin, so go for flesh-flattering shades instead.

Share a shrink with her mate? No way. She wrote the dictionary entry on privacy, and knew that even professionals can spring a leak. Besides, in her day, men were much less apt to go there. A word to the wise: Couples work can be enlightening, but if your pro slips and refers to your secret crush on your boss, there's no going back. So have and hold a doc of your own.

Chapter 4

The Art of Attachment:

Lessons on Sex, Marriage, and
Men of Consequence

> "I don't think there are many men
> who are faithful to their wives."
> —JBKO

As the daughter of a rakishly handsome bon vivant and as the wife of two husbands with the means to philander on multiple continents, Jackie knew men. She could intuitively court them, befriend them, summon them to her various causes. Some within the Kennedy clan may have jokingly called her "the Deb," but Jackie—who could tease out the playful side of characters as disparate as Nureyev, Kissinger, de Gaulle, and Brando—often managed to have the last laugh. A demure interloper, she navigated a masculine world with greater skill than most men.

As can you.

Some might find it reassuring to know that Jackie wasn't always the picture of confidence—she suffered from a healthy dose of self-doubt early on. In high school she fretted that no one would ever marry her and that she'd be lost in a world of ordinariness. Upon graduating from Miss Porter's, her life ambition as stated in the class yearbook was "not to be a housewife." Patrician looks, spiffy riding habits, and beautiful manners made her a girl to watch, but Miss Bouvier was as blind to her own charms as any young woman.

College, international travel, a stint as a photojournalist—and trysts in stylish automobiles—honed her natural talents with the opposite sex. On the surface, men were drawn to her whispery voice and geisha-like composure. On a deeper level, she learned to quietly wield her power as an intellectual equal. Such skills, however, couldn't protect her from romantic hardship. As scenes of Camelot filled the national imagination, Jackie would have to compartmentalize her emotions to handle the constant specter of infidelity. While she didn't always make choices other women could live with, she did stick to her convictions and carried on with strength and guile (albeit with a hint of "I'm watching you through my sunglasses" naughtiness).

◆ ◆ ◆

"You always hear these stories that Jackie spoke quietly
so men would lean in. So I do that every now and again,
just to see, are they going to? But no, they turn away!"
—JOAN RIVERS, COMEDIENNE

◆ ◆ ◆

ACQUISITION TACTICS 101

Unlike her classmates at Vassar (which, mind you, was the all-female equivalent of Harvard or Yale in her day), Jackie had little use for giddiness when it came to men. A fierce competitor who accepted only winning, she treated the acquisition of suitable men as both an art and a business—a discipline to approach with the utmost seriousness. One might fault her father, John "Black Jack" Bouvier, with giving her such an unromantic view of the male species.

Yet it was his cocktail of womanizing, drinking, money woes, and vanity that ironically prepared her for the less attractive side of men. In fact, her father convinced her that cheating was in a man's DNA, a lesson that helped her never to take such behavior personally.

Jackie's arsenal of wooing weaponry was vast. Among her more successful spearing techniques:

Use flaws to your advantage. Women today, obsessed with ridiculous beauty standards, often strive for a measure of sameness. Pity how these copycats don't recognize—as did Jackie—an opportunity to leverage their beauty marks, Roman noses, and generous behinds as a way to stand out from the crowd. In an essay that won her a prestigious *Vogue* magazine prize, a young Jackie wrote, "I am . . . 5'7" . . . with brown hair and eyes so unfortunately far apart that it takes three weeks to have a pair of glasses made." The lady doth protest too much. As we all know, Jackie would later become famous for wearing a pair of those supposedly awkward (sun)glasses. She also managed to turn her uglyduckling hair into an international phenomenon, "the Swan."

Don't spook men needlessly. Although she was curious and well read, a young Jackie opted to deflate her smarts around bachelors, feigning nervousness, for instance, about exams or her ability to finish coursework. As she astutely understood, an independent woman can afford to reveal her true, strong self to a man over time. So don't overwhelm your dates with early shock-and-awe tactics (trilling in Russian over dinner, for example, or gloating over high grades). Give them a chance to appreciate your other, more womanly arts first.

Speak softly (and carry a good lipstick). Jackie made a concerted effort to temper her conversational voice sometime during college. She willed herself to speak sotto voce—typically drawing out the S in words like "yesssssss." Gentlemen callers found the trait seductive; it also afforded her the kind of attention a conspiratorial whisper can conjure. Even as a young man, admirers such as Thomas Guinzburg (a college-age friend of Jackie's and later her boss at Viking) "found that pretty attractive."

PEARL

Since this breathy technique compels a man to lean closer to hear you (thus bringing your mouth into greater focus), be sure to have your lips primed with a flattering—and preferably unflavored—color.

Don't scoff at matchmaking. Jackie was by no means a fan of the practice, but it is how she and Jack got together. Be particularly open to matchmaking overtures when the fixer-uppers know you and the gentleman equally well. To make the rendezvous worth your while, arrange to meet over lunch or dinner—not just drinks or coffee. After all, a girl's got to eat. And beverage-only dates are an early sign of commitment issues or, worse, cheapness.

Be detached, and tune out all reality "dating" shows. Jackie's father had firm opinions about how a woman should capture a man: "Play hard to get!" he'd admonish repeatedly. She took his advice seriously, preferring to exude nonchalance rather than commit quickly or easily. Admirers complained that it was tough to get a chaste kiss out of her, let alone anything more. Women today, who often fret that their dates have an abundance of bed partners, should take heed. After JFK proposed to Jackie, she took off to Europe for several weeks to supposedly mull over the merits of such a union. Upon her return, the young Kennedy was waiting for her at the airport. Her refusal to let him take her for granted, even after a yearlong courtship, sealed the marriage deal.

Make him the epicenter of your universe—at least until dessert arrives.
Always appear intensely fascinated by the man you're with. Never look
bored, never glance over his shoulder, and always draw him out with
endless questions. The side benefit, and perhaps the real art, is that
this tactic allows you as a woman to remain enigmatic by staying
mum about yourself. And few men can resist such a flattering amount
of interest. When all else failed, Jackie was able to hold forth on certain subjects—animals and art in particular—but her (soft-spoken!)
reporter-like questioning was a strong offensive. So talented was she
that Jackie even made a party crasher—writer Bob Colacello, who
showed up at 1040 with Andy Warhol in the late seventies—feel special by sharing her glass of Perrier with him when the waiter couldn't
be found. "It's *ours*," she purred.

When three's a crowd, make it four. Remind a roaming man that he
isn't the only one with outside love connections. In early 1968, during
her courtship with Ari Onassis, Jackie went off to Mexico with Roswell
Gilpatric, an old acquaintance from her Washington, D.C., days—
even though he was still married. (Subtext: As long as they are eligible,
divorcing men are not necessarily off-limits.) They went so far as to
kiss and flirt in public, and their exploits became fodder for a story in
Women's Wear Daily.

Cozy up to the family kingpin. Many women seek to win over a man's
mother while overlooking the parent who may well hold more influence over him (not to mention the reins of the family fortune). Thanks
mainly to her grandfather, Jackie knew how to handle older powerful
men—especially her father-in-law Joe Kennedy, who favored her and
her smart spunkiness over his other daughters-in-law. She worked her
magic on him, knowing how influential he'd be in getting his son to
move toward a proposal. If a ring is your goal, get to know your prospec-
tive father-in-law's favorite sports teams, car models, liquor brands, and
hobbies. Carry relevant periodicals and scalped tickets in your purse
as necessary. Above all, dare to flirt a bit. Jackie did.

It isn't over until the altar. Practical to her core, Jackie had no qualms about keeping her options open during her first—yes, first— engagement, to John Husted in 1952. She went about town with, among others, a dreamy journalist who had been at the *Washington Times-Herald*. Was this good-girl behavior? Probably not. Did she follow her gut instincts, and eventually land a future president instead? You get the idea: An engagement is a quaint plan, yet one that is subject to change if you happen upon a more suitable mate. The real dance, dear, begins at your wedding reception.

PICKING A DATE VS. A MATE
(and Recognizing the Difference)

It is unwise to hook up with men who are merely outwardly eligible— i.e., the multitude of socially inept bankers and lawyers and admen who stuff themselves into custom-made Italian suits but have no interest in seeing Rome; or who purchase season tickets to the opera only to dash out at the first curtain. You'll do far better to choose a successful, broad-minded man who not only looks good (albeit not *too* good— more on that shortly), but can give you the platform you so richly deserve.

Business leaders, entrepreneurs, politicians, artists, and other (employed) intellectuals are all fine candidates. So, too, are emotionally balanced men with trust funds—as long as they have some cause or activity to keep their time, and minds, occupied.

Jackie understood these precepts perfectly. She judged men as much on their professional prospects as on their looks, their minds, and their bank accounts. She gave preference to suitors who had great physical presence (even if squat—Ari Onassis was nearly a head shorter than she) and were masters at flattery.

A Note about Deflowering

The lone—albeit unsubstantiated—account on this topic is that Jackie lost her virginity at the age of 20, in France, to the son of a famous writer. The Paris interlude allegedly took place in a stalled elevator (or *ascenseur calé*, which sounds far more glamorous). Her reaction to the business: "Oh, is that all there is to it?" Whether it was a romantic myth of her own or others' creation, the lesson is the same: If you have yet to yield your maidenhood, remember that it's best done in memorable fashion. Boozy post-prom encounters are out of the question. After all, this is an occasion where pomp and storytelling count. Details of the rite (time, place, duration) are key. Given our digital age, so, too, is your partner's potential "Google factor." This demands you choose your man with posterity in mind. When typing his name into a search engine twenty years from now, you don't want to recoil at what pops up (worst-case scenario: "Your search did not match any documents").

◆ Know Where the Boys Are ◆

As Jackie didn't much believe in matchmaking, she would probably subscribe to the dictum "sell thyself." It is therefore recommended to get on a meaningful social rotation. The following are some choice venues, along with symbols to denote the financial implications for each.

§§§ Onassis bucks, or super connections, required
§§ Worth saving for
§ Jackie on a budget

Swell parties. Defined, for these purposes, as those events likely to draw a group of people who are more attractive than boorish, and are worth knowing for at least three hours. Soirees with dancing—a seductive art Jackie mastered through lessons—make particularly good pickup places. Men love a woman who sways her hips to a good rap or rumba beat (the latter was Jackie's fave). §§

Concerts. Meaning those staged in auditoriums with plush seats—not the plastic kind typical of sports arenas. The logic here is simple: A higher seat fabric grade is likely to attract a higher grade of man. The ballet, opera, and symphony pack in a wealth of connected, cultured types. (Jackie was a trustee of the American Ballet Theatre.) And yes, these bastions of old money are fast attracting more young and single fans. To make the best use of intermission time, bring opera glasses and do a quick pan and scan before the lights go down. §

Smart cafés (particularly those in foreign cities). There's nothing like the roar of a Ferrari pulling up to an Italian café—especially when the object of the driver's attention is you. Wear dark shades, tote plenty of reading material, and cross your legs, ladylike, at the ankles. Lap up pastries and other local delicacies (as did Jackie) as a way to express your appetites to those foreign swains. And do so in the before- and after-work hours and on weekends, when the *employed* swains surface. Incidentally, Starbucks does not qualify as a "smart" café, which must always have table service. §§

Any embassy. As Jackie discovered in India, it is easy to stand out in places populated by people with different accents, cultural norms, and complexions. If international travel isn't imminent, embassies and consulates are good bets. The diplomatic service attracts adventurous single men who are gifted in several tongues, and functions held at these splendid places often have favorable male-to-female ratios. Getting in shouldn't be a big problem. Shoot for a holiday fete, such as Sweden's pre-Christmas St. Lucia festival. The partying natives will be flattered to indulge your curiosity for their unusual customs. (In this instance, singing Swedish Christmas songs as a flaming-candle wreath burns atop one's head.) §

Church events. The Catholic Church was central to Jackie's strict upbringing. Assuming the blue-haired crowd at the after-service coffee hour just depresses you, head for off-peak and nonecumenical events sponsored by the church. If your own place of worship doesn't have a healthy roster of pottery classes and John Donne poetry readings, it's okay to recreationally stray—to a church in a wealthier zip code. §

Schools you couldn't get into. Finding a good man is like discovering precious ore—you have to pan from the richest tributaries. No need to let campus boundaries hinder you, then. Since Vassar was a women's college at the time, Jackie and her crew naturally made social forays to other learning labs. (Her favorites were Yale and Harvard.) Cross-campus dating permits you to discreetly try on multiple men for size while never being too available (i.e., seen at the library every night). Crashing foreign gates also puts you in the ranks of "the other woman," driving your female competition wild and making you a bit of an exotic catch to men. §

Antique fairs/auction houses. Not just haunts for gay men, these places are a magnet for straight art-history types with a taste for finer things— i.e., furniture and *objets* of the pre-Pottery Barn era. With any luck, you just might bag a diamond dealer like Maurice Tempelsman, Jackie's loyal, post-Ari companion. §

At and around the office. Throw away the company manual on this one. If Jackie used her work environment to cast about for a mate, why shouldn't you? She viewed her first paying job, as the *Times-Herald's* "Inquiring Camera Girl," as a great way to seek out men. Of course, she kept her lens well trained outside the scope of the newsroom. They don't call her favored reporting technique the "man-on-the-street interview" for nothing. §

Yacht clubs, hunt clubs, nightclubs. Any venue, in other words, where the group is bound by a common passion and where limb-loosening booze is readily available. Most women mess up the order, heading to nightclubs as ingénues. Wrong! Unless you want to meet only players, head to the tonier sanctums in youth—country clubs and the like— when, under their parents' watch, young men are apt to be on their best behavior. Save the night-crawling (Jackie ducked into scenes like El Morocco and Studio 54 in the seventies) for later, when you'll be better equipped to weed out the poseurs. $-$$$

On the tennis court, at the riding stables. In a sports context, far better to find a mate on the field than on the sidelines—no matter how novice your skills. As Jackie once advised her sister-in-law Joan, why worry about your prowess at the game "when men are attracted by the feminine way you play?" A disclaimer: Avoid picking up men at your regular gym. By definition, that must fall under the category of private space/time, and should therefore be left as a neutral zone. $$-$$$

PLAY WITH THE BOYS, BUT CHOOSE A MAN OF SUBSTANCE

Do you choose your Jimmy Choo shoes more carefully than your relationships? Are you stymied by the mind-numbing reality of an era in which TV shows goad strangers to the altar, and ordinary men seem to have astonishing access to supermodels?

Few women today could claim a broader range of gentlemen callers—and rich scenarios—than Jackie. Other than a handsome president and a "squiggly" (as she called Ari) shipping tycoon, her quarry included Warren Beatty, producer Mike Nichols, and journalist Pete Hamill.

Male Type No vs. Male Type O

Male Type No

- Men who weigh less than you do—or who have smaller feet
- Dentists from New Jersey
- Men who can't dance
- Men with a sense of entitlement
- Philanderers who make no attempt to hide their infidelity
- Pretentious playboys (in the style of *Le Bourgeois Gentilhomme*)

Male Type O

- Men with keen minds (who aren't intimidated by yours)
- Enthusiastic flatterers
- Men who know how to wield a soup spoon (scoop outward)
- Men with pedigrees
- Men who like your children
- Men who know quality (i.e., you) when they see it

Such diversity was testament to her open, creative mind (as well as one prone to human folly: She did, after all, carry on with a few married men). Intrepid Jackie may have kept the mix interesting, but she did so with a long-term view that favored substance and practicality above all else.

The art is to sort men by type as easily as you would your winter clothes from your summer frocks.

Consider:

Put men in their proper place. In Jackie's case, we can identify several distinct male strains. JFK represented what we can call the PT (Presidential Type, as in charismatic and ambitious to a fault). Ari was the BBT (Bootstrapper Billionaire Type), and Maurice Tempelsman stood for ULT (Unconditional Love Type). Punctuating the journey were her lowercase pts (as in playboy types). Assign labels to the men you are most attracted to and then ask, how best to use them? It would've gone against Jackie's principles, say, to daydream about marrying Warren Beatty or to casually date a man with senatorial potential.

Make sure he is age-appropriate. Chronological age should make little difference. However, assuming you want to go the distance with a man, he does need to act his age. A few hints:

Any man over thirty who considers clubs and bars to be his main social outlet falls solidly into the playboy/dunce category. It doesn't matter if he's got a Harvard MBA. Also not ready for prime time are fortyish men who lie about their age, dye or goop up their hair, and have never been married. Steer clear, too, of men over 50 who pine for a Porsche or other fast car they couldn't afford in their youth.

Jackie swerved around all such men, as she equated maturity with dependability. A man who pitifully clings to his glory days is stuck in Act I and is not ready to proceed to Act II—i.e., serious courtship, marriage, and fancy prams. Keep these guys around for fun—for the occasional ego boost, free meal, etc. Any extended contact is at your own risk.

Wandering hands, yes; wandering eyes, no. A man needs to have you ever fixed in his mind, his gaze, his arms. In her younger days, Jackie gave points to men who noticed the smallest details about her, physical or otherwise. And she prized the moments when JFK flattered her (telling her on Inauguration Day, for instance, that she never looked lovelier). As she matured, she came to cherish a man's constancy even more.

Choose admirers who are happy—dare we say grateful?—to be with you. Men who get too excited in the presence of other beauties or who make you feel like an Interchangeable Woman (see "Daily Bred," p. 11) in any way are best left on the shelf.

On a related theme, jettison men who don't treat their mothers with respect. That mom could be you in twenty years' time. Jackie took note of JFK's maternal solicitousness during an early trip to Hyannis Port: When Rose Kennedy called him in from the ocean for a meal, he came forth like a jubilant little boy. In other words, he passed.

Test his platform. Ideally, your other half should open up a second world of opportunities to you. For some, that connotes wealthy circles; for others, it may mean exposure to an intellectual crowd, rich cultural experiences, new places and ideas. Decide early what's important to you, go after it—and don't rule out relocating. After returning from the Sorbonne, Jackie headed to Washington, D.C., to continue her college studies at George Washington University and find a job. She chose the nation's capital over New York because at the time, it was the epicenter of power and social activity. Known as the "Conversation Capital," it brimmed with eligible men.

Notice what he keeps close at hand. Your man's environs provide important clues about his values, passions, and overall True Worth. Does his home contain books (hardcovers get more points than paperbacks), an indication of curiosity and scholarship? Does he subscribe to *The New Yorker* or *Maxim*? Has he spent more money on the ties in his closet than on artwork to adorn the walls? How about photographic evidence of friends, family, favorite trips? A sterile, anonymous environment often means that the man himself is stale.

Jackie's men may have been light-years apart aesthetically (Ari's boat had barstools covered in whale testicle skin; Jack's prized possessions were his books). Still, each expressed himself with aplomb and wit. You don't have to agree with a man's taste—just make sure there's some interior logic to the stuff he does have around. And that he's open to a little reshuffling. (See "En Suite Home," p. 131.)

Love vs. Money

Let us not for a moment denounce the power of true love, but let's also be honest enough to acknowledge that a little extra dough in a man's pocket can help a girl get to "yes." There's nothing wrong with admitting this—to yourself and to friends who may be in a position to set you up. As Jackie herself said, while pondering mates post-JFK, "I can't very well marry a dentist from New Jersey."

Her desire for money and security wasn't necessarily shallow. Having watched her father struggle financially left her worried about her own future. And her mother set the tone by marrying the incredibly well-to-do, old-money Hugh Auchincloss the second time around.

Jackie, who always felt like an outsider in such WASP circles, wasn't about to set herself up for a life of hardship. Many close to her felt that the Kennedy money and later the security afforded by Onassis's fortune were big motivators in her male selection process.

And why shouldn't trust funds, Swiss bank accounts, offshore holdings—you name the financial opiate—at least urge the heart in a more practical direction?

The key is knowing your limits. If you're content on a beer budget, God bless. If, however, you aspire to a truly haute lifestyle, don't indulge in sentimental attachments with men who can't provide ski chalets and yachts. And don't blame us ten years from now when you're well dressed but not in love—every choice comes with trade-offs.

Love vs. Money
(Or, the Art of Staying Above the Line)

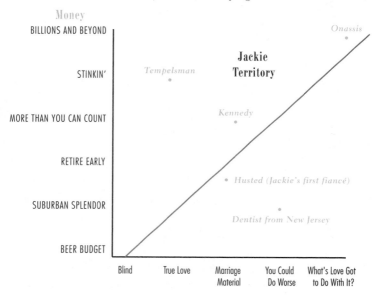

If you're irrevocably drawn to powerful, rich, charismatic men, you'll have some challenges to face that most women won't. But then, who wants to be average? Although blessed with an athletic body and occasionally raunchy sense of humor, Jackie (thanks to her own code of ethics) wasn't in Jack's league when it came to sexual experience. She learned, however, that timing is everything (they apparently loved to have sex in the middle of the day—the illicit-rendezvous scenario). And they were known to gossip about others' sex lives and foibles, or venture into discourse on the Kama Sutra at dinner parties.

Was the gal adventurous? She had to be to share a bed with JFK; but she also must have subscribed to his belief that there are two kinds of women: those you marry and those you sleep with. Above all, she insisted on privacy when it came to matters of her bedroom—a good strategy for every woman. Public displays of affection in the Kennedy years were rare, although later with Ari, she learned how effective a well-placed PDA could be for getting some positive media attention.

◆ ◆ ◆

"Hand-holding in public is so bourgeois—
Jack and Jackie never did that."

—OLEG CASSINI, FASHION DESIGNER,

COUTURIER TO JACKIE IN THE WHITE HOUSE

◆ ◆ ◆

◆ Prelude to Bliss ◆

Although Jackie preferred to be tight-lipped about her premarital escapades, during her three pre-commitment phases (pre-Jack, pre-Ari, pre-Maurice), there was nothing less than a cologne-scented swirl of males around her. She didn't survive all those years on a diet of chaste kisses alone. And neither, we suspect, will you when you decide to take your relationship to the horizontal level.

On giving it up. While it would not be very Jackie-like to dictate volumes on sexual morality, there are a few other topics just too ripe to leave untouched. The most obvious being . . . when to give "it" up? This question becomes rhetorical, of course, in a just-fooling-around, one-night-stand context. Upon more serious play, Jackie's "Inquiring Camera Girl" skills are quite useful—and help create a practical timeline.

Make sure, for example, that you visit his place at least a few times before permitting yourself to be tossed about on those 300-thread-count (or higher) sheets. Jackie (on JFK's arm) canvassed Ari's floating palace, the *Christina*, before they hit the White House. Does he keep his little black book (BlackBerry) out for all to see? Have photos of ex-girlfriends on display? A condom basket by the bed? Detail-oriented Jackie wouldn't put up with such carelessness. It's also wise to meet the neighbors/roommates beforehand. That way, you've penciled yourself into the landscape, allowing for an easy, respectable exit after the deed.

On shacking up. These days, couples waste precious little time before sharing beds, toilets, addresses. We posit—and believe Jackie would concur—that cohabitation is best left to post-grads and old folks. Jackie never lived with a beau before marrying JFK; preserving mystery was always her goal. And if you're an erudite, modern woman, there's something to be said for having a room of one's own. Why fumble over the newspaper, the TV remote, the last shards of soap until you have to? The biggest exceptions come with age. After husband number two, Jackie—long blessed with kids, real estate, and other marital bounty—didn't feel the need to wed again. (Which was prudent, as her boyfriend Maurice was still married, albeit separated.) A bonus of shacking up in your twilight years: You won't face stinging judgment from your parents. They'll be too old (or dead) to care.

On pillow talk. Conventional wisdom holds that single women should be mute on the subject of past loves. Jackie offers a contrary lesson. While not one to blather on about her romantic history with men—talking of conquests is decidedly male—she did wistfully drop an amorous reference here and there. The implication, of course, is that you are acutely, fabulously in demand. Another tip: Always speak well of former dear hearts when you mention them in that coy manner. Dwelling on bad experiences not only is unattractive but also inspires pity—an emotion for which Jackie had little use.

◆ Infidelity Bites ◆

Given all the tumult of her love life, it was infidelity that dealt Jackie the sharpest blow. Still, she armed herself as ably as possible. If you should suffer a similar fate (and statistics suggest you well may), do as Jackie did: Decide whether to stay or go. But don't waffle, and refuse the role of weak, defeated woman. Take pains to look smashing throughout the messy business (red is an appropriate "go to hell" color). If you choose to stay with the cad, learn from a few Jackie-esque coping methods:

Artful revenge. If you must fight fire with fire, be sure to use an emotional accelerant. Rather than scream in public or smash the White House china to bits, Jackie employed Machiavellian tactics with her first roaming husband. Tired of sidestepping his antics, she made international headlines in 1962 by going sexy-swimming with Fiat chairman Gianni Agnelli on the Amalfi Coast. The gesture wasn't lost on an irked JFK, who sent a terse cable to Italy: "A little more Caroline and less Agnelli."

Her response? She went scuba diving with the Italian magnate — in a smashing Oleg Cassini one-piece, thank you very much.

Marital psyops. For the truly bold, it can also be rather effective — or at least satisfying — to place yourself in harm's way. This requires you to steel yourself against the emotions of the moment and make a premeditated move to disrupt your man's interludes. Cell phone records and credit card receipts can be handy leads to follow, but in Jackie's case she had the benefit of the international press covering Ari's every move. After a Paris tryst with his longtime love Maria Callas was documented by the foreign papers, Jackie made haste to Paris and cleverly had Ari take her to dine at the same *boite*, sitting at the same table as he had with Callas. A few lens men were called to the scene as well. The deft move not only forced Onassis into the role of bad dog by rubbing his nose in it, but also crushed Callas's ego in the process.

Dis(appearing) acts. In any marriage, it is essential to spend a certain amount of time apart to keep one's habits, friends, sanity. In relationships marred by infidelity, absence and distance can serve an entirely different purpose. By fleeing the scene of the crime, you may spare yourself the need to pop sedatives—and handily rip away your man's cover of a happy marriage. Suddenly, business colleagues, visiting relatives, and the dry cleaner all require explanations—triggering stress for him and sympathy for you.

When Jackie tired of too many blond poolside guests at the White House, she would repair to Glen Ora or to the Kennedy compound in Palm Beach, leaving the president to host dignitaries alone.

Shop. When Jackie grew distraught over Jack's shenanigans, she'd sometimes do what the best of us do: spend money. Designer clothes, jewelry, home renovations—no expense was spared, despite the president's constant harping on budgets. Best to do your retail rounds on credit, so your mate will be forced to see exactly how much you've spent on those limited-edition La Perla panties. (The ones you won't be modeling for him anytime soon.)

Avoid unhappy returns. How awful to come home to a sweaty sofa surprise. Never willing to risk finding JFK in illicit acts, Jackie was known to cable him with details about any possible early return from a trip abroad. Reach out with your e-mail, BlackBerry, cell phone, whatever, to preempt ugly scenes.

Maintain a brave exterior, but also seek wise counsel. Do make every attempt to exorcise your relationship demons through therapy, yoga, sisterly solidarity, or whatever else works for you. Even intensely private Jackie knew not to obscure her every emotion. For balancing, she visited a New York psychiatrist regularly. She also bonded with women who suffered similar strife, including her Kennedy sisters-in-law and Carly Simon, whose marriage to James Taylor was on the rocks.

ON SEXUAL AIDS AND ELIXIRS

Porn (Yes to X-Men). A little pornography can be good for a marriage. Just don't make your appetite for the genre too public. Jackie learned this lesson in 1969, when she accompanied Onassis to the X-rated Swedish film *I Am Curious (Yellow)*. Upon exiting the theater early, she was captured by photographers.

Multiple Positions (Be O-So-Flexible). Even a First Lady must be open to mild acrobatics, so limber up. Jack used to brag that he hadn't had a woman until he'd "had her three ways."

Backseat Sex (Park to Pet). Just make sure that the steel steed is a cool or current model. During their early courtship, Jack and Jackie were known to do some surreptitious groping—in Jack's Buick.

Tantric Sex (Don't Be Sari). It's possible that Jackie picked up more than a few rubies on her trips to India. After all, this was a woman who pursued medical advice to get in touch with her erogenous zones and better please her first husband. Eager for sexual know-how (and ever keen on exotic cultures), Jackie would probably embrace the Tantric techniques that are so in vogue today.

♦ ♦ ♦

*"It's utterly brilliant that Jackie sought help to learn
about her female anatomy. It's about vulnerability.
Where else would she have learned about her vagina?
People weren't pulling out manuals. Talk about
metaphors—that you need to consult a pro to get to
know the center of yourself, your soul."*

—EVE ENSLER, PLAYWRIGHT, ACTOR, ACTIVIST,
AND AUTHOR OF *THE VAGINA MONOLOGUES*

♦ ♦ ♦

Viagra (Empty That Pillbox). A chest-thumping Ari claimed
that he and his younger wife enjoyed as many as five couplings per
night. That's a lot of work, even for a man who was said to have
taken sheep-cell injections for virility. Surely Jackie would've preferred him to pop a little blue pill over the *Animal Farm* routine.

Mile-High Sex (Take It Off Before Landing). Mr. and
Mrs. Onassis liked to make love in odd places—especially aboard
luxury craft. These included a converted section of an Olympic
Airways jet (Ari owned the carrier) and the dinghy of the *Christina*.

HAVING YOUR WAY WITH POWERFUL MEN

In her days as an editor in New York, Jackie once remarked that she
wasn't "into power." Whether she meant as a book subject or in her own
personal life, or both, remains unclear—and a tad suspect. However,

we do know that Jackie had cunning ways with men in lofty places. Whether they were unreliable (like her father), self-made (like Ari), or born into dynasties (JFK), she definitely knew how to throw her delicate weight around to get what she required.

◆ Give Him a Baby Nickname ◆

In their downtime, many a powerful man wants to be fawned over. In what might be described as mild domination, Jackie both tamed and thrilled JFK, the most powerful man on the planet, with a baby nickname: Bunny. No fool, she was known to utter it only once in public.

◆ Offer Your Opinion, But Let Him Think You Didn't ◆

Jackie knew how to impose her will on unsuspecting types—husbands included. Her ruse was to do so in a manner that was matter-of-fact, never confrontational. Jackie and JFK loved to discuss the vicissitudes of human nature. While this was mostly social-hour banter, Jackie would latch on to the human-interest angle in order to occasionally comment on national policy. When Jack was hard at work drafting his book *Profiles in Courage*, a stealthy Jackie, who studied government at Georgetown University, was said to have helped foment the work's thesis. Gently, of course.

◆ Make Your Boyfriend the King of Your Castle ◆

On many late-in-life occasions, Jackie asked Tempelsman to play party host at her Fifth Avenue apartment. In the absence of a wedding band, such license gives a man a sense of control—even when his name is not on the mortgage. The arrangement worked well for Jackie and Maurice. Over the years, he picked up more influence in the household, and his presence signaled his stature in Jackie's life to all guests.

EXIT STRATEGIES:
Drills for Bowing Out

An exacting woman knows how to remove herself from circumstances that no longer suit her purposes. As such times are apt to arise, it is best to prepare for—even script—them in advance.

Jackie would condone this sort of choreographed pas de deux. An avid organizer, planner, and scheduler, she was rarely caught off guard. Say you've given a suitor adequate time to win your charms (tap, tap, tapping on your Cartier Tank Française), yet he still fails to move you.

Or maybe the roles are reversed and the fool (inexplicably!) dumps you on your 29th birthday. No matter. You must exit the situation as elegantly as you entered it, causing a minimum of pain and embarrassment as you turn away. Jackie was known to detest messy vocal overtures. Leave screaming and other dramatic maneuvers to the less highly evolved (or to opera stars).

❖ Exit Strategy No. 1 ❖

Draft a standard response for casual bow-outs. Got a man who calls you for dinner, but just isn't your dish? Try a slightly vague rejoinder, one that will suit you time and again. Something like, "Oh, I'm afraid that won't be possible." Or, "Oh, you're so thoughtful, but I'm terribly busy these days." A smart man gets the picture quickly. These are the sort of polite turn-downs Jackie used with with groveling guys as a Washington, D.C., ingenue.

❖ Exit Strategy No. 2 ❖

If you break it off, spare words to spare feelings. Don't get into a whole to-do about why things didn't pan out or who's to blame. Jackie worked on the theory that scarred emotions heal more quickly this way. To nullify her engagement to Wall Streeter John Husted, she simply placed her engagement ring in his pocket.

✦ Exit Strategy No. 3 ✦

Marry (much) older, to increase the odds that your husband naturally precedes you in death. Jackie and Ari were roughly a quarter of a century apart in age. After six years of marriage, rumors had it that the two were considering divorce—an event that turned out to be unnecessary upon his demise, of pneumonia, in 1975. Widowed for the second time, a youngish Jackie, only in her mid-forties, still had plenty of years for happy romance.

OTHER USES FOR THE OTHER SEX

Well before short-listing Ari as second-husband material, First Lady Jackie and sister Lee Radziwill packed their Capri pants and boarded the Greek tycoon's yacht for an island vacation. During the Mediterranean romp, it was somewhat unclear who was courting whom (Lee had been romantically involved with Onassis for months.) The Greek tycoon, though, ended up bestowing the more lavish parting gift— rubies, of course—on Jackie.

We all know where those innocent sparks between her and Ari eventually led. But don't overlook the broader lesson: With the possible exclusion of gay friends and first cousins, every man in your social set (or above, darlings) is a potential mate—either now or in the future—and must at all times be treated as such. That said, it can pay to harness the resources of your male coterie for more immediate endeavors.

To negotiate delicate matters. By some accounts, Jackie summoned a bevy of male advisors to tend to the awkward business of a prenuptial agreement. Ditto upon Onassis's death when negotiations for a settlement with Christina got hot. Call upon male acquaintances to avoid messy confrontations yourself. This might be anything from haggling with a chauvinistic car dealer to telling the parish priest that you really do mind when he pats you on the backside.

To remind your man that you're still a hot number. Jackie kept a number of would-be gentlemen callers at arm's length during her marriage to JFK. Notable among them was Robert McNamara, JFK's secretary of defense. The two would dine together, read poetry together, and often talked as close friends. Jackie was drawn to his charm, warmth, and intellect. McNamara was impressed by her intelligence, and said that with him, "she was flirtatious."

As vehicles to places of privilege. On occasion, even a young Jackie needed a social lift. The Debutante of the Year may have been a fine student, but she turned to her Uncle "Lefty" Lewis, Hugh Auchincloss's brother-in-law, to recommend her to the prestigious Paris Sorbonne. Her studies there, and her subsequent travels through Europe, did much to shape her appreciation for art and literature.

For bestowing rainy-day gifts. Jackie had no qualms about accepting spoils from all manner of men—relatives to potentates. During her White House years, she racked up jewelry, artwork, and even a couple of well-bred horses. And early in her second marriage, she adored finding the diamond-studded bracelets Ari would hide on her breakfast tray. The key here is not to get overly sentimental about such material riches, because someday you may need to "monetize"—i.e., pawn or exchange—the goods. As her tastes evolved, Jackie was known to sell off her bounty to acquire things she liked better (see "Goal Digger," p. 217).

As escorts/travel companions. It was no secret that Jackie had more male than female friends. Whether married, gay, or substantially older than she, they often made for excellent travel companions (see "Building Your Inner Temple," p. 170). Former Deputy Secretary of Defense Ros Gilpatric was one, illustrator Charles Addams another. She didn't mind speculation about their intimate involvement. A big advantage to taking off with men rather than women: You won't have to worry about dressing competitively (as Jackie did when traveling with Lee).

As decoys. Simple creatures, men are most interested in the woman who is least available. Rather than go to a party or dinner with a gaggle of girlfriends, or by yourself, solicit a platonic male friend to accompany you when you're on the prowl. After Ari's death, Jackie kept erudite males such as *The New Yorker* writer Brendan Gill on call for just this purpose. To make others gaze at you over their martini glasses, your man must be a convincing, attentive date: Whispering, drink-fetching, and cackling can all be a part of your harmless ruse. Remember, the best accessories never come cheap. So pay your beard's way if you must.

Would Jackie . . .

- **Engage in Internet exploits?** To a certain degree, yes. Lord knows she had the pick of any litter she wanted, but such sites as match.com would've piqued her curiosity—at least about the female competition. We can also imagine her exploring (anonymously) the realms of the soft, um, sexual sites. The Paris Hilton video would've fascinated her.

- **Take female Viagra?** Absolutely. She was said to join Ari in getting live sheep-cell injections, so swallowing the women's version of the little blue pill for some heightened gratification would have been a simpler pleasure.

Date interracially? Yep. Being a woman of the world practically demands a few cross-cultural exchanges. And think about it: A Greek, a Jew—these were the equivalent of mixed relations in Jackie's day. She was also defensive of intermarriages at a time when they were socially shocking, including the union of Sammy Davis, Jr., and his Swedish wife, Mai Britt.

Flirt with a teacher? Sí, sí—and did, with her dashing art instructor while traveling in Venice as a young woman with Lee. Just be sure your motive is to raise your culture quotient—not your grade point average.

Inform an ex of her intention to marry someone else? Yes, as it's the thing to do—especially if you've remained on good terms, the affair was recent, and the ex is still loitering in Singlesville. When Jackie became (temporarily) betrothed to John Husted, she sent a crisp note to an ex to let him know directly that she was altar-bound.

Tell on people having affairs? No. Jackie never spilled the dirt on her voraciously womanizing father to her mother, stayed mum on JFK's antics, and stood by Ari, despite his ongoing affair with Maria Callas. She had lived with the pain of too much information, and therefore wouldn't inflict it on others.

Bust up a couple? Since all's fair in love and war, yes—although not always intentionally, and never in a calculated, mean-spirited manner. There was Roswell Gilpatric, whose wife left him after Jackie's affectionate correspondence with him got leaked to the press, and Maurice Tempelsman, who remained legally married throughout his time with Jackie. To name only two.

Chapter 5

En Suite Home:

Perfecting Your Domestic Pitch

> *"I do think every room should have a purpose."*
> —JBKO

From the White House to 1040 Fifth Avenue and Martha's Vineyard, Jackie's residences (more than a dozen during her adulthood) were the product of an unerring eye: grand rooms humbled by a copper pot of flowers; Greek alabaster sculptures mingling with plebeian baskets from—could it be?—Pier 1. The spaces were also intensely personal, a reflection of both her public and private journeys: Loot from the Presidential days as well as her favorite books and artwork were always on display.

Jackie believed that overt formality—Versailles, Trump Tower, take your pick—had little place in the modern abode. As she learned from a trusted style mentor, the über-wealthy Bunny Mellon, no individual thing should stand out; the tableau of paintings and furniture and tchotchkes should make both the owner and the visitor feel at ease, never put upon.

Expressed another way, you want a home that oozes sophistication, but also foils would-be thieves. As decorator Richard Keith Langham observed about Jackie's Fifth Avenue lair: "Her taste was so quiet, that, unless you had some knowledge, you would never notice how fine the pieces were. There were a lot of French and Italian Old Master drawings and watercolors. It felt like a family apartment—cozy, warm, friendly."

Homefront hauteur, of course, doesn't develop overnight. Jackie was an avid sampler of decorative ideas, particularly during the early years of her marriage, when she was prone to jettisoning color schemes and furniture pieces, to JFK's chagrin. Jackie's ephemeral design sense was such that she changed the living room of their N Street Georgetown house three times within almost as many months.

Ever theatrical, Jackie also viewed the home as a grand set: a malleable, working stage on which to play out the daily sketches of life, from inveterate hostess (cocktail tray, please) to doting mother—even a sometimes cook. In the building process, aptly, she rehearsed: When planning her oceanview Martha's Vineyard home in the late seventies, Jackie plotted the architect's renderings in the sand in order to feel the scale of the rooms.

ART DIRECTING YOUR PALACE

The staging of your home should commence right away, before the boxes are unpacked and post-moving inertia sets in. Jackie immediately got to decorating her residences, including the White House. In fact, she began brainstorming for the *Maison Blanche* restoration well in advance, while recuperating in Palm Beach after the birth of John Jr. Just two days after marrying Onassis, she flew society decorator Billy Baldwin to her side.

✦ ✦ ✦

"So many clients want to create a façade—an interior that presents the face of who they'd like to be, using references they don't understand. Jackie would never do that."

—THOM FILICIA, INTERIOR DECORATOR, AKA
THE "DESIGN DOCTOR," *QUEER EYE FOR THE STRAIGHT GUY*

✦ ✦ ✦

Figure Your Budget Ratio

Don't wonder "How much shall I spend?" but rather, "How much is warranted?" One solution is to calculate a simple house-cost-to-design ratio, a loose approximation of how Jackie managed her own gyrating budgets.

The Kennedys' second Georgetown home, a three-story brick Federal affair, cost $82,000. Jackie spent an additional $18,000 decorating it. Cost-to-design ratio: about four to one.

The ante increased considerably a decade later, at 1040 Fifth Avenue, her most permanent residence. That swanky 15-room apartment cost about $200,000, and she was thought to have spent an additional $125,000 gussying it up. In this lofty abode, notice how the cost-to-design ratio soared, to about two to one.

Mind you, we're only talking decorating costs here—furniture, painting, accessories, window treatments, etc. Interior demolition jobs and renovation projects technically fall under a different budget line. If, however, you encounter resistance from a mate, gently explain that you are restoring vs. redecorating the home. This was Jackie's clever way of casting the White House redo, which was really a grand interior design project. She knew that the public wouldn't balk at such a scholarly notion.

Temporary residence—be it in the White House or a rental—is a poor excuse to scrimp. You may not care to invest as much as an owner, but if you operate in frat house/transient mode, your place will feel more like a way station than home. Perhaps that's why Jackie freely spent $10,000 to trick out an estate in Virginia hunt country called Glen Ora, which the First Family rented for two years.

Assuming you do plan to add wallpaper or change the hideous plastic toilet flush handle, be sure to get permission from your landlord and be prepared to return things to their original (even if less grand) state upon your exit. When the Kennedys left Glen Ora, they complied by repainting and removing slipcovers from furniture that had offended Jackie's eye.

◆ Call In a Design Doctor—or Two ◆

Why? Because you don't want your place to seem as if it's been decorated "by a wholesale furniture store during a January clearance"—which is how Jackie described the sad state of affairs at 1600 Pennsylvania Avenue before taking matters into her own hands, forming the White House Fine Arts Committee to properly refurbish the place.

Pros generally know more than you do—about period styles, color schemes, and symmetry. They can talk you out of Formica countertops, leaving wisdom and discounted Carrera marble in their wake. Jackie, who studied interior design herself, had a direct line to the world's snootiest society decorators (Billy Baldwin, Sister Parish, Stéphane Boudin, and Keith Irvine, to name a few). But today's populist design community is more accessible than ever, from shelter magazines like *Dwell* to tube obsessions such as the Home & Garden Television channel. Interior decorators and consultants are also available for hire by the hour, or by the room.

Take the time to screen several and "pick their brains." That's what Jackie would do: According to Joseph Karitas, who served on the White House staff, "She always liked to get someone else's ideas first before she would commit herself to any definite plan."

If possible, court multiple decorators at once. This pits them against one another competitively, and can set off price wars in your favor. While applying her touch to Onassis's homes in Greece, Jackie had her design squad scrambling. Decorator Keith Irvine recalled, "I found out . . . that she was asking Billy Baldwin and me for all the same things, and whoever got it cheaper or got it there first got the sale."

To better understand their choices, put decorators through their paces. Challenge every sconce, carpet, and doggie bed, asking, "Why would you do that?"—a favorite refrain of Jackie's, according to Irvine.

Besides, you're too clever to hang on every morsel of advice. When you've got conviction—about why something looks brilliant in a different color or in another corner of the room—go with it.

Jackie defied the decorative decree of none other than connoisseur-collector Henry du Pont, the White House Fine Arts Committee chairman, who advised her that still life paintings were—*tsk, tsk*—appropriate only for dining rooms. A mock-contrite Jackie, having hung pictures of flowers in the White House's Red Room, said, "How awful of us not to know. . . . We're so ignorant. Thank goodness you've told us. They'll be down right away." The paintings disappeared temporarily, but were quickly put back where they'd been.

Shuffle Your Stuff

A home should always evolve, yet not necessarily with new sofas, sconces, and tables. The best way to keep your look lively? Do a massive (or mini) reorganization from time to time. "Jackie understood that you don't buy or live in a set room," says decorator Irvine. "You move things." At least every few years, recruit a few friends—and maybe even a pro—to redistribute everything from pictures and rugs to chaises. You'll be surprised by the magical transformation.

DEFINE YOUR "TREASURES" AND "HORRORS"

Set some basic decorative ground rules by defining the things that you absolutely love and absolutely abhor. Though her taste certainly morphed over time, Jackie kept a running list of what she called "Treasures" and

"Horrors." For her, no-nos included Victorian mirrors; anything French and ending in a Roman numeral was typically a keeper.

Make your own list clear to all potential interior decorators, roommates, and husbands. Men, it seems, don't cotton to the actual legwork required to beautify a home. A survey by the American Furniture Manufacturers Association reported that 78 percent of women respondents loved decorating more than almost any activity; 74 percent of men said they loathed nothing more.

◆ Avoid the Overly Matched Look ◆

This may suit a hotel, but the effect can be awful in your living spaces—especially when applied to upholstered pieces. Jackie flatly rejected entire sets of like-colored chairs, saying that such a palette "gives a suite look which I hate." In planning for a set of ten side chairs for the private Yellow Oval Room in the White House, she had six covered in a gold silk brocade, and four done up in a brown fabric. (Notice how she didn't do five and five—that would have been too Hilton-esque.) Curtains and wall treatments, on the other hand, can be simpatico, to create a sweeping, seamless effect.

◆ Rescue Old Gems ◆

The White House restoration had Jackie digging through back rooms and warehouses for improbable treasures long hidden: heart-backed chairs used by Rutherford B. Hayes; an ornate (and noisy) crystal chandelier purchased by President Grant. She even went so far as to peel battle-scene wallpaper from a Maryland house under demolition and install it (cost at the time: $12,500) in the family dining room.

Your search-and-rescue expedition may go only as far as your mom's attic, or the thrift shop, where you may find a battered but beautifully shaped chaise and recognize its reupholstered potential. A lovely chair with good bones may cost only about $700 to re-cover and replump. That's a fraction of the price of a quality chair you'd find in a decorator's showroom.

Whose Stuff Where?

You must never attempt to remove all of the "horrors" from your mate's favorite spaces—key advice for folks over 30, who can get very touchy when their decorative sense, or lack thereof, is challenged. Think of this as your own Nuclear (Family) Test Ban Treaty: You agree not to banish his velour La-Z-Boy recliner, and he won't challenge your selection of a custom-made Swedish platform bed.

Learn to compromise, and suck up some defeats. In the White House, Jackie conspired to take away JFK's back-comforting rocker, but lost the battle, eventually reupholstering it instead. She didn't, however, even attempt to interfere with his choice of bedroom wallpaper (a blue-and-white toile covered with angels).

The lesson continued on Skorpios, with her second husband. By tolerating his beloved over-the-top yacht *Christina*—whale scrotum-skin barstools and all—she gained considerable leverage to shuffle the décor elsewhere. Even as Jackie picked apart Ari's "Pink House" with the help of Billy Baldwin in 1968, she knew enough to heed her husband's single request: to have a long sofa by the fireplace.

There's an argument, too, for letting kids have their say, assuming they are old enough to articulate their opinions and/or pay for some items themselves. Jackie indulged Caroline's adolescent taste for more modern décor at 1040 Fifth Avenue, even though she had already selected some dainty French furniture for her daughter's room.

◆ Poach Ideas from Others' Abodes ◆

Awed by your friend's casa, cabana? Imitation (or, ahem, reinterpretation) is perfectly acceptable, as long as you give credit where it's due, and mix things up just a bit. Jackie once took a sample of her friend Jayne Wrightsman's shower curtain and had window treatments for the White House breakfast room made up in the same fabric.

Eyes roaming again, she later asked pal Marie Harriman for permission to copy her Georgetown bedroom in her own Fifth Avenue apartment. After getting the nod, Jackie swathed her boudoir in Harriman's glazed cotton floral fabric, called Tuileries. She never strayed from the pattern, which she touched up several times.

◈ Mix Period Styles ◈

A home that sticks strictly to one design period—be it Bauhaus, mid-century modern or Victorian—can quickly become sterile. So don't be lulled into the notion of interior "purism" espoused by certain decorators and architects. Fix on the styles and lines you like, then go further afield to leaven the look of your place. You might be surprised, for example, by how smashing a Lucite chair looks with a Louis XVI desk. Or how magically a resin genie-bottle Jonathan Adler lamp illuminates an Art Deco bed.

If you fear you're walking a fine line between creative and catastrophic, bring in a design doctor. Barring that, ask one of your very well dressed, very design savvy male friends to come over and take a look.

When it came to mixing it up, Jackie first got her groove on during the White House restoration. Operating within the confines of American and French furnishings, she managed a harmonious blend of pieces from several periods, including Federal, Classical, and Empire. Of course, she had the assistance of some of the most noted decorators and curators—not to mention wealthy patrons. But she had the confidence to rely on her own eye for the final placement of chairs, pictures, and rugs. Later, in her own homes—which spanned from the New England country look to understated Gallic—Jackie let painted Swedish furniture and battered wooden benches mingle with her precious Louis loot.

Don't Overrate Practicality

Whether it's white furniture or stainless steel cabinets, don't always sacrifice the details of your dream for something as dreary as practicality. As long as you're getting durable goods—even white Ultrasuede stands up to drooling toddlers—and commit to the necessary upkeep, indulge your whims at least some of the time. This applies to even the smallest details, like hand-blown Murano glass wall tiles that may need more than Windex to stay perfecto.

When the White House staffers installed a dark wood molding around Jackie's bedroom baseboards, they did so to be practical—the idea was to save the walls from shoes and carpet sweepers. Such a protective ring around the room may have been prudent, but it displeased the First Lady, who had it painted off-white to blend with the cream walls. At 1040 Fifth Avenue, Jackie cloaked her master bathroom walls in fussy ivory silk.

◆ ◆ ◆

"Even though my aesthetic is different from hers, Jackie's decorating style has influenced me greatly. She personified a new standard of non-pretentiousness that is alive and well today."

—IAN SCHRAGER, HOTELIER

◆ ◆ ◆

NECESSARY OBJECTS

If you're well beyond college age, you should be headed up the design chain, casting off all dormitory-level items as you go. These include, but are not limited to, framed cheap Monet posters, synthetic wall-to-wall carpet, gooseneck lamps, and almost all furniture from department stores (it made Jackie shudder—she'd surely prefer Ikea's sleeker, near-disposable stuff).

This doesn't require that you study at Sotheby's, as Caroline Kennedy did. But you should school yourself enough to know Porthault from Pottery Barn; that a serigraph is something you hang on the wall, not a document you've signed; or the telltale sign of machine-made vs. blown glass (dimpled pontil-mark on the former's bottom). Mastering such minutiae makes you an aspirational sort, someone who appreciates the very best—and can intuitively spot the next-best thing (more on that later).

◆ Always a Collector Be ◆

Punctuate your space with objects that are interesting, mixing price points as well as periods. Things don't always have to be expensive, although many of Jackie's were, of course. A Hellenistic terra-cotta horse is interesting, but so too is a beautiful, art-quality map of the world (Jackie hung one in her dining room at 1040 Fifth Avenue as a way to educate her kids about geography). Even a Swedish wool throw purchased during your travels (to the Ice Hotel?) makes a great conversation piece.

To be clear, interesting objects are not mass-produced. So if plucking things off the racks at Restoration Hardware or Crate & Barrel is your sole means of accessorizing, get a new strategy. You'll have better luck, for example, at a flea market or collectibles fair, where whole categories of items—like German pottery—may throw you into a trance. (One of Jackie's early collector cravings was for nineteenth-century Sandwich Glass.) Should you feel lost in the secondhand sphere, ask your zany aunt (everyone has one) to show you the ropes. And don't forget to raid her attic.

◆ . . . Or Know the Next-Best Thing ◆

If originals are out of your realm, go for good copies of furniture, art, and objects—always making sure to get the best reproduction or facsimile possible. For art, this perhaps means a limited-edition print or poster, as well as copies of gallery pieces found at cool museum shops like the Museum of Modern Art Store. If mid-century modern furniture's your thing, select designs made by the current licensee (Saarinen for Knoll Studio, Eames for Herman Miller) rather than any old eBay knockoff. Jackie, after all, had plenty of French reproductions—always of impeccable quality.

Well-chosen stand-ins are also a great way to rein in your decorating budget. In doing up the White House, Jackie cried poverty on many fronts, having depleted the $50,000 government appropriation to revamp the personal quarters in just two weeks. In a letter to one decorator, she expressed her love for highfalutin glass, but went on to rave about her much cheaper substitute: "Now I really love my West Virginia wine glasses all so very much—like Baccarat—and one-millionth the price." (The glasses, it turns out, were also politically fashionable, as the First Family's purchase helped bring attention to poverty-scarred West Virginia.)

◆ Rough Up the Furniture, Walls, Floors ◆

Except for neon-contemporary looks, furniture should never smack of newness. There's something a bit ne'er-do-well about a sofa that looks never rested upon. Or an Art Deco dresser that's been over-restored to gleaming perfection. Similarly, a shiny new Steinway is vulgar unless you can dash out Chopin's complete works on it. (Jackie's baby grand was slightly more lowbrow—the Henry F. Miller piano, which graced her Fifth Avenue dining room, was also appropriately banged up.)

Jackie was known to rough up fresh-from-the-factory items—to make a sofa or chair look "like it had been used, you know, been lived with," recalled White House staffer Karitas. One way to "age" furniture: Use various staining and scraping techniques to muck up a too-new finish. For walls with instant history, apply heavy paint with a glaze, as Jackie ordered up in the White House. She also had workers apply imitation distress marks—with crayon!—to wood paneling as a final, faux-aging touch.

To keep the heirloom look intact, never clean fine pieces of furniture—true period pieces that are possibly worth a bit of money. Instead, wipe dust from the surfaces, but don't polish to Pledge perfection. That kind of "care" may cause items to lose their proper patina, and depreciate in value to boot.

◆ Hide the TV; Show Your Spines ◆

It's a common impulse to conceal the things of everyday life, from televisions to books and other personal effects. Go ahead, tuck away the tube and any unsightly electronics and gizmos. But when it comes to books, there should be no hiding place.

While visiting Jackie at her Fifth Avenue apartment in 1993, Hillary Clinton was amazed to see how she had books "piled so high in her study that she could rest her plate on them," wrote Clinton in *Living History*. The former First Lady went home and attempted to tap this spinal logic, but "Ours never look quite as elegant."

Jackie preferred open bookcases for her dining room library and—except for special tabletop tomes—avoided arranging them with institutional precision. Books look best slightly mussed, as if someone groped reflexively for Byron's letters, toppling a few titles in the process.

In more formal spaces, you might group some of your most striking hardcover volumes by color to complement the room. A bored Jackie once shelved only red books and photo albums in her Fifth Avenue drawing room—a technique that brought out the cherry chintz.

PEARL

Books should serve as decorative accessories only if you've actually read them. Thick glossy volumes may look brilliant on the coffee table, but you'll seem idiotic when a guest cracks open *Greek Art and Architecture* and you're unable to expound on Attic black pottery and Lekythos vases.

SAY IT WITH FLOWERS

Flowers about the house should never seem formal, rigid, or funereal—casual and serene is the way to go. Jackie's taste in blooms ran from dainty blue cornflowers to plump peonies. No stuffy, overdone bouquets, and—gasp!—no honking red Valentine's Day bouquets, which Jackie snubbed as "florists' roses" (she also disliked snapdragons and gladioli).

Go for seasonal sprays whenever possible—petite dianthus, freesia, tulips, peonies, White Majestic daisies. These have that just-picked-from-the-garden Flemish effect that Jackie so loved. Even a single, perfect stem can make a big statement in the right vase.

Recruit unlikely vessels, such as copper pots and straw baskets, two of Jackie's favorites. One of her decorators, Sister Parish, liked the assortment of whimsical (and inexpensive) baskets at Pier 1. In the White House, a floral arrangement was always tucked into a handled Lowestoft mug.

Recycle your blooms from one day, or soiree, to the next. A Jackie White House tactic: Refrigerate your arrangements after an event,

OBJECTS OF DESIRE

Jackie would beseech you to have at least one from every category:

Tabletop Treasures: Lovely china, glassware to be used every day. Jackie had a glorious peony-patterned Spode set from 1820.

Jet-Set Souvenirs: Leopard skin may be endangered, but how about a Russian sable throw for your sofa?

Lovers' Loot: Let gifts remind you of your romantic bounty. Some of Jackie's more sculptural jewelry, such as 22-karat Greek gold cuffs from Onassis, was worthy of display.

Something Old: Jackie adored her nineteenth-century Cream-ware candlesticks so much that they actually stuck around longer than many of her possessions. She spotted and fell in love with them as a newlywed.

Luxurious Helpers: Even the most banal household items can be uplifting, such as Jackie's 26-foot Tiffany sterling silver tape measure. And how about cashmere pillows? Jackie's three-ply covers made reading spells comfy.

Original Artwork: Sargent, Rodin, and many other important names graced Jackie's homes. On a more accessible level, she also loved photographs and prints of animals.

Heirloom-Quality Furniture: Anything named Louis or collected by early settlers was worth passing down in Jackie's book.

Items with a Personal Theme: Many of Jackie's belongings, such as a watercolor by Peter Tillemans, featured equestrian scenes reminiscent of her ribbon-winning glory days in the saddle.

Something Purchased at Auction: Where better to score a truly unique find? At Jackie's estate auction, her monogrammed J black enamel lighter went for $85,000. She'd have approved: In 1961, she bought a mirror once owned by Byron.

Anything with a Great Story: Jackie cherished a whimsical painted plastic model of Air Force One inscribed to her from the crew.

A Musical Instrument or Weapon: Joy, pain, it can all be the same. Jackie's guests in New York could make music on her baby grand, or war with a fabulous antique sword.

A Real Timepiece: One with a mechanical, not a quartz, movement—for authenticity and tick-tock sake. Among Jackie's table clocks was a gold-and-gem number from Van Cleef & Arpels.

then pick them apart the next day, selecting a stem here and a bloom there for smaller bouquets to go in surprising places—such as the guest bathroom.

Document flower arrangements with a photo record (these days, digital snaps are easiest). This way you'll be able to recreate all the scrumptious bunches sent by admirers without having to take a course in horticulture. Jackie used this trick to memorialize bouquets from State dinners.

Bring the outdoors indoors. Budding tree branches—quince?—are simply smashing in a living room environment—especially when they're plunked unexpectedly atop a baby grand piano. In the spring, Jackie liked to feature such earthy arrangements.

MANSE MODES:
Country vs. City Living

Perhaps the best thing about having a place in the country is that you can let it all hang out: You can dress down or streak naked on your private patch of land (or beach—Jackie had nearly 5,000 feet of oceanfront on Martha's Vineyard)—and revel in unsightly rituals (she applied a layer of Pond's cold cream on her face before plunging into the water for a vigorous swim). But country homes also give you a chance to explore new adventures—gardening! Home Depot!—that city living too often excludes. Plus, you can basically have more of everything: more space, more pets, more chintz, and more chimneys.

Lard on the extras that are just too impractical or decadent for the city. A Jacuzzi tub, a three-car garage, a walk-in closet with motorized racks. Jackie made sure to pile on a few perks in her nineteen-room Martha's Vineyard home: She had a sixteen-burner stove in the kitchen, and eight fireplaces that stayed ablaze even through the summer.

JACKIE DOS, JACKIE DON'TS

Do reuse good materials. No need to discard perfectly good fabrics, picture frames, or other things that have second-life potential. After purchasing pricey draperies from a London atelier, Jackie decided not to hang them in New York. Rather than stuff the curtains into a closet, though, she had the dark coral fabric refashioned into fab upholstery covers.

Do make firewood a decorative item. Did it ever occur to you that even firewood could be a chic accent? It did to Jackie—she stocked huge, porcelain ginger jars with perfectly hewn logs, which stood at attention like giant matchsticks on either side of her Fifth Avenue dining room fireplace.

Do keep your memories tidy. Arrange old photographs in decorative boxes or binders, marked by event and date. (No need to paw through old boyfriend pics when your date wants to see photos of you as an adorable teenager.) In New York, Jackie preserved pictures in lovely red Moroccan leather volumes.

Don't over-reflect. A few well-placed mirrors can be useful devices to open up small rooms and help refract light in dark spaces. Too many mirrors, on the other hand, make for a cheesy funhouse look. Jackie preferred gilt Louis XV–style mirrors—one hung over a fireplace in her Fifth Avenue apartment.

continues . . .

Don't accept design help from "creative" relatives who think they have a superior eye. Jackie learned the hard way. After allowing her younger sister Lee to dictate an early Georgetown design scheme—mostly in beige—she ended up redoing almost every nook and cranny with Sister Parish.

Do think of house hues in terms of nature. To Jackie, a favored shade of green was "citron," and a slightly faded red was "raspberry." Doesn't that sound so much better than dressing your walls in green or red?

Don't skimp on fabric for curtains, tablecloths, or upholstered furniture. Rather, err on the high side of the yardstick by about 20 percent "just to be on the safe side," as Jackie used to say. For example, she liked to order ten yards when told she'd need just eight. Better to be over than under, since a reorder may take months and fabrics can be discontinued.

Do make it yourself. If Jackson Pollack can splash a bucket of paint on a canvas, what's stopping you? Jackie loved to paint, and both she and her family cherished her original sketches and Homer-esque watercolors as much as they did their Old Masters.

Do accessorize defensively. Assuming you want to keep your house beautiful, why not have two sets of *objets* on hand? One for your appreciative and careful guests, another for the relatives and folks with clumsy toddlers you must dutifully entertain. It may not seem all that egalitarian, but it sure is practical, which is probably why Jackie sometimes replaced White House objects depending on who was expected. Good ashtrays, for example, went into hiding, only to reappear once the second-string guests had said good night.

Don't mess with the neighbors. City neighbors must be endured. Country neighbors are to be obscured—with fences, trees, anything you can think of. Although she was certainly friendly to local folks, Jackie's long, rustic driveway discouraged nosy neighbors or would-be visitors from approaching her place up on the Vineyard.

Pretend you run a B&B. Suddenly, houseguests are charming in the country. You'll want to perform little niceties—during and after their stay—to draw them back (see "Having Houseguests," p. 29). When fashion designer Valentino once spent beach time with Jackie, he left his sunglasses behind. His hostess returned them in an envelope containing a bit of sand and some seashells.

Be a model citizen. Bad behavior rarely passes in the country, where you're likely to be viewed as a carpetbagger anyway. Jackie had to comply with local rules and zoning laws, and didn't always get her way right away. To appease the picky locals, she politely concealed a 34-foot chimney with tall trees.

Give yourself a land grant. Who can resist the urge to spread out and grab up all the land they can to create a fabulous country retreat? When Jackie moved into Red Gate Farm on Martha's Vineyard in 1981, she had about 400 acres, but needed a drop more: the roughly 1.5 adjoining acres that belonged, technically, to the Wampanoag Indian tribe. Jackie went to court and spent ten years haggling with the Native Americans, eventually managing to score the land by buying the Wampanoags a separate, larger tract.

Seek out "junk-tique" bargains. Mine offbeat shops for home décor deals. Let's face it—shoppers are apt to pay a premium for furniture and accessories in big cities like New York. But a few exits away in the "country," small stores and yard sales can save you a fortune. Jackie loved to dart into such dives with decorators like Richard Keith Langham. At one Paris, Virginia, "junk-tique" shop, as Langham calls them, she came across a baker's table and paid just $270 for it. Years later, at Sotheby's, it went for the price of a BMW.

HABITAT HABITS

Looks aside, what's the tone of your home? Even if the walls and floors are bare, your place will still project a distinct attitude—an invisible set of messages that tells guests, relatives, and neighbors how you process all manner of details.

Never Be a Stiff

You won't be able to truly relax in your own home unless you permit those you care about to do the same (within reason, of course). Jackie felt so strongly about this rule that she allegedly parted ways with Sister Parish after the decorator suggested that Caroline not put her feet up on the upholstery. "I don't ever want a house where I have to say to my children, 'Don't touch,' " Jackie once famously said.

Think twice about insisting guests remove their shoes before entering your place (unless you offer them chic Turkish slippers), or banning red wine from the living room. Fuss enough, and you won't need funny house rules for lack of guests.

Go for a House with a Name— Preferably One You've Picked

Rather than refer to your place generically as "home," why not christen it with a proper name of its own? This also helps clarify matters when you need to specify one of your multiple residences.

Jackie was very big on houses with names. Shortly before leaving the White House, she dubbed her second Virginia country house "Wexford," in honor of JFK's family, who'd emigrated from Ireland's

County Wexford. Other of her homes had equally patrician-sounding names: Glen Ora (the rental in Virginia—which already had been named by its owners); Hickory Hill (in McLean, Virginia); Red Gate Farm, which she also personally christened; and Brambletyde, the Kennedys' place on Massachusetts's Squaw Island.

Note, however, that it is unacceptable to live in a place that bears someone else's name—Zeckendorf, Bloomberg—unless he or she is long dead. Jackie would find that gauche.

Be Curious About the Way Others Live

How can you be certain that your home is fabulous if you haven't scrutinized the way other people live? More importantly, how can you know whose ideas you'd like to import to your own place if you haven't traversed the entryway of many diverse homes?

Never assume that you can't learn a thing or two from folks of lesser means. Jackie was astute enough to know that it isn't always über-rich types who have the best put-together sense.

Visiting the Manhattan apartment of the interracial Fales family in the 1970s, Jackie roamed with wide eyes. "Our apartment (on West End Avenue) was perfectly nice, but not super impressive by Park Avenue standards," recalls Susan Fales-Hill, who describes her childhood home as "Euro-eclectic"—a mélange of eighteenth- and nineteenth-century pieces mixed with plainer items. When Jackie came calling that night, she politely asked to be shown all around. Says Fales-Hill: "Here was a woman who had seen everything, and she was as curious about our place as she would be about Versailles."

Beware House Cooties

Maybe it's the bad feng shui, or perhaps the *rat-a-tat* of upstairs neighbors. If a place doesn't feel right, even for some inexplicable reason, turn tail. Could you ever rest comfortably in such an abode? Jackie initially got the heebie-jeebies from Camp David, pointing out that the very missionary Eisenhowers had enjoyed it. She finally came around,

A Room of One's Own?

Jackie agreed with Virginia Woolf: It's a good thing to have space that's yours alone. A separate bedroom, that is. Complete with leopard throw, a tented canopy bed, and a fanciful trompe l'oeil wardrobe—all items found in Jackie's White House boudoir.

Should you go so far? Times now are different, of course. But Jackie would implore you to at least carve out a dressing room or "office" for yourself. Separate baths are de rigueur. That division spares your spouse, and your guests, from overhearing private business. (Rose Kennedy was said to be amused that Jackie would turn on the bathroom tap to drown out any less-than-ladylike sounds.)

Another plus of a special sanctuary: It gives you the privacy to apply your makeup, tend your tresses, and obsessively try on outfits—precisely the things a man doesn't need to see. Thus, the mystery lives on.

but only after the President shelled out money to rent Glen Ora, a country retreat with a more pleasing aura.

In this spirit, you have every right to ask a man to change residences, so as to avoid the ghosts of paramours past. Jackie refused to live in one of Onassis's Skorpios homes because he'd shacked up there with other women.

HOUSE HELP

How are you at managing the folks who manage your household? If it's true that you can tell a lot about someone's breeding by how they treat others in general, then you can deconstruct their soul by observing how they are with the help.

Jackie, no surprise, was fortunate enough to have spent all of her years with servants. Omniscient observers of her richly textured life, they ironed her pink silk bed sheets, picked her stockings up off the floor—and rarely ratted to the press.

◆　◆　◆

"Jackie would hate how clients today spend so lavishly on kitchens—silly, cutting-edge kitchens. They're like operating theaters, and have nothing to do with food. Spend the money on a good cook instead! —KEITH IRVINE, PARTNER, IRVINE FLEMING INTERIORS, AND DECORATOR TO THE KENNEDYS

◆　◆　◆

Consider Your Successors

Leave behind useful tidbits of information for the folks next in line to inhabit your abode. When vacating the house on Georgetown's N Street, a gracious Jackie thought to make a list of the electrician, gardener, grocery stores, florists, and other essential neighborhood contacts for the new residents.

What About Houseguests?

No matter how spacious your quarters, you needn't feel obliged to take in houseguests, especially if they aren't relatives. Fib as necessary, and go to lengths to spare their feelings (i.e., make sure any white lies don't backfire).

Jackie was a hostess par excellence—when she wanted to be. In his memoir, White House usher J. B. West recalled how a glib Jackie once uninvited an overnight visitor to the manse. According to him, she explained that the rooms were under renovation, which indeed

HOME COOKING:
HOME COOKING:
Learn to Produce Authentic Kitchen Smells

No full-time cook or caterer can ever replace the feminine allure of you swaying over a shiny, steamy pot (just think of the movie *Chocolat*). This allows you to avoid life-draining criticism from relatives, as well as warm the tum of any man. If your mother didn't give you any kitchen confidence, go out and learn—maybe taking a cooking lesson like Jackie once did to make Ari's favorite Greek treat (*dolmades*, stuffed grape leaves). Along the way, it's perfectly okay to take a few culinary shortcuts, like using frozen cookie dough or pre-chopped garlic. Jackie and Ari absolutely adored cake mixes from Duncan Hines.

When you find a restaurant dish that makes you particularly giddy, ask the owner or chef for the recipe so you can duplicate it at home. Just don't go for anything too elaborate.

In the eighties, Jackie liked to frequent Elaine's, the media watering hole on Manhattan's Upper East Side. One night, while taking supper at her preferred table—in the back, against the exit door, where she could see everyone but few could see her—she asked proprietor Elaine Kaufman for her yummy fettuccine recipe. "I didn't know that she cooked!" says Kaufman, who happily handed it over. The ever-thoughtful Jackie later sent her a handwritten note saying how much she enjoyed preparing it.

✦ Jackie O's Favorite Fettuccine, from Elaine's ✦

Ingredients: 1 lb. egg noodles, 3 oz. butter, ¼ tsp. finely chopped garlic, 1 cup plus 4 tbsp. heavy cream, 4 egg yolks, 4 oz. (or more to taste) Parmesan cheese, salt and pepper to taste.

Method: Cook pasta in 6 cups boiling salted water. While the pasta is cooking, heat butter in a large sauté pan over medium heat and add garlic; do not brown. Add 1 cup of the cream and bring to a boil. Mix the egg yolks with the remaining 4 tbsp. of cream. When the pasta is cooked al dente, add to the hot cream and toss well. Add the egg and cream mixture and continue to toss, adding the Parmesan cheese, and seasoning with the salt and pepper. Toss until the sauce is very creamy, approximately one minute. Serve and eat immediately. Yield: approximately four servings

they appeared to be: She had created a fake, frenzied decorating scenario—complete with ladders and paint cans—to demonstrate the rooms' unavailability.

A similar but less complicated ruse: Tell would-be guests that your hot and cold water have inexplicably gone dry. Another tactic: Decorate your guestrooms in such a jarring fashion as to discourage visitors in the first place. Jackie may have been using this logic at Wexford, where she acknowledged that guests were apt to hate the festive red, orange, and green paisley wallpaper.

Drill down on the details. Jackie's helpers were hardly the anonymous "little people" of Leona Helmsley's twisted palace. She made sure to learn not only their names, but also those of their spouses, children, and pets. She sometimes surprised people with her penchant for details. Arriving at the White House, the newly minted First Lady approached a staffer and exclaimed, "Good morning, Mr. Pierce." (Note her use of the surname, not assuming familiarity too soon.) Recalled Pierce: "It surprised me very, very much because . . . I had never been introduced to her. I didn't realize that she knew who I was."

Thou shalt not bark commands. Helpers respond best when they are made to feel like consultants, not servants. Rather than order that a job be done, Jackie would say, "Do you think you could . . ." or "Would it be too much trouble if . . ." But those subtle requests were as good as commands. The staff knew to jump—high—when she suggested something.

It's also pertinent that you use the same tone with your staff as you do with your friends and family (for Jackie, that was the famous whisper-voice). Otherwise, they're apt to pick up on any madam-of-the-house inflection and resent you for it.

Offer token gifts and other perks. Find small, meaningful ways to show appreciation for your doting crew. Arrange rides to and from your home, especially when you've worked them like Ben-Hur; and offer more than cash when they go above the call of duty. Jackie, for instance, sent a cymbidium orchid corsage to Karitas's wife after he pulled an all-nighter. She gave her ever-loyal maid Provi Paredes month-long access to her house in Hyannis Port; her son Hector got JFK's hand-me-downs, including a custom-designed gray tweed suit.

Personal introductions are another way to express gratitude—to a good doctor, your mortgage broker, etc. Just don't pat yourself on the back too hard. Jackie went so far as to set up meet-and-greets between her staff and several dignitaries. She made sure that Paredes, a Catholic, had her own appearance before the Pope; English nanny Maud Shaw got to meet Queen Elizabeth.

Seek multitasking help. Why not hire housekeepers and gardeners who can perform more than one task? Jackie was careful to surround herself with help that could take on several roles. Paredes was responsible for, among other things, looking after Jackie's extensive wardrobe, and also managed updos and roller-sets when necessary. She could make last-minute clothing repairs, too. Nanny Marta Sgubin segued from babysitter to fantastic cook. Today's must-have? A technology-savvy helper for when your wireless Internet connection poops out.

Make sure they like your kids and your pets. It's clear enough why they should get along with your kids. But why the emphasis on the little furry ones? Well, for one thing, house help who grow accustomed to your animals make handy surrogates in the event you need to give any away.

After JFK suffered an allergic reaction to Tom Kitten, Jackie sent Caroline's beloved cat to her personal secretary Mary Gallagher's home. Upon leaving the White House, she handed over Pushinka, a Russian canine from Khrushchev, to Irvin Williams, who was the manse's chief gardener and the dog's most ardent admirer.

Remember them in your will. It would be especially kind of you to offer a parting gift to loyal types. Nothing brings on tears at the reading of a will better than a clause about a bequest to a faithful servant. Jackie remembered Paredes with a $50,000 gift.

Fire annoying help. These days it may not be just incompetence, but also odd behavior, that prompts you to write a pink slip. Acceptable firing offenses include any habits or actions you find inappropriate and/or untenable. Jackie relieved one of Onassis's charges after hearing him sing the words to *Jesus Christ Superstar* in Greek. Another Greek maid got the boot after getting caught twirling around in one of Jackie's Givenchy gowns.

Would Jackie . . .

   Display animal skins/fur in the house? Yes—so chic! She had large throws fashioned from leopard and sable pelts, which she

On House Pets

Those loyal souls who serve as companions and foot-of-bed warmers can do their part to elevate the home tone, too. In the best of all possible worlds, they would even blend into your home décor.

Summering at Hammersmith Farm, a plucky young Jackie suggested that dark-haired dogs would best complement the Newport, R.I., estate's white walls and crimson carpets. Her advice apparently stuck, as black and brown became the hound hues of choice.

Affection should come first, of course, when selecting a pet. Trends next. Over the years, Jackie acquired a virtual menagerie for her kids, adopting everything from ponies, hamsters, and dogs to fish, goats, and birds. Today's more advanced home zoos include oddities like ferrets and chinchillas.

To help pets feel at home, they should have routines. A White House German shepherd named Clipper had a specific daily regimen. He attended dog school on Thursdays and lapped up a special diet, which the house staff had written down.

If pets spoil your home pleasure, it's time for them to go. Jackie asked Caroline's teacher at Convent of the Sacred Heart to take back a mouse—even after she'd acquired a fancy Chinese cage for the creature at Bloomingdale's. The reason: "The mouse is killing my social life," said Jackie, who explained it was stinking up her Fifth Avenue digs.

used in both bedrooms and living rooms. Risk offending your PETA friends to get your own wild look.

◆ **Purchase a home listed on the National Register of Historic Places?** Alas, no. Despite her love of pedigreed things—and access to these listings online—Jackie would pass for the obvious reason: Government rules limit the amount of tinkering you can do to the properties, both inside and out.

Take tips from Martha Stewart? No. The two ladies did meet, but Jackie never quite understood all the fuss over Martha's product-driven advice, which struck her as terribly obvious. Plus, the jail thing would've just freaked her out. If possible, glom on to one or two people whose tastes you admire, so as to get the benefit of exclusive, not mass, advice.

Display a honking portrait of herself? Yes, so long as the image is up to scratch, and even then, only in an appropriate setting. Generally speaking, it's tacky to tack up an image of yourself— unless it is Whitney-worthy. Jackie did exhibit a lovely abstract pen-and-ink drawing of herself by artist-friend Franz Bueb, in her Hyannis Port living room.

Watch home improvement shows for ideas? Yes (even though she wasn't much of a channel surfer). Not that she'd cotton to the froufrou colors and slapdash built-ins that the current spate of design shows promote. Or relish the idea of strangers invading her privacy to make over her home. But Jackie's intense desire to stay abreast of decorative trends—she collected fabric samples and visited design showrooms just for kicks—would make her want to see what others covet. And she'd be intrigued by some of the creative quick-fixes. Just remember: The best design solutions often cost a bit more but will earn their keep over time.

Chapter 6

Building Your Inner Temple:

The Art of Self-Enrichment and Fulfillment

> *"As we strive to fulfill our vision, we must make the most of every living moment."*
> *–JKBO*

A master's degree and a passport bursting with visas are pointless—vile in fact—if you neglect to amass further learning, more adventures. As Jackie said to her sister Lee before embarking on a trip to Europe in 1951, "Don't you ever want to meet fascinating people or just spend your time with your dreary little American friends?"

Indeed, it is terribly easy to spot a dullard, someone who ruins a dinner party faster than a drunken debutante. This is why you must never pass up the chance to attach yourself to intriguing people, experiences, causes—venturing outside your own comfort zone (and zip code) to find new levels of depth.

Jackie was famous for levitating above and around her own day-to-day milieu. In 1975, she emerged from behind the famous sunglasses and appeared in public to help fight against the proposed razing of New York's Grand Central Terminal. The campaign to save the Beaux-

Arts building went all the way to the Supreme Court, and earned Jackie a reputation as a gloved fist.

Though she lost much in life, there were certain treasures that no one could take away from her. This was her secret stash—the bounty of her Inner Temple—that she would call upon time and again for emotional shelter. From travel (chic or introspective) and charity work to the intense solace provided by books and scholarship, these pursuits were what made Jackie so fetching from the inside out.

YOU ARE THE MISTRESS OF ALL YOU SURVEY–AND MORE

If Jackie vowed to "not be a housewife" as a teenager, her ambitions grew substantially by the age of 21, when she declared she would like to be nothing less than an "Overall Art Director for the Twentieth Century," presiding from a chair in space.

Each decade, she pushed herself to learn more. In the fifties it was writing and photography, in the sixties it was couture style and historic preservation, and in the eighties, how to pair authors with book projects. The cumulative message: Don't squander your precious time with half-baked efforts. As Jackie's friend Claude du Granrut observed, "When she was doing something, she was doing it completely."

✦ Promote, Adapt the Fabulous ✦

What utterly original, mind-bending thing have you done lately? Fascinating people are constantly in social excavation mode, mining their surroundings for anything that might solidify their place as a first-mover/adapter (and get snapped in their newspaper's Style section in the process).

Other than her famous fashion influence, Jackie was an irreverent mark-maker on many fronts. In 1960, after a rousing ticker-tape parade through Manhattan to celebrate JFK's campaign close, Jackie shrugged out of her formal garb and stalked off with an artist friend to go check out avant-garde paintings at a progressive gallery. Two years later, she invited black mezzo-soprano Grace Bumbry to give her first major U.S. performance at the White House as a way to further the singer's fame, which was already considerable in Europe. When American wine buffs were still sipping Chablis, Jackie moved on, and helped to popularize Rieslings.

As evidence of Jackie's keen eye for design, she glommed on to the work of the architect I. M. Pei. By choosing Pei, who was credited mainly for building low-cost housing projects, to design the John F. Kennedy Library, Jackie "made me as an architect," said Pei. "Until then I was not known at all."

Even if you're not in a position to anoint the next Frank Gehry, you can always outclass celebrity gawkers by nabbing season tickets to the architect's Walt Disney Concert Hall, new home of the Los Angeles Philharmonic. (You might even help your friends to pronounce the name of the group's yummy conductor, Esa-Pekka Salonen — Ess-ah Peck-ah Sal-o-nin — by praising his fine baton stroke after yoga class.)

Jackie would most certainly have made a beeline to the temporary Museum of Modern Art, used until late 2004, even though it was housed in an outer borough. Given her penchant for art-house films — she screened movies such as *Jules et Jim* at the White House — she would have been one of the first to schlep downtown to see what Robert De Niro's TriBeCa Film Festival was all about. To wit, De Niro was awarded the Jacqueline Kennedy Onassis Medal in 1997 by the Municipal Art Society of New York, one of Jackie's favorite causes.

◈ Preen Your Hobbyhorse ◈

Whether you learn to knit G-strings, play baroque harpsichord, or join Cirque du Soleil, challenge and mastery are what promise to make you an EFP (eminently fascinating person).

To follow Jackie's lead means becoming a full-immersion hobbyist, letting your passion and interests surround you from every (flattering) angle possible. Don't just go to films by Stanley Kubrick. Read his biography, go visit his hometown. If you play the violin, retune your love of the instrument by giving lessons on the side and hoarding every obscure volume ever written about bow position — in addition to applauding great new talents on the scene.

Jackie so loved ballet in youth that she not only practiced the art, but also collected books on the subject. In New York, she spent more than twenty-five years on the board of trustees at the American Ballet Theatre (the organization named a school after her in 2004). As a book editor, she commissioned works from no fewer than three famous dancers — Judith Jamison of Alvin Ailey, Martha Graham, and Gelsey Kirkland.

Forget about dabbling. Like a lover or mistress, lifetime hobbies also demand that you be honest about your commitment level. In other words, how much are you really willing to give of yourself?

Jealously guard the time you set aside for your passion, and don't let bores distract you. Jackie didn't permit anyone — not even Judy Garland — to take her eye off her painting, another soul-cleansing pursuit. When the actress burst in on her one day in Hyannis Port, Jackie looked up from her watercolors and asked the starlet to let her be. "Watch if you like. But no one talks to me when I'm painting," she said.

◆ Snuggle Up to Old People ◆

Candid elders help you sharpen your wit, widen your perspective — and often have an uncanny ability to size up no-good friends and boyfriends. They also will inspire you with their wonderful storytelling, retro collectibles, and wardrobes — the latter of which they undoubtedly will loan (or bequeath) to you for your own enrichment.

During a visit to Italy in 1951, Jackie and her sister Lee were excited to drop in on the sage art historian Bernard Berenson. They were already jaded by all they'd seen, heard, bought, and eaten — but were still quite taken by the white-bearded man's advice. "Don't waste your time with Life Diminishing people," he told them. "Seek the company of Life Enhancing people. . . ." Hear, hear.

Cozy up to in-laws, school professors, and distinctive characters you meet during your travels. Jackie did all of the above. Other than her most famous old-school crush, Joe Kennedy, a favorite elder was Prince Serge Obolensky, a public relations man and former Czarist officer whose company—and tales about pre-Bolshevik Russia—Jackie preferred to the banal soliloquies of East Hampton boys.

(His influence obviously stuck: At Viking, one of her most important projects was *In the Russian Style*—a book about the costumes of Czarist Russia.)

◆ Reject Monotony ◆

"Dreary" is how Jackie would probably describe the prison of habits that make some of us repeat the same routines, day in, day out. Treat the activities of your day as if they're charged atomic particles, apt to burst from your calendar, they're so in flux. This is a key to living always in the present. A big believer in mixing it up, Jackie said, "the only routine with me is no routine at all."

If you like to jog daily, take a different path, soaking up different scenery, real estate, and marriage prospects along the way. And seek out new aids to further your freewheeling cause, such as the random-tune iPod shuffle.

◆ ◆ ◆

"I'm thinking about taking piano lessons again, maybe to learn some show tunes. Jackie, if alive today, would encourage me to try a new tack instead of playing the same old classical music." —JOAN B. KENNEDY

◆ ◆ ◆

◆ Trill in Tongues ◆

All those horrid hours spent learning to conjugate verbs and develop a convincing accent pay off big time when you glide into an Italian store and order your Parma ham like a native. Or when you sweep your Swedish neighbor off his feet by cooing, *Jag tala din sprak* (I speak your language) as his American girlfriend stands by, bewildered.

Jackie spoke French, Italian, Spanish, and even a little Greek— skills that would help her navigate plenty of diplomatic moments. We've all heard the stories about how she dismissed JFK's translators in France, choosing to interpret between the President and Charles de Gaulle. She also used her linguistic savvy to beckon potential lovers, and even to protect her cherished privacy: She assumed fake voices to get rid of unwanted callers to her home and her office, often employing a Spanish accent.

Jackie so believed that different languages are essential to our creative expression, she made sure her children's nannies spoke French. Never, by the way, use the excuse that you're too old to learn a new tongue. Out of respect for her second husband, Jackie took Greek lessons and she insisted that her children did, too.

BE A CONSPICUOUS (CULTURE) CONSUMER

If the last stage performance you attended was one you were in (back in high school), or the only museum you've strolled through gave you a child's rate, consider yourself in serious cultural turnaround mode.

Remedial skills on this front simply do not cut it. An EFP always knows the must-see plays, operas, and other goings-on about town. She seeks out the best current literature, and revisits old favorites. She drops in on her friends at work, who just happen to be curators at small, but important, galleries. She learns exotic dances (Jackie mastered the Greek *syrtaki*). And just when she thinks her head will burst from it all, she has a sudden thirst for more—auditing grad school classes, hiring a coach to polish her Middle English, or traveling to Hawaii to study Chinese painting, as Jackie did in 1966. (Disclaimer: The Learning Annex and online "correspondence" gigs don't count.)

◆ ◆ ◆

"[Jackie] was devout about the arts. And yet she knew you couldn't dissect them verbally. If you're in front of a Picasso and try to say anything interesting, it sounds phony immediately." —CARLY SIMON

◆ ◆ ◆

❖ Know Your Pablos ❖

First things first. If your arts vocabulary (or that of someone you know) is lacking, spend the next six months—yes, six months!—correcting the deficiency. Attend concerts (or don the headphones at Tower Records) to check out things like great works for the cello—perhaps tuning in to renditions by Pablo Casals. Also head to a museum that houses fine paintings, seeing how well you cotton to another Pablo—Picasso.

First Lady Jackie felt obliged to set a cultural example for her American Bandstand public by inviting performers such as Casals and violinist Isaac Stern to the White House. In another such feat, she convinced French Minister of Cultural Affairs André Malraux to bring the *Mona Lisa* to the U.S. for a brief visit—one of the few times her crooked smile was seen outside France.

It doesn't matter if you end up hating every concerto, every impressionist's stroke. Exposure is the point—so that you can at least have an opinion of your own. If country music or jazz is your thing, don't feel the need to put on classical airs just to please or impress others. Jackie wouldn't modulate her taste for somebody else's sake. She once told her White House handlers to steer some visitors away from a Kentucky student group that was performing on the lawn, suggesting that their "hillbilly" concert wasn't her cup of tea.

Try to Stick with the Program

Hate Wagner? *Nixon in China?* Resist the urge to do a disappearing act at live performances. For truly refined sorts, criticizing not-so-great stage acts (scrawling "tenor was fat and off-key" in the program margins) can be as satisfying as an encore.

If you detest what's going on, you may want to stay simply to savor the boos at the end. Do you really think that Jackie—who invested thousands of hours and wrote lots of checks to support causes like the American Ballet Theatre—would ever scoot out in the middle? Okay, maybe. But only when the lights dimmed.

Form Your Own (Cultural) Brain Trust

Though well schooled in art and history, Jackie relied on a bevy of advisors to ratchet up her culture quotient. Malraux, *Vogue* editor and museum curator Diana Vreeland, and Bunny Mellon were perhaps her most important soothsayers—her own Gang of Three for all things sublime.

Conveniently, Jackie didn't have to pay for their tutelage (or for the services of the Fine Arts Committee, which collected objects for her famous White House restoration). And ideally, neither should you have to shell out big bucks to open fresh artistic avenues. One good option: Put together your own collection of cultural ambassadors. This could include the colleague at work who has a fascination for Outsider Art; a friend's aunt who plays with the local symphony; a neighbor who heads up the regional theater.

You may find that such experts are delighted to share their knowledge with you, as artistic passion tends to be contagious. Having your own culture klatch is also an excellent way to score free or discounted house tickets to events.

Know Your Way Around the Stacks

As in, the library. Because a) Google just isn't enough and b) that's what people of substance do. Besides, there's something slightly romantic about getting lost in the musty rows of an important collection. And you just might find it titillating to be scolded—or praised—by a stern librarian.

Jackie got a kick out of dragging authors to the rare book rooms at the New York Public Library. She also prowled research facilities that could benefit any of her book projects, such as the slide library at the Metropolitan Museum of Art's Costume Institute. And as Jackie showed, there's no need to pretend to be a know-it-all in such hallowed halls.

Visiting the latter library in 1976, she blew away the staff with her inquisitiveness. "She managed to go around the table and ask questions that involved us all," recalls one former assistant, Joannie Danielides. "What was most impressive was that she asked so many, many questions—some simplistic and some very thoughtful and intelligent. She was learning, taking it all in—she had a great curiosity and wanted to educate herself."

Read, Don't Skim

In a time when it's so damn easy to cut corners and substance—TiVo your favorite TV shows, find a vintage Pucci on eBay, get a concise history of modern art by tapping online—there is still no substitute for sitting down and paging through a book.

Everybody has literary lapses, which is no crime. The misdemeanor happens once you go on permanent book leave. Another thing to watch out for: people who don't read at all. Be very suspicious of anyone who does not have books at home or in the office, or who stammers when you ask them about the last thing they read.

Jackie, of course, loved a good page-turner, a lovely line—a gift she inherited from her paternal grandfather, "Grampy" Jack, who raised her on a diet of Shakespeare. (She later consumed as many as ten titles per week.) Jackie's library included thousands of books, and no two people will ever have the exact same literary taste. But if your interior decorator dared stock your place with fake, hollow volumes, consider swapping them for a few of Jackie's shelf staples.

Jackie Reading List

Books/Plays:

The Memoirs of the Duc de Saint-Simon

The Odyssey, Homer

Richard III, William Shakespeare

Henry V, William Shakespeare

Age of Reason, Thomas Paine

Lost Cities and Vanished Civilizations, Robert Silverberg

Pilgrim's Way, John Buchan

Shadows from India, Roderick William Cameron

Poems:

Ithaca, Constantine P. Cavafy

I Taste a Liquor Never Brewed, Emily Dickinson

The Negro Speaks of Rivers, Langston Hughes

The Sonnets, William Shakespeare

Ode on a Grecian Urn, John Keats

Death, Be Not Proud, John Donne

in Just, e.e. cummings

CAUSES:
CAUSES:
How to Choose Them and Use Them

◆ ◆ ◆

*"Jackie chose [organizations] that were important to her
and she stuck to them. If you spread yourself too thin, you
can't do it all—she understood that. I think she'd say
pick two or three things you're passionate about,
that have real meaning to you, and work on those."*

—BLAINE TRUMP, PHILANTHROPIST, SOCIALITE

◆ ◆ ◆

When it comes to charities, too many people get it wrong. They hope involvement with a cause will somehow serve them—by plumping their social status, their calendars, their couture closet—rather than the other way around. This helps to explain why some budding philanthropists spread themselves thin, plying various groups with money in anticipation of being in a perpetual charity-ball whirl.

In this area, Jackie was both generous and restrained. And yet she loathed the idea of being on the charity "circuit," where pretentious airs can quickly get out of hand. Of course she attended premieres, served on boards, etc., but she was never one to support a group, a cause, or a charity just for the sake of doing so. To her, the party part was often a bit painful.

Is it your responsibility to get involved philanthropically? Jackie would certainly say "yes." A few things to consider when duty calls:

◆ **Support what moves you.** The size of your donation doesn't matter. Just make sure your interest level in the cause is grand.

Jackie was able to give both time and money to groups—always selecting those that resonated with her passions and beliefs. She was a longtime supporter of organizations such as the New York Municipal Art Society, the Metropolitan Opera, and the American Ballet Theatre.

Go up against mice, men. Sometimes, a picket sign or demonstration is what it takes to get the job done. So make sure you're willing to assist in any capacity. Jackie was certainly up for all manner of brawls. Before helping save Grand Central Terminal, she had battled in 1962 to preserve Washington, D.C.'s historic Lafayette Square. Three decades later, she was horrified by the idea of Disney building a theme park near horsey Middleburg, Va., and helped bankroll efforts to foil the fantasy. "I pray against Disney every night," she told her friends Eve Fout and Charlie Whitehouse.

Don't let a cause rub you the wrong way. If the local orchestra is overly excited about your mansion (for parties) or your celebrity boyfriend (for the news-generating attention he generates), go *piano, piano.* Jackie knew that her famous name could give a cause or organization a distinct edge, and thus allowed herself to be used—but only up to a point. She totally recoiled when hospital board members from Cedars-Sinai Medical Center in Los Angeles showed up at her New York apartment building seeking to be photographed with her. Without further ado, she cut ties to their forthcoming event.

Tout your charitable deeds selectively. Serving on the board of the ballet or public theater is admirable. As a side benefit, your affiliation could also put you in good stead with a tough co-op board. Should you mention it? Sure. Just tout your deeds selectively, and never make a pledge for the specific purpose of getting ahead. As Jackie was well versed in the name-dropping necessary to snare a Manhattan residence, she would urge you to mention your genuinely passionate roles.

CAFTAN IN A KELLY BAG:
How to Travel Beautifully

Traveling to faraway places is a way to tap into our deepest curiosities and fantasies—a concept Jackie would implore you to explore at full tilt. "I know that to visit Seville and not ride horseback at the fair is equal to not coming at all," she once said.

Destinations should be more than notches in your passport; amass them as reference points to a richly textured life. For Jackie, some places—Paris, Jaipur—became old friends she'd visit time and again.

Unfortunately, too many travelers today hit the road in hurried fashion, relying on tour-bus excursions, two-for-one deals, and other pre-fab jaunts likely to rob you of a truly fabulous (and occasionally naughty) time. So get thee gone in a manner that suits the wondrous, enterprising creature you are.

◆ Do a Cultural Deep Dive ◆

How gauche to just parachute into an exciting new destination, armed with little else than your spanking new Goyard travel case! At least brush up on the language, history, and terrain of a place *en avance*. (One tip: Ask your host or concierge to supply you with current periodicals and translations of recent, native works.) Not only is such study practical, but it can also help ignite daydreams—of being "discovered," Fellini-style, near Rome's Trevi fountain, or being picked as the next Chanel muse while strolling the Tuileries in Paris.

Jackie "was a great historian, fascinating to travel with," says her stepbrother Hugh "Yusha" Auchincloss III. "I got a better education listening to Jackie than I did going to Yale."

Training in youth helped. Jackie took intensive French lessons before going to study at the Sorbonne during the equivalent of her junior year in college. She also passed on the common dormitory digs in favor of living in a much more interesting atmosphere. Her hosts were a "countess" and her brood who lived on Avenue Mozart. (Monsieur had perished under the Germans, and Jackie had to take cold baths and eat lots of stew, so the Dickensian storytelling factor was quite high.)

Jackie always said she profited from the more proletarian, anti-dorm experience—one you can replicate by choosing to rent an apartment abroad rather than book a hotel; or staying with old (as in elderly) friends or friends of friends. They're more likely to have a large home than your younger acquaintances, and they'll be happy for the company to boot.

Your cultural plunge may not be complete without, well, exactly that—and a splash of romance. When Jackie traveled to the Yucatán peninsula in 1968, her companion, former Deputy Defense Secretary Roswell Gilpatric, noted how "she wasn't content just to see the Mayan ruins by car in the daytime," as the average tourist would. Instead, "she also insisted on seeing them by moonlight, on horseback, to get the feeling of the way it was the day before yesterday. And once she tossed herself into a pool near the ruins with all her clothes on."

Choose Your Travel Beaus Carefully

Since every gondola ride, each trek through ruins, and every al fresco meal will be forever etched in your mind (if not your digital camera), it is imperative that you choose any male traveling companions wisely. It's one thing to be with a girlfriend who commands more than her fair share of stares and gawks. You can survive that. But the horror of kissing the wrong man, a cheap man, a dull man, atop the Eiffel Tower is simply not recoverable.

Here, Jackie would again let practicality prevail. On her many trots around the globe, she often took a squire—or met up with one upon arrival. In each case, she chose a man of impeccable taste, knowledge, and means, even managing in one case to snag a beau with access to a helicopter to swoop her away on dates.

In November 1967, it was former British Ambassador Lord Harlech who escorted her on a quasi-political junket to Cambodia. Though she was not romantically smitten with the wealthy Brit, rumors swirled about their impending marriage. The photos of their journey suggest Jackie was simply content that he enjoyed trekking through ruins as much as she did, and that he was thoughtful enough to dress in complementary fashion (trim khaki pants, crisp white shirt, low leather boots).

Four months later, she was off to see those Mexican ruins with Roswell Gilpatric, a still-married, much older man whom she found both riveting and romantic.

Notice that these men weren't all necessarily available, or even sexy—but they each fit the bill perfectly in that they augmented the scene by being attentive. They looked good for the camera, and each was as curious about their surroundings as she. In short, Jackie chose pleasingly benign guys who were unlikely to mar her travel memories with regrets.

◆ Create Advance Buzz for Yourself ◆

After your tickets and reservations are secured, it's time to start whipping up some local excitement over your imminent arrival. This is especially important if you're traveling to a place you've never been, but where you have some respectable half-acquaintances.

En route to Europe aboard the *Queen Elizabeth*, a young Jackie and her sister Lee bragged about "cables arriving steadily every day all day long . . ." By the time they arrived, they indeed had all manner of parties, lunches, and concerts to attend, including one soiree packed with "THE SENATORS!!," as the sisters squealed in their journal.

To spread the word about your own coming, dispatch e-mails to your friends and colleagues in the city you plan to infiltrate. Suggest, of course, that you'll be very busy, but would love the chance to meet up with their gang if time allows. Also latch on to any family acquaintances, since they'll feel obliged to hook you up with appropriate partners and diversions.

And even once you arrive, keep the attention focused on you. It's nice, after all, to have admirers on foreign soil. As she toured Europe in 1950, Jackie was sure to leave teasing messages for Demi Gates, the smitten brother of a friend from Vassar, prompting him—of course!— to trail her as she traipsed about Scotland and England with her stepbrother Yusha Auchincloss.

◆ Never Pass Up an Impromptu Adventure ◆

The best trip is often an unexpected one—a journey that has you packing just moments after you promised to dog-sit for the neighbors. No fool, a young Jackie jumped at a last-minute chance in 1953 to sail to Queen Elizabeth's coronation. She also didn't hide her (mock) disdain for those who didn't take full advantage of their overseas opportunities. When a Vassar friend squirmed out of their planned adventure to study at the Sorbonne (to wed, of all things), Jackie expressed herself in verse: "Instead of boating on the Seine, alas, Puffin's floating down the drain in Pittsfield, Mass."

Because the real adventures begin only after you arrive, it is essential that you consider all offers for dinner, drinks, music lessons— and perhaps most importantly, rides in fast cars.

Any woman, married or not, who has the chance to hop in a sexy sports car and tear down a stretch of beautiful European highway had better do it. There's nothing like whipping through Austrian asparagus fields in a muscle-bound Ferrari. A dashing man at the wheel—and clothes that stand out against the car—complete the fantasy. In June of 1961, when Jackie traveled to Greece, she donned a white silk scarf and a bright orange dress before pouring herself into HRH Crown Prince Constantine's blue Mercedes convertible for a spin through the countryside. When it's your turn, toss your head back, laugh uncontrollably— and hold on to your headgear.

✦ Travel High and Low ✦

From 900-room palaces to mansions on the Rhône, jet-jockey Jackie pretty much saw it all. But "swanky" travel, as she liked to call it, is only cool if you temper it with more raw and exotic experiences.

Despite being armed with an American Express letter of credit (today's equivalent of a platinum card), a young Jackie and Lee made sure to stay in plenty of third-class European hotels, and to blend in when they wanted to. ("Oh we're not at all what you think we are — we've traveller's checks and a little car. . . .") the girls wrote in a 1951 travel journal later published as a book. Smartly, they clung to native types who showed them how to revel in their sub-swank time.

"We spent most of our days with Fazzini," wrote Jackie, who divided her time between Rome's glamorous boutiques, great museums, and bohemian adventures with the young man. As much as the shopping tours, she relished how their local friend/guide took the sisters to "coffee in a bamboo-curtained cafeteria," and to a studio "where he taught Lee to make ceramic jewelry in one corner and drew pictures of me in another."

It's easier than you think to achieve some of Jackie's swanky style on a budget. One of her favorite things to do in Paris was to get all dolled up (clothes, hair, and makeup), and zip over to the Right Bank for cocktails at the Ritz Bar, where she knew she'd be able to mingle with a mix of monied, expatriate, and aristocratic lads.

Alas, sometimes nonstop luxury can prove tiresome. Once, while traveling to the small Greek island of Hydra, Jackie requested to take the regular boat with locals and tourists, rather than go by private craft. During the hour-and-a-half sail, "Jackie sat in a chair, facing the ocean, happily engrossed in a book," recalled Kiki Feroudi Moutsatsos, Onassis's secretary.

Is It Jackie-Fabulous Travel?

- If a hotel has more than 400 guest rooms, an ice machine on every floor, an ATM in the lobby — it's not fabulous.

- If a diplomat has never stayed there — it's not fabulous.

- If the bed sheets are less than 300 threads per inch — it's not fabulous.

- If a cruise ship looks more like a mall than a boat; if it has a Vegas-style casino on board — it's not fabulous.

- If you've traveled by plane more than twelve hours to reach a remote locale and there's no good shopping — meaning flea markets, open-air bazaars, and other such haunts where you can purchase native crafts, etc. — it's not fabulous.

- If the toiletries in the bathroom bear the same name as the hotel (Hilton) rather than the name of a luxury brand (Bulgari) — it's not fabulous.

- If the staff does not remember your name after you've entered and exited the premises more than twice — it's not fabulous.

◆ JACKIE DOS, JACKIE DON'TS ◆

Do wear a good piece of jewelry in your passport photo to give your face an expectant, patrician glow. A simple adornment (such as a 16-inch pearl strand or retro-chic pin) will melt steely customs agents. It also says, "Bump me up to first class instead of *her*." For an early passport shot, Jackie sported a gold four-leaf clover brooch.

Do plan your en route getup. If you want to join the leisure class, forget your leisure togs (or Juicy Couture equivalent) and wear something more civilized. Wrinkle- and sag-proof fabrics (such as cashmere/stretch blends) are a good bet, and still allow you to be chicly anonymous amid the cartoon T-shirt crowd. Always assume you will happen upon someone from your past or future, so don't wear anything you wouldn't want an ex-flame or potential boss to see you in. A fastidious Jackie was known to change outfits before disembarking from an airplane.

Don't fret over tonnage. For trips where you'll need major baggage— like the ten suitcases Jackie once hauled for a four-day shopping binge through Manhatttan—go ahead, indulge by bringing ten Prada bags and twenty pairs of Jimmy Choos. But given today's tight security procedures, you'll do well to send at least some of your stuff beforehand, using express mail. Ditto on the way home. So what if you must fork over extra for excess baggage? Jackie paid more than $100 in such fees (about $700 today) when returning from the queen's coronation loaded with books and other finds.

Do go explore your family's "roots"—but hurry and do so before someone has the chance to ruin any quaint notions you may have about your ancestry. Jackie first traveled to France thinking that she'd been descended from French nobility. Her author-cousin John H. Davis later revealed that she'd actually been hewn by French carpenters and cabinetmakers.

Don't overlook regional shopping. Explore all the local boutiques at every port of call, searching for outfits (custom, if possible) that will have your friends scanning the racks back home in vain. In Greece, Jackie had Athens boutique owner Roula Strathis stitch up made-to-measure skirts and blouses.

Do bring back a few dance moves as well as souvenirs—as Jackie did following a trip to Marrakech. Returning to the White House, she proudly showed off her ethnic bumps and grinds to her friends.

Do suck up to people with private craft. You'll notice that Jackie always managed to roll with a jet/yacht/helicopter-ready crowd. A few cabin access ideas: Take flying lessons to meet a) instructors who pilot the big birds in their day gigs and b) the novice pilots who are probably already shopping for their first Piper. If boats rock you, assume your very own inquiring reporter role, and charm your way—in the name of nautical journalism—onto yachts docked at a pier near you.

HEAD ROOM:
On Privacy and Personal Boundaries

Perhaps no one prized, or fought for, privacy more than Jackie. Though it meant being part Houdini, part Garbo, part CIA agent, her daily battle for anonymity, especially in the post-White House years, was essential to preserve her own sanity and her family's safety.

Assuming there's no swarm of paparazzi outside your door (and that you haven't hired the pseudo-variety now available in some cities to give you a fake celeb halo) consider yourself lucky. Yet with all the increasing ways for the world to encroach—from spam and instant-messaging to on-demand video chats—achieving a measure of privacy can seem as tough today for the average person as it was for Jackie. So be sure to get your fair share of oxygen.

Perfect your stare-through glare. Nothing says "leave me be" like a stone-faced mug. No need to affect an angry or mean look, of course—Jackie's go-to-hell-gaze was ever so benign. By refusing to visually engage or acknowledge people, you are telling them to stay out of your orbit.

But since that won't always work . . .

STICKY TRAVEL SITUATIONS

Sticky Travel Situation No. 1 You're checking in for your international flight, and the clerk winks as he slips an upgraded boarding pass to you—but not your travel companion. What to do?

♦ Plead the case of your companion to gain another upgrade. "Of course, we're together. Would it be possible?" Barring all else, take the seat, but get your companion to give you permission to do so by pretending to put the matter in their hands. "My, I'd so hate to leave you alone back there. But it would be such a shame to waste this wonderful opportunity. What shall I do?" Jackie often deflected questions, and problems, in this rhetorical manner.

Sticky Travel Situation No. 2 You've been flirting with a dashing European man over e-mail and during heady in-town interludes. He invites you to, say, Cape Town or Saint Tropez, but the details are vague. What to make of it all?

♦ Make certain he'll put out all the way, both financially and (if you wish) sexually, stoking those romantic flames that have been searing your computer screen in the process. Just be sure to gently press for the details up front—a way to employ the

continues . . .

Jackie-esque technique of not appearing overly eager to travel to see a man. Even her father warned her against the dangers of being too geographically available.

Sticky Travel Situation No. 3 During your travels, you acquired some pretty spectacular loot: rubies here, dhurrie carpets there. U.S. customs permit you to bring in only a pittance-worth of goods, and you've far exceeded the limit. What to do?

◆ Er, err on your declarations form. Our girl didn't seem to have a problem making certain large gems purchased overseas disappear in mid-passage. Private jet travel generally makes it easier to slip things over the border unnoticed. To decrease your chances of a customs confrontation, book your flight through an airport where the agents are apt to be less savvy. In New York, JFK agents can sniff out Prada, for example, but in Detroit, a fashion sting isn't as likely.

Line up your physical barriers. Jackie's preferred block-and-tacklers included the large sunglasses she popularized in the late 1960s (make sure yours are big enough to obscure at least a third of your face). She also made effective use of giant, house-shrouding shrubs, bodyguards, remote islands, even court injunctions. A few democratic equivalents: headphones (the large, not dainty, kind) to discourage stranger interceptions on the street and on planes, potholed driveways that are difficult to traverse, and a very big dog trained to bare his teeth in the back of your SUV.

Have a fake-out voice and getup. Even though caller ID often spares us from unwanted conversations, the false voice can come in handy when you trip up, or fail to recognize you ex's phone number. Have a name and inflection on standby for such occasions—your cousin from Atlanta, maybe?

Also be prepared to slip into a fictional guise, perhaps using a costume when circumstances warrant it. Shopping for apartments in New York, Jackie once went incognito, letting her friend Nancy Tuckerman assume the role of wealthy purchaser while she loped along pretending to be a British nanny.

Put friends and family under oath. If you're super-persnickety about your privacy, you'll need to enlist your friends and loved ones to guard your business too. Jackie gently laid down the law in this regard, sometimes cutting off those whose loyalty she perceived as less than up to snuff. Even in her will, Jackie asked her children to consider her right to privacy in death. Disclaimer: By telling loved ones to hush around others, you may compel them to do exactly the opposite. It's called human nature.

Beware "user switching" and other privacy-zapping technologies. Your spouse may think that it's cool to gain control over your personal computer screen. But do you really want him—or anyone—to know what you harbor there? Jackie was so guarded about the details of her life that she famously left no memoirs. And she learned the hard way that private letters can end up in public hands (some of hers made it to auction). With so much of our correspondence on computer today, Word files and e-mail are a reality for most of us. Just do your damn best to keep those most sensitive documents where they belong—away from the eyes of your boss, your spouse, and anybody else whose mouse is too close for comfort. And password-protect the spiciest stuff.

Shred—or burn—the past. A shredder is necessary to gnarl all sensitive documents beyond recognition. Love letters and other highly private papers, however, you may prefer to toss into a fire—the dramatic value peaks with the certainty that they're being consumed by flames, and not other eyes. Jackie employed this utterly romantic gesture near the end of her life.

In the "me" hours. The surest, Jackie-esque way to carve out precious time alone is to bill yourself as a serious hobbyist. Broadcast to all friends, colleagues, and loved ones that your very sanity depends on your ability to pursue riding, knitting, or whatever it is that takes you away from the frenetic world. You'll find that declaratives like "I must exercise my gelding" or "I'm way overdue to finish that baby blanket" buy a lot more leeway than "I'm off to go shopping!" (and who's to know what else you may do between trots and purls?). For those times when the walls really start to close in, allow yourself the occasional fib indulgence. To get out of dull White House commitments and escape to the fresh country air of Virginia, Jackie wasn't above feigning illness.

Learn to love being alone. "Me" time, of course, isn't always self-enforced. So for those periods when you find yourself unexpectedly *tout seul*—whether you're between lovers or dining at a table for one—don't stiffen. Learn to savor the extra breathing room instead. Jackie, a solitary sort even as a child, had a leg up here—she had no qualms about eating, painting, traveling by herself. As she once declared, "I'm happiest when I'm alone." Going effortlessly solo in public can be a particular badge of glory—a woman who strolls a museum gallery, or takes herself to the opera, is a creature of mystery, beauty.

HEAVENLY JACKIE:
A Celestial Account of
Why She Lived as She Did

Just what do Jackie's stars reveal about the complex Mrs. O? We asked Los Angeles-based celebrity astrologer Margaret Fitzgerald, author of *The Lost Gateways*, to deconstruct her chart.

Jacqueline Kennedy Onassis was born on July 28, 1929, at 2:30 P.M. in Southampton, New York. At that moment, the Sun was in Leo in the ninth house—the house of truth—with Scorpio as her rising. No one can shine in the limelight like Leo the Lion. Her Leo side craved attention: Her public persona fed an intense desire for acknowledgment.

Her rising in Scorpio, however, made her deeply secretive, sensual, and passionate beneath the glamour. She shared her true nature only with the few people she trusted. Scorpio—a water sign—made her extremely sensitive and protective. Scorpio also connects to the accumulation of money and wealth—especially other people's money. Her choices in wealthy partners speak to that: Kennedy, Onassis, and Tempelsman all possessed extraordinary financial resources.

Her moon, which rules the heart, was in Aries in the fifth house, which also rules children. She was destined to be in the spotlight with her offspring. Once again, Jackie was always balancing the public and the private sides of life and raised her children

continues . . .

to be able to do the same. The Moon's influence in both the fifth and sixth houses of creativity and daily routines respectively would have made her a maternal force to be reckoned with.

Overall Personality. Neptune, which rules glamour and mystery, is at the mid-heaven of Jackie's chart, indicating a strong emphasis on public life and making one's mark in the world. This is one of the astrological elements that created the halo of mystique around Jackie. With Sagittarius on the cusp of her second house of values and Taurus on the Descendent—which represents the solid and dependable energy she craved in a partner—it is interesting to note how her first marriage to JFK would have been such a personal struggle for her. However, this makes sense when you see that her "nodes" (karmic lessons that play out in relationships) were aligned with her Ascendant and Descendent. No wonder she was so drawn to what looked like the reliability and safety of her second marriage.

Love. Venus in Gemini would indicate that Jackie was easily charmed: Say the right words and she'd be hooked. Simultaneously, she would have had a way with words herself when it came to the art of seduction. Given that Pluto, the planet of authority, is in her eighth house of joint resources, it is not surprising that Jackie would have married prominent men. She also has both Venus and Jupiter in chatty/flirty Gemini in her seventh house of relationships interacting powerfully with a sextile to Uranus in the fifth house of love, knocking her off balance with infidelity as a potentially consistent element of her love life.

Wealth. Saturn in the second house of finances can indicate a seemingly endless supply of money—and in Jackie's cases suggests the burdens of enormous wealth and the challenges that came with it. Saturn in Sagittarius and retrograde would make her extremely practical in some ways and extremely frivolous in others, though she probably had clear boundaries about when it was okay to spend and when it wasn't. With this Saturn placement, she also would have prized high morals, truth, and knowledge.

Health. Chiron, an aspect in Astrology that tells us of where our wounds lie, is in Taurus in the sixth house of body and health. Jackie's indicates that she would have easily tired under the strains of public life—so much so that she would have felt their effects physically. However, with Aries Moon in her sixth house of daily routine, she'd likely have had the get and up and go to start each day—as long as what she was doing was to her liking.

Career. With Mars (the planet that rules work) in the tenth house of career in Virgo (the sign that rules details), Jackie was well suited for the publishing industry. Her Mars was in a trine relationship with the Taurus energy of her sixth house of everyday life and routine: Work would have been her best medicine. She had Leo and Virgo very closely cusping her tenth house, which means she had access to both the powerful Leo creative energy as well as the drive associated with Mars in detail-oriented Virgo—perfect for explaining her impressive oeuvre at Doubleday.

Would Jackie . . .

Sneak into first class? You bet, because it became her—as it will you. You'll see just how much so when you dart through the curtain or gate separating you from the engraved luggage caste. A bold approach is required here, so act as if you truly do belong. Your best chance for class-hopping on airplanes is aboard international flights, where larger cabins make good hiding places and a worldly crew is apt to admire your moxie.

On the *Queen Elizabeth*, a young Jackie and Lee regularly slipped into first class from third. Though they deemed it good fun, it certainly also gave them access to better food and drink—not to mention some hot dancing partners.

Listen to books on tape? Although she'd surely prefer to consume her words the old-fashioned way, she would also make some exceptions for certain titles and circumstances. We think she'd love the idea, for example, of listening to the dreamy voice of her friend Bill Clinton, who narrated his autobiography, while ripping down the highway in her BMW. And if she really liked a book, she'd stock her library with the hardback original anyway.

Sneak food into the movies? Why, of course, since at least half the enjoyment of a film may be contained between two slices of yummy homemade bread. Jackie got a kick out of spiriting more than just snacks into the theater. She brought entire picnic baskets. At a time when movie tickets are costly, and theaters force you to view endless ads and promotions, why should you have to buy their overpriced dogs and corn? So long as your foods aren't particularly redolent, and you tidy up during the credits, go ahead.

Join a church for the purpose of being able to perform certain rites there? Yes. Every city has but a few prestigious places of worship. And plenty of folks want to celebrate baptisms, weddings, and funerals there. Of course, this often requires membership. Jackie, who clearly saw the need to have more than one place to pray—fancy and plain—would understand.

Though she mainly worshipped in New York City at the modest Church of St. Thomas More, she preferred the more patrician St. Ignatius Loyola for big celebrations and rites. She was christened, confirmed, and eulogized at the latter church, on Park Avenue.

Chapter 7

Career Whirl:

Pearls for Getting Ahead

> *"People who work themselves*
> *have respect for the work of others."*
> —JBKO

P erhaps you are young and scrappy, beginning the arduous climb through your chosen field. Jackie was there. Maybe you have impressive professional or "life experience" credentials (elegant elephant rides count) and are looking for the next challenge. Jackie was there, too. Or possibly you are entering—or reentering—the professional world later in life. Yes, Jackie did that as well.

A naturally driven worker and networker, Jackie racked up some unusual and compelling experience from which you can learn. Even though her journey was circuitous and her official career as a book editor didn't begin until she was 46 years old, she was hardly a slouch. She balanced short-term agendas with long-term vision, motivating those around her all the while. She latched on to mentor figures and hoarded contacts like so many precious collectibles.

INSERT YOUR
KITTEN-HEELED SHOE IN THE DOOR

Rule No. 1:
◆ Savor Passion Fruits ◆

Be true to what naturally interests you—and be brave enough to turn an obsession into a profession. Jackie was always drawn to books; she digested Chekhov's short stories as a preteen. Later, she helped JFK pull together *Profiles in Courage*. It's widely known that Jackie served as de facto editor on Mary ("Molly") Van Rensselaer Thayer's two biographies of her (she approved pages as Molly submitted them, and even secured a publisher). In 1974, Lee published her and Jackie's European travel journal from 1951, *One Special Summer*.

And so by the time she sat down in 1975 with Thomas Guinzburg, then president of Viking, to discuss a job in publishing, her ultimate calling had already played a transforming role in her life. But what Jackie really did—and you shouldn't be shy about considering—is reinvent herself time and again. Her public popularity had plummeted during her Onassis phase; her book editing career made people love and admire her once more. As she wrote in *Ms.* magazine in March 1979, "You have to be doing something you enjoy. That is a definition of happiness: 'complete use of one's faculties along the lines leading to excellence in a life affording them scope.' "

Think you'd make a successful antiques dealer? Try selling a few items on eBay or participating in a local flea market first as a reality check to determine whether the world of old objects truly calls to you—and vice versa. Suspect you have a talent for product development but you are stuck in a sales job? Befriend the creative arbiters within your company or use your college's alum services to network with other execs outside your day-to-day milieu. If you're clever and make a First Lady–like impression (see "Daily Bred," p. 11), they may be conduits to new positions, if not mentors. Jackie always assessed her abilities realistically: She loved dance and the American Ballet Theatre, for instance, but knew better than to try to pirouette her way into a pro dance career.

Rule No. 2:
◆ Listen to Backseat Drivers ◆

Call on your friends and family to do the unthinkable: catalog your strengths for you. This is not an exercise in ego-building (or demolishing), but rather a helpful analytical tool. If three different loved ones praise your people skills—and you work alone—maybe it's time to summon the manager within. When Letitia Baldrige suggested over lunch that she seek out a job in book publishing after Onassis's death, Jackie was at first surprised. All she could focus on was her lack of experience—and all Baldrige could see seated in front of her was a book lover with an extraordinary sense of organization.

Rule No. 3:
◆ Don't Let a Little Inexperience Stand in Your Way ◆

Of course, you don't want to lie about your qualifications (padding is for bras, not résumés). However, if a job you covet requires a particular skill you lack but can master quickly—then by all means claim it. As long as you fib with intent, this counts as projecting into the future, not deception. Jackie used this logic, no doubt, in her first job as a photojournalist for the *Washington Times-Herald*: When her boss-to-be asked her if she could use a contraption called the Speed Graphic camera, she talked up her limited photographic experience—and then rushed out to take a crash course in news photography from a staffer to fine-tune her skills. And when she parachuted into publishing without any official experience, she did so as an on-the-job apprentice. In fact, that's the title she initially suggested for herself at Viking.

Rule No. 4:
◆ Connect the Dots ◆

Screen friends and family for any possible contacts in your chosen profession—and then liberally apply all your charms. Don't fret over the appearance of nepotism or cronyism—no one has since the 1980s. The merit part kicks in only when you start to work. Absolutely any edge you have is worth exploiting.

Jackie was a master at flicking her bitten-down nails through a Rolodex, looking for six (or five or four) degrees of separation. One example: She talked her stepfather, Hugh Auchincloss, into calling his friend Arthur Krock, chief of the *New York Times*'s Washington bureau, to telephone Frank Waldrop, editor of the *Washington Times-Herald*, so she could get a job there. And then she wisely accepted the position as the Inquiring Camera Girl, a gig that provided a bit-writing part. She figured that once inside the paper, she would have more of a chance to look for bigger reporting opportunities.

Similarly, when she finally agreed with Tish Baldrige that book publishing might be just the ticket for her, Jackie had Baldrige call up Guinzburg to plant the idea. He, too, had known Jackie since before she married JFK, so the ties were already there.

Rule No. 5:
◆ Don't Take Lip for Starting Late ◆

Hey, since these days 50 is the new 30, embarking on a novel endeavor later in your professional life isn't as tough as it was in Jackie's day. "Jackie was a trailblazer for women to be independent and do what brings them pleasure rather than [bowing to] how society defines their choices," says Faye Wattleton, head of the Center for Advancement of Women. "By entering publishing later in life, Jackie broke with that defining role that we had all put her in."

Chances are, in fact, that with a few extra miles on your odometer, you'll be more credentialed and capable of tackling a new field.

But you may also endure more-than-average push-back from your colleagues at first. Exhibit some well-bred backbone—and line up a few strong defensive moves. Jackie was well aware that she raised some eyebrows—both because of who she was and also because of her age—and showed some chutzpah: "It's not as if I've never done anything interesting," she said to a friend. "I've been a reporter myself and I've lived through important parts of American history. I'm not the worst choice for this position." To prove her point, she attended all manner of editorial meetings, from idea pitching to budgeting, and made it her business to contribute.

Rule No. 6:
◆ **Focus on the Position as Well as the Pay** ◆

Whether you need the money or not, being offered a healthy salary is an extra vote of confidence from your employer. Up to a point, there's always some negotiating room; be sure to sharpen your bargaining skills beforehand. At the same time, don't underestimate the value of a good title: It's what the world sees and how future employers will assess you. So when you hit the wall on moola, try for a better label.

When Jackie agreed to take a job at Viking, she did so for only $10,000 annually, but with the lofty-sounding moniker of Consulting Editor. Said Guinzburg, "I explained that that could be just about anything one might want to define it as . . . somebody who didn't have what we call 'line responsibilities,' they're not assigned books, they don't even necessarily have to work out of the office. Their primary job is to acquire books."

Even at Doubleday, her next publishing job, where she oversaw dozens of books over sixteen years, she started with a salary of $20,000 and never hit six figures. But her ultimate title—Senior Editor—at once established her as an active, pencil-wielding publishing pro.

FIRST CAREER:
First Lady

There are more skills lurking in your day-to-day grind than you might imagine. Take a hard look at the way Jackie ran her (East) Wing of the White House, and you'll spot a Fortune 500 exec cloaked in a ball gown. She had an iron-fisted grasp of marketing, customer service, and management. With thousands of letters pouring in from around the world, delegations to host, frequent travel, expenses to oversee, and a screaming bunch of kids upstairs in the White House school, Jackie was nothing less than a CEO.

A few other titles she earned during her tenure at 1600 Pennsylvania Avenue:

VP of Human Resources. No matter how good you are, you can't go it alone—so identify underlings who can further your cause. According to those who worked with her, Jackie was a great manager: "It was inbuilt in her," says Baldrige. "She was a good delegator; she wanted every task done right away and perfectly. And she discovered all these people with power—like White House usher/concierge J. B. West—and she used them, thanked them, and gave them credit."

Chairman of the Board. Got a big dream? Then act like it. Pull together a board of experts to help you mastermind your vision. Jackie orchestrated an expensive and difficult renovation of a public landmark, recruited a world-class group of cross-disciplinary luminaries to help (and soothed their egos), and solicited big-ticket donations from wealthy patrons (see "En Suite Home," p. 125). All this, mind you, after personally persuading members of Congress to pass a law defining the White House as a national monument.

Chief Operating Officer. Multitask like a master. To do so requires that you grade tasks in order of importance—without letting the minor details dangle. Jackie kept a cool eye on all daily functions, from seating at dinner parties and speechwriting to how much the kitchen staff spent on asparagus. She and Baldrige developed a folder system; red-hot items went into a file marked "priority." Jackie would decide and respond to those issues within two hours. Less urgent queries—did Jackie want a twin- or a king-size bed on her next trip?—went in regular manila folders, which she would answer within two days.

Chief Financial Officer. Fear them not: The only way to work (or massage) the numbers is to know them intimately. So roll up your sleeves, grab a calculator or mouse, and dive in. While her beloved father-in-law, Joe Kennedy, paid for Jackie's exorbitant clothing bills during the White House years, she and her staff were still responsible for other expenditures, such as keeping the Kennedys' personal bills on food and entertaining separate from the official state T&E budgets. Jackie was also on the hook for tallying the complex and expensive White House Restoration project—a feat requiring some impressive spreadsheet skills.

Creative Director. Don't let politics and heaps of hubris deter you from your long-term goals. Take charge and be imaginative

continues . . .

about how to keep the team on task. During the White House restoration, Sister Parish grew so irked at the encroaching role of rival decorator Stéphane Boudin that she threatened to quit. When competitive pressures peaked—Parish frowned on the Frenchman's idea for window treatments—Jackie ironed out tensions: She allowed the draperies of Boudin's choosing, but adhered to Parish's installation preference, which called for less fabric.

Public Relations Director. When even the best-run ship goes aground, trot out your interpersonal skills—and if things really go wrong, blame the staff (just don't name names). If Jackie caught wind of a mix-up on her crew's part, she would step in to diffuse the situation. When literary critic Lionel Trilling sent her D. H. Lawrence's *The Rainbow,* for example, and in return got a typed letter thanking him for short stories, Jackie fired off a handwritten note: "Dear Mr. Trilling, You are not the first to receive a letter thanking you for the wrong thing from the snake-pit which is my office in the W. House . . ."

◆　◆　◆

"A smart, beautiful woman like Jackie has a lot of advantages in business today. But one very admirable thing about her publishing career: She wasn't the boss. She went to work because she loved books and loved the opportunity to make them. She could have found a place that would have named her queen, and she didn't do that." —STANLEY BING, MEDIA EXECUTIVE, AUTHOR, AND *FORTUNE* COLUMNIST

◆　◆　◆

HOW TO ADVANCE GRACEFULLY

Once you're settled in your job, scan the cubicles to see who's getting kudos and who isn't—and for what. Although every office culture has its quirks, there are some universal tricks you can tweak to further your cause.

Fire your inner prima donna. Even if it isn't in your job description to update the group meeting calendar or tidy up around the copier, do it anyway—in full view of colleagues. It'll give coworkers the impression that you don't think you're above the menial stuff and they'll like you better for it. At Viking, Jackie did her own doll deeds, from typing to copying, and never relied on gofers. Later, as a full-fledged editor at Doubleday, Jackie continued to make her own phone calls and personally greeted her guests in the reception area. She also graciously accepted a tiny interior office when she first started, saying, "Oh, that's all right. I've lots of windows in my home." In an act of low-wage solidarity, she "decorated" with a single ballet poster.

Show a little muscle. It's vital that the troops see you take a strong stand from time to time. Whether it's supporting a controversial idea or setting a public goal for yourself, showing some guts (without drama, please) makes you promotable. During her publishing years, the normally reserved Jackie would occasionally flaunt her successes: After *The Power of Myth*—a hard-won Jackie project—flew off shelves, Jackie used it as leverage to get the green light on other proposals. "With all the copies of *The Power of Myth* that were sold," she'd ask in meetings, "don't I get a couple of books that I want to do?"

Jackie's determination helped push through other ideas. She convinced the Viking editorial board that she needed to go in person to the Soviet Union to see costumes worn by Nicholas and Alexandra for *In the Russian Style*. She also campaigned for Doubleday to publish George Plimpton's quirky book on fireworks. No one but Jackie thought it would do well. It did.

Be your own most fabulous boss. Don't be so naïve as to assume that bosses will be thinking of you first and foremost; they have their own job security and shrink appointments to fret about. Track your own progress, and ask for feedback well before your annual review. (It's always better to hear a negative comment in a timely fashion and work on fixing it.) If you feel ready, request more responsibility. When she started at Viking, Jackie hounded Guinzburg for new challenges; she rightly believed it was the only way she was going to learn the inner workings of book publishing. Said Guinzburg, "A couple of times she wrote me a letter saying, 'Don't be so lenient with me. I may not be a professional publisher, but I want to learn, and the only way I can do it is if you give me more to do.'"

Grab that (platinum) ring. When a great opportunity presents itself, don't think twice—it may never come again. If you're a journalist and you run into a big-deal publisher at a party, boldly introduce yourself and get busy; cocktail napkins have a long history of being jotted on. As an editor, Jackie dipped into her contacts going as far back as her school days. As Jackie's friend Carly Simon observed, "She knew that it's very important to consult with other wise people to become great yourself."

A little sleight of hand is all in a good day's work. It's okay to occasionally get creative with the boundaries of office propriety—when it saves your neck. If a flirtatious coworker won't take the hint, for instance, slip a solitaire ring onto your left hand (spectacular fakes are OK) and let him assume you're spoken for. Or if an out-of-line competitor asks you a confidential question at a trade show, feign ignorance. Jackie was the master of such moments: To throw off journalists—e.g., those who called her office to confirm rumors that Jimmy Carter was going to appoint her ambassador to Great Britain—she would answer the phone in a Spanish accent and say, "Mee-sess Onassis *no está aquí*."

Suck up when there's payoff potential. Swallow hard and do what it takes to score what you want—but only if the payoff is tangible and sizable. Recruited in 1983 to help Michael Jackson—yes, the King of Pop—write his first book, *Moonwalk*, Jackie traveled to see him in California. After they cut the six-figure deal, the Elegant One allowed the Gloved One to escort her to Disneyland. Pirates of the Caribbean must have been painful for her to endure, but we can surmise what wafted through Jackie's mind at the time: The celebrity book would be a huge commercial hit (it reached No. 1 on the *New York Times* best-seller list) and score her points as a rainmaking editor. (It did.)

MAKING YOUR WORK FIT YOUR LIFE

◆ Flex Your Flextime ◆

Pity the nine-to-fivers—so predictable, so dull. Seek out a profession that either tolerates—or, better, promotes—flextime, and then use it. Even if it's not among your company's formal offerings, ask for it. Lots of people get flexible hours as a side perk. Whether that means working from home on certain days or working a four-day week, it's an ideal opportunity to have more time with the kids, peruse the next great American novel—or just check out the Hermès sample sale.

Jackie was an early adopter of flextime: When she moved to the White House in 1961, she allowed her personal secretary, Mary Gallagher, to work three days a week rather than lose her (Mary had two young children at home). And throughout her book publishing years, Jackie herself usually went to the office three or four days a week. But during her off-hours she wasn't idle: She used the quiet time she had at 1040 Fifth or on the Vineyard to pore over manuscripts.

If the Job Doesn't Fit—Reject It

To bask in the flattery of a job offer is glorious. But if the position feels like an awkward fit, reject it—even if you discover that only after you've accepted. The longer you wait to admit you're in the wrong spot, the harder it will be to right your own course, and the worse off all parties involved will be.

Before she could get ink on her hands at *Vogue* in 1951, Jackie quit. Some versions of the story say she did it because she realized that she would be working with mostly women and gay men and that the fashion magazine was no place to lengthen her list of eligible males. Other accounts point to her mother, Janet, who may have wanted to keep her away from her father, then living in New York. Either way, Jackie surveyed the scene and then told the editors that her mother "felt terrifically strongly" about keeping her at home.

Don't Let Others Use You

As tasty and enticing as an offer may be, look behind, above, and below it for others' ulterior motives. Jackie refused numerous offers from LBJ, including appointments as ambassador to France and Mexico. While the positions were prestigious and would have appealed to Jackie's cultural interests, she suspected that LBJ was trying to use her for his re-election effort.

How to Take (and Give) No for an Answer

Count on your colleagues and contacts to shoot down some of your ideas, suggestions, requests. Rather than brood under the spectre of rejection, take such lumps as an opportunity to thicken your skin. Jackie certainly heard "no" often enough: She approached many noteworthies, including Queen Elizabeth and the Duchess of Windsor, hoping to publish books about them; she got the royal boot in both cases. Despite such high-level rejection, she never cowered. Other glamorous

Men vs. Women in the Workplace

You know the difference: You are smart (but not too smart) and simpatico with your female colleagues. You're clever, charming, and more overtly competitive with your male coworkers. This dichotomy is not a bad thing; it's simply honest. Jackie cleverly played each gender's tune at work. After all, she had had decades of practice in diplomacy and getting what she wanted. She knew to disarm a woman by calling her "pretty," and that her breathless powers over men were unequaled. A few pointers:

Women and Work:

◆ *More nurture, less vulture.* No matter your age, show the women that you are maternal and caring. They'll feel comforted, less threatened—and will confide in you more readily. Jackie, knowing the effect her persona had on her coworkers, chided colleagues at Doubleday for not wearing hats in winter and admonished them to take her favorite cold remedy, TheraFlu.

◆ *Hop into the backseat every so often.* Admitting you aren't perfect resonates with other women—they feel at once compassionate and a bit superior. Let them. In front of female colleagues at Viking, Jackie implored boss Tom Guinzburg to "ask all the hard questions" while on a conference call with an author.

◆ *Be a straight shooter.* Sometimes guilelessness is the best policy with a female coworker. Jackie was at once disarmingly straightforward and unemotional when she asked Lisa Drew,

continues . . .

then her direct boss at Doubleday, who was pushing for celebrity autobiographies, "Is there anybody else you'd like me to try and get?"

◆ *Let loose.* Women with real power can unbutton that well-tailored jacket and work shoulder-to-shoulder with the troops, who will always remember such gestures. When *Town & Country* editor-in-chief Pamela Fiori collaborated with Jackie on a photography book, she remembers with surprise how Jackie deformalized their first meeting in early 1994. "She was incredibly gracious, offering us coffee and pastries, and then she plopped right down on the floor right at my feet and started spreading pages out," says Fiori. "She was intensely serious about the design, and I immediately respected her for that."

Men and Work:

◆ *Speak-a their language.* Guys like a little dramatic overstatement: It shows you have cojones. At Doubleday, an editor mentioned during a meeting that he was trying to snag a Hunter Thompson book. Jackie slipped a note to the colleague next to her: "I would give up food to publish Hunter Thompson."

◆ *Whip out your soft side.* Delivering a critique to an ego-inflated male? Just drop your voice to a Jackie near-whisper or throw in a few self-defacing comments to lessen the blow. At the beginning of a long letter outlining many manuscript changes to author Louis Auchincloss (a cousin by marriage), Jackie wrote, "The most uncomfortable thing I have ever had to do is edit your immaculate writing." She was also fond of signing business letters with "much love" and "affectionately"; who could resist? She even disarmed the feisty *Rolling Stone* founder Jann Wenner in a heated meeting about the cover of *The Best of Rolling Stone: 25 Years of Journalism on the Edge* when she breathily said, "You're such a bully!" He turned to putty.

◆ *Pump them up.* And they'll be on your side forever. According to Richard de Combray, a non-fiction writer and novelist whose books Jackie edited at Doubleday, "It was enormously appealing sitting opposite this woman who, with all this baggage she carried, this fame and fortune, whatever, was totally absorbed by whatever it is you were saying to her." Such a professionally beguiling manner is a sure-fire hubris enhancer.

◆ *Show them the money.* Guys really relate to the bottom line, so demonstrate that it's in your crosshairs, too. Jackie gained a reputation at Doubleday for effectively projecting numbers on a book's eventual success. She also knew when to dangle the dough with writers and agents: In a letter to Hugh Fraser, for instance, she wrote: ". . . We then take [your idea] to the top and get lots more money. . . . I can't wait to see you in November, when we can count your money and invest it in diamonds."

rejecters: Lord Snowden, Greta Garbo, Elizabeth Taylor, Brigitte Bardot, Katharine Hepburn, Bette Davis, Barbara Walters, Prince, Ted Turner, and Frank Sinatra, among others. Later she tried to persuade Princess Diana and Mia Farrow to do books (she was fascinated by the Farrow/Woody Allen/Soon-Yi Previn saga), but again was unsuccessful.

All the turn-downs didn't make Jackie any more sympathetic to those trying to get her to talk. She continued to refuse interviews about her own life, even by her close friends Aileen Mehle (gossip/society columnist "Suzy") and George Plimpton, who offered to write her story for her family's consumption only.

UPSTAGING OFFICE POLITICS

Every office has 'em, few people like 'em—and a handful of crazies thrive on 'em. No matter which camp you fall into, be careful not to let them swallow you whole. Jackie was skilled at sizing up people and situations, but she disdained politics—which meant she had to work particularly hard to fit into the clubby publishing world.

Don't Be the Office Mascot

Whether you're female, black, a celebrity—or all three—you shouldn't let your coworkers abuse your status. Help break the pattern. Be confidently nonchalant if asked to PowerPoint for the big boss, for instance—but beware if you are always the one put on display. Jackie, the token celebrity, managed to be low-key with her publishing cohorts, asking everyone to simply call her Jackie. But if anyone treated her like Mrs. Kennedy Onassis, she shattered the pattern by freezing them out—and they at once knew that they had just made a CLM (Career Limiting Move).

Get to Checkmate Before They're at Check

It's worth doing some extra homework before a big meeting—especially one in which you hope to win support for a project. Before a definitive editorial powwow at Doubleday, at which she knew a few adversaries were going to attempt to shoot down her idea for a book with Tiffany's design director John Loring, Jackie called the author and prepped him. "We have to psych them out on this one," she said. It worked: She let the naysayers prattle on—and then let fly an argument so compellingly in her favor that no one could stonewall her further. "She knew how to tip the balance at the right moment in a meeting," said Loring.

❖ Dispense Praise High and Low ❖

You may know all the answers, but at least give your coworkers the il-
lusion that they have some say. A few kind words about their abilities
in meetings and to others will show that you are a keen observer and
may help fend off back-stabbing types. Jackie made a habit of passing
along comments from top editors to her authors. It made her look terribly plugged in—and if authors didn't like a remark that another editor
had made, at least they knew it wasn't coming from her.

Jackie also knew how to manage the creative temperament: According to Eugene Kennedy (no relation), author of two novels Jackie
edited, "She understood that writers, like fine china being prepared
for shipment, need to be packaged gently and supported strongly for
the long journey from blank paper to publication day."

❖ ❖ ❖

*"I'd love to have Jackie on my board of advisors
today. Who [in business] would have not
wanted her on their letterhead?"*
—FAYE WATTLETON, PRESIDENT,
CENTER FOR THE ADVANCEMENT OF WOMEN

❖ ❖ ❖

ON MENTORING:
How to Look Up and Down

Casting about for the ultimate career boost? Enlist a small group of
people whom you admire—and, more important, who believe in you—

to act as your own personal Board of Directors. You'll want to hit them up from time to time for advice on tactical and strategic planning, and for feedback if they work with you. Jackie collected such types at every stage of her life—she had a virtual boardroom full of them by the time she entered publishing. Both Viking's Tom Guinzburg and Doubleday's John Sargent shepherded her through the industry.

In her later years, Jackie herself was a mentor to several young people. At Doubleday, she doted on the young editors and editorial assistants around her, including Bruce Tracy and Scott Moyers, giving them advice on everything from career to personal matters. Said Moyers, "[She was] a profoundly generous woman, a sort of mother figure to us all, with a lot of empathy."

Tracy remembered going to Jackie with a quandary that his travel-obsessed colleague could certainly relate to. Having scheduled his maiden voyage to Europe, Tracy realized he would surely miss the launch of an important book. When he brought the issue to Jackie, she implored him to go. "Life comes first."

There is a lot to be said for being a mini-mentor, too. If a new talent comes along, but you can't directly help, grease his or her path as best you can. You'll have the satisfaction of doing a good turn, and who knows? He or she may even remember to thank you after making it big. Jackie liked to help authors place their book ideas with other publishers if her own editorial board turned down the proposal. In fact, she championed several such projects.

One was a novel, *The Hunting Ban*, by Spanish author Eduardo Garrigues, which Doubleday rejected. Jackie contacted literary agent James O. Brown to persuade him to help the foreigner along. "I wouldn't waste your time with all of this if I didn't think Eduardo was capable of producing something interesting. . . ." she wrote. "If another house jumps at his proposal, hooray—but if a good novel emerges eventually, I can do much better with it the second time around at Doubleday. . . ."

PLOT YOUR OWN PERKS

Free books, travel, or meals out on the company offer a chance to balance long hours and low pay (this is especially true in "glamour" jobs such as book and magazine editing). Just don't ever be too enthralled by the graft, or it'll come back to bite you.

As early as her first job at the *Times-Herald*, Jackie could suss out a good perk or two. When friend Aileen Bowdoin's mother suggested that her daughter sail to England to the queen's coronation and take Jackie, the Inquiring Camera Girl turned it into an assignment for the paper—and scored herself some great front-page clips in the process.

Much later, although Jackie's Doubleday salary wasn't great, she managed to make up her own perks. She adored the travel the job required at times. On top of her trip to Russia for *In the Russian Style*, she also trekked to China, the Middle East, and other exotic destinations. Visiting Russia, she persuaded museum curators to let her try on Alexandra's fur coat. In France, she sweet-talked her way into Versaille's non-public rooms in the name of research.

Perhaps her favorite publishing perk, however, was the tradition of lunching about town—"festive lunches," as she called them, at such places as Le Cirque and The Four Seasons. At the latter establishment, recalls managing partner Julian Niccolini, she reveled in the scene—and always kept her cool around competing editor and publisher types, such as quasi-nemesis and *Women's Wear Daily* boss John Fairchild.

Would Jackie . . .

   Hire a male assistant? Yes—and did. At Doubleday, Bruce Tracy and Scott Moyers were both her editorial assistants— she had long shown a flair for handling men. An extra plus of having the other sex handle your filing? They present no wardrobe competition.

Quit without notice? Yes, as long as the excuse is very, very good. When Viking published a novel about the assassination of a fictional President Ted Kennedy, a review in the *New York Times* insinuated Jackie had had something to do with the book. She quit at once—much to Tom Guinzburg's dismay and against his wishes. She disagreed with his version of the story—that she had known about the project all along—and refused to discuss the matter with him.

Put up with a little flirting or innuendo from a male colleague? No—and why should she, especially if it put her job security at risk? More women than we'd like to admit face unwanted attention from coworkers, and it's particularly harmful coming from a superior (who holds promotions and pay in his clutches). Given her desire to blend in professionally and her occasionally litigious nature, she'd likely be inclined to have the offender fired. Especially in the face of formal/professional matters, Jackie was nothing if not conservative; she was taken aback when President Carter innocently kissed her on the cheek at the Kennedy Library opening—a gesture few would have questioned.

Accept lavish gifts from work acquaintances? In certain circumstances, she'd find it tough to keep her hand out of the goody bag. That said, steering clear of the quid pro quo stigma would be of utmost importance to her, so she'd likely consider any such bounty on a case-by-case basis. Jackie is said to have accepted a watch from Michael Jackson for her work on *Moonwalk*. Her comfort level in doing so was probably based on the notion that she wouldn't work with the pop star again. And besides, his wealth—and hers—would have rendered the gift a trifle. It's doubtful, on the other hand, that she would accept a big-ticket thank-you from an author whose work might land on her desk again.

Be a slave to her BlackBerry? She'd absolutely have one and use it—with her travel schedule, she would have been as addicted as the rest of us to PDAs and cell phones. And given the fact that she fired an assistant by phone once, she'd also recruit it to deliver bad news; its real-time messaging would have been a draw to the correspondence-crazed Jackie. But she'd be discreet about its use: Just because it isn't ringing, don't think it isn't incredibly rude to thumb-type under the conference table during the boss's presentation. One drawback? The tiny keypad would be tough on the big-handed and wordy Jackie.

Hitch a ride on someone else's wireless Internet connection? Yes, considering her penchant for bumming more tangible things—a smoke and a light were common requests—as well as a naughty voyeuristic streak. If a strong signal from a neighbor wafted into her bedroom, she'd use it as a backup. Of course, as a mainstay, she'd have her own password-protected account.

Help herself to office supplies? Sure—within reason. Smythson stationery, after all, is pricey stuff, and even Jackie loved to economize. That may help explain why she frequently wrote personal notes on Doubleday letterhead. To assuage any guilt, give back by making sure your candy bowl is always full— Tootsie Rolls and plain M&M's were Jackie faves.

Chapter 8

Goal Digger:
Making Your Money Matter

> *"If one has to be trapped and unhappy,*
> *maybe it's better in sables after all."*
> —JBKO

Jackie's relationship with money holds some especially potent lessons. Her financial ups and downs (mainly ups) began as a child, when her beloved father lost much of his Wall Street fortune. Growing up the stepdaughter of wealthy Hugh Auchincloss wasn't enough to make her an equal in that trust-fund clan, and Jackie took to Washington an uneasiness about money that would, on some level, linger forever.

Yes, she had wild days of excess—which peaked during the Onassis years—speed-shopping her way through six figures' worth of shoes, jewelry, and entire couture collections. Those sprees, though, abated with age, as Jackie the editor largely muted her extravagant urges, taking taxis to work and lunching on foil-wrapped turkey sandwiches.

The original "Money Honey," Jackie knew how to maintain proximity to major moolah, how to extract pleasure from it and summon its curative powers. "I think that shopping to give yourself a lift is a valuable form of do-it-yourself therapy," she once said. In death, Jackie used money as both a gift and a diss—revealing her complex feelings for everyone from her loyal maid Provi Paredes (to whom she bequeathed $50,000) to her sister Lee (who got nothing). Speaking of the latter directive, half brother Jamie Auchincloss says, "It was definitely a shot from beyond."

MONETARY ATTITUDE ADJUSTMENTS

How to benefit from such tangled fiscal sensibilities? Let's start with two key monetary attitude adjustments (MAAs) that Jackie would surely condone:

✦ Yes, It Can Pay to Splurge ✦

A little extravagance can be defensible, so long as you buy the right things, appraising them for their payoff potential. Ask yourself, "Can this object, in *any* way, be construed as a life investment?" By "life investment" we mean something that will not only appreciate monetarily, but that will also a) save you money in the long-term, or b) grant you status, cultural enrichment, and/or intense pleasure.

Of course, stock or real estate qualifies as an investment. So, too, under this rule, as often applied by Jackie, is a first-rate dressage horse (to boost your competitive edge) or a fine musical instrument (to harness your creative energy). Keep in mind products that offer lifetime warranties (Calphalon pots and pans, or items that come with superlative service, such as a Lexus). Even over-the-top feminine accoutrements can occasionally be considered an "investment." So the next time your beloved wails over the AmEx bill—perhaps those $1,800 custom-made lizard sling-backs?—point out not only that they are timeless and well crafted, but how they have eradicated the desire to buy the four lesser pairs you eyed at Saks.

When Ari Onassis complained about Jackie's plain panties, she immediately appealed to designer Halston to stitch up more than $5,000 worth of unmentionables—a move she surely deemed necessary to boost her intimate prospects. Priceless, wouldn't you say?

✦ Disregard Labels Like "Old Money" ✦

Growing up, Jackie was drawn to patrician types with pedigreed fortunes. But when it came to wooing monied folks later in life, she had a more egalitarian approach. Onassis may have been nouveau riche, but he was also ne plus ultra rich. Diamond dealer/financier Maurice Tempelsman didn't have generational cash; he earned his own, gemsational cache, which was more than enough for her in the end.

Such logic—that money is money is money—resonates even more powerfully today. Surely you've noticed how even *Town & Country* has bulked up its coverage of post–Bill Gates millionaires? So ignore any tacit class rules that "WASP-y" types may wish to invoke. Don a spectacular hat and twirl about the Hamptons Classic horse show (even if you've only ever had a pony ride). March into the important auction houses—Sotheby's, Christie's—to check out the magnificent gems during their pre-jewelry sale viewing periods, making it your business to coax the biggest, bling-est baubles from their cases (try-ons are free, *bien sur*). It doesn't actually matter if you can or can't afford the ice—let everyone whisper and wonder.

✦ ✦ ✦

"For a woman who has money as Jackie did, the question is how to hold onto it. It's so important to be educated about where your money is, what's coming in and going out. Get over the fear— it's not brain surgery—it's easier than you think."

—MARIA BARTIROMO, CNBC ANCHOR

✦ ✦ ✦

"TIT FOR TAT" AND OTHER USEFUL MONEY-SAVING WINKS

Feel free to accept any side dividends for favors or projects you take on. This might mean free Thin Mints from the Girl Scouts for donating time to their cookie cause. Or first dibs on all the couture cast-offs at New York's annual charity Posh sale (yes, some volunteers have been known to bag the choiciest loot long before the public opening).

❖ Make Secret Barter Deals ❖

Lack of funds shouldn't necessarily prevent you from acquiring the things you so desire. Who has what you want, and vice versa? Bartering gets what you covet without bleeding your own bank account. It also gives you power by handing off something that may be a trifle to you, but a hot ticket to the other party. Jackie profited from this technique with portrait painter Aaron Shikler.

While dating Onassis, she had the artist draw more than 30 studies of her children—without any explicit agreement that she would buy the works. She adored the sketches, but balked at paying for them. An opportunity presented itself when Jackie asked Shikler to paint her official White House portrait—a commission that brought him considerable notice, and the offer of a lucrative writing assignment from *McCall's*.

Knowing that she would frown on any publicity over the topic, he approached her with a deal: "Let's make a tradeoff," he said. "You give me permission for the article. You can look at the article before it's printed. . . . You keep the [children's picture] studies, but I get the article." Jackie had already tried, and failed, to get Onassis to buy some of the works. So with the arrangement, she got her beloved art, and Shikler got his payday.

On a similar note, in the late fifties, Jackie and her sister Lee agreed to model high-fashion clothes for *Ladies' Home Journal*—provided the fashion-obsessed women could keep the expensive outfits. Though some reports have claimed that the magazine frowned upon the terms, the editors of the publication say it wasn't so: "Tit for tat, don't you know, which we were glad to do," is how coeditor Bruce Gould recalled the deal. (Disclaimer: Such graft isn't acceptable to take if you are professionally involved in the field. Had Jackie been a fashion journalist, the plot wouldn't have been proper.)

If you're a style maven, offer to perform a makeover for your rumpled realtor in lieu of paying a hefty broker's fee. As a publicist, you might lend your talents to a travel agency in exchange for a trip to Turkey. Bear in mind that not everyone cottons to a trade, so be prepared for rejection, which stung even Jackie. When she asked a contractor whether he would like to be paid, or receive a signed photograph, he tersely replied that he preferred an autographed check.

Re-Gift to Save Time, Money, Storage Space

Imagine the budget-boosting cheer of receiving a gift, then passing it along for others to enjoy! Let's dispense with any mock horror over the idea. Everybody does it, with a wink and a nod. Jackie did, too. During the White House years, as presents flowed in from around the world, she made it her business to send art, dolls, and hand-knitted Peruvian caps to needy folks at hospitals and charities. She also screened packages for items that could be re-gifted as presents for friends, relatives, and staffers.

There's no stigma here, so long as the goods you re-gift are lovely to begin with. If you're blessed with a surfeit of leaded crystal and sterling serving pieces, why not give them to a grateful new owner? Jackie would shudder only at the more common re-gifting ruse, which involves playing hot potato with truly awful stuff. Handing off ugly sweaters with reindeer—from taste-challenged Secret Santas—is never acceptable.

• PEARL •

Take the same care in doling out re-gifted items as you would
with first-generation presents. That set of Mahler symphonies
is all wrong for your tone-deaf friend; men tend to abhor ginger-
scented candles. Also, re-wrap your re-goodies in paper that
reflects your own taste.

◆ Never Overpay, Not Even for Veggies ◆

Dare to part with serious dollars for the material things that matter
most to you in life, but never overpay for all the rest—not even produce. Jackie, to say the least, was hardly a penny-pincher when it came
to home decorating or wardrobing (her clothing expenses for the
month of January 1962 were about $5,000, or the staggering equiva-
lent of $31,000 today). Yet she exhaustively saved dollars and cents on
all other manner of purchases, going so far as to return vegetables to a
store when she found a better deal. She implored White House usher
J. B. West to buy booze and food from wholesalers, and sent assistants
scurrying to discount stores to comb for gifts. (Jackie was thrilled when
personal secretary Mary Gallagher found cute sweaters for $8.95!)

◆ Charge It to Uncle Sam ◆

Have you considered how Uncle Sam might tip his hat to your fanciful lifestyle, swooping in to pick up the tab for an indulgence here and
there? Granted, this demands both creative and accounting smarts,
something you and Jackie no doubt have in common.

Ever financially enterprising, Jackie took pains to figure out
whether certain White House parties could be deducted. She also at

least mulled how she could score a possible farm tax deduction for Glen Ora, the retreat she shared with JFK in Virginia's hunt country. After all, cows and horses *were* roaming about! If it was worth a try then, what's stopping you now?

As magnates like Steve Forbes know, certain state farm write-offs can apply to Beverly Hills types, not just hillbillies. In New Jersey, for instance, the farmland assessment program gives huge property tax breaks to "farmers"—folks who devote as little as five qualified acres to raising anything from Christmas trees to cattle—so long as they generate $500 or more in annual revenue.

Have a way with words? You can perhaps cover your jaunt to Paris by penning an article about your adventures. Publish the work and a write-off is yours, as a cost of doing business, or an un-reimbursed business expense. SUV fans may be able to take advantage of an odd IRS rule that allows a hefty write-off for some vehicles—provided you operate a business and meet certain limitations. Hybrid cars, like Toyota's Prius, also score you a one-time tax break. So check with your accountant.

SLIP YOUR (ELEGANTLY GLOVED) HAND INTO OTHERS' POCKETS

The best kind of money is other people's money—especially when you manage to magically transfer it to your bank account or cause.

Asked to participate in the 1991 festivities surrounding the reopening of Henri Bendel after the Manhattan specialty store had been acquired and relocated by Leslie Wexner's Limited Brands Inc., Jackie agreed. She hosted an opening event, and smiled for the cameras as the wealthy Wexner basked in her glow. The underlying beneficiary of this fashion moment: The New York Municipal Art Society, one of Jackie's favorite causes.

KA-CHING!

How to Haggle and Hoard Like Jackie

In a Jackie world, prices are negotiable and sources are replaceable. Intoxicated by a good bargain, she was known to press for reductions on even the smallest items, and she was always on the lookout for newer, cheaper vendors. Shopping for flowers on New York's Madison Avenue one day, Jackie ran into interior decorator Albert Hadley. Turning to him, she said, "Albert, have you been to the new shop up the street? Well, it's very good and they're much less expensive."

♦ *Count the change.* Jackie appreciated how money that jingles adds up. She made sure she got what was coming to her, even when the margin was oh-so-small ($3.75 back on a 1960s furniture purchase; a $2.97 tax refund in 1984).

♦ *Name your price.* When searching for goods or services of any kind, consider the price tag as the merchant's opening bid, and paddle down from there. Today, even department stores may cut you a side deal if a garment has a slight flaw, and Web sites like bizrate.com can arm you with the latest low-price information. Tip: Jackie sometimes had others inquire for her. Despite today's digital resources, this old-fashioned tactic is still smart in some cases—especially with car purchases, where women often get a raw deal.

◆ *Increase their customer base.* With contractors, Jackie often talked up how she could help them drum up more business—so long as they gave her a "special price." When it's time for your kitchen or bath redo, gain some leverage by casting about for others in similar renovation mode. Then plot a possible group deal.

◆ *Be on alert for adjust-o-matic rebates.* Since Jackie had no qualms about returning goods to stores—she even sent things back to Hermès in Paris—we're sure she'd love the idea of a price adjustment. Once you've made a purchase, keep your eyes peeled for subsequent markdowns. Many stores, even tony ones such as Bergdorf's and Barneys New York, will give you cash back to reflect an item's new price—just be quick about it.

◆ *Don't discount coupons.* They arrive in our mail and in our newspapers, and yes, most of us toss them. Jackie wouldn't. At least scour for treasures, like the $50 rebate Home Depot sometimes offers on appliances—for as much as a 10 percent savings. Jackie giddily collected trading stamps, and redeemed them for practical purchases as well as gifts.

◆ *Run up a tab.* Jackie didn't always pay for goods and services right away—she had house accounts. If you're a frequent customer at a shop (and your Equifax report is clean), perhaps you can arrange this kind of courtesy credit. It's the equivalent of charging on plastic, without the hefty interest rates.

continues . . .

> ◆ *Be a fashion doll.* Look good enough, be seen enough, and you may be able to score clothing discounts for being such a hardworking mannequin. Knowing that she was endlessly photographed—and that her fashion choices could wipe out store inventories overnight—Jackie sought price breaks at places like Bonwit Teller, a now-defunct specialty store. If you're not in that league, try a simpler approach: Ask. Many big-chain salesclerks—at Macy's, Bloomingdale's, etc.—will slip you a discount at the register if you sweetly inquire. Instantly redeemable coupons can save you 10 percent or more.

It's all in the execution, you see. Jackie took stock of her "show and tell" value to others, and used it accordingly. The logic: If you're being used, feel free to use back.

Consider Jackie's stance during a trip to Iran in 1972. In her zeal to soak up the local culture—and take her wealthy hosts' generosity at face value—she scooped up six-figures' worth of clothing, jewelry, and *objets*, charging the booty to the oilman Reza Fallah (at his insistence, of course).

Even if you're not so bold, do accept all invitations from well-to-do acquaintances—factoring in the cachet you bring to the table. (Perhaps they like to brag about their friendship with you, the weapons inspector!) And if your hosts are kind enough to pick up dinner or spring for a ski outing, be your best gracious self and leave behind a thoughtful gift.

Use matter-of-fact flattery ("Oh, I so love your Miro!") to score additional windfalls. Jackie effortlessly gave praise to folks, whether the remark stood to reward her or not (she was known to trill over people's decorative choices, such as Mary Gallagher's wallpaper). Other simpatico acts—like the time she rode horses with Ayub Khan of Pakistan in 1962—won her huge bennies. Arriving home after the trip, she was pleased to find that Sardar, the gelding she'd so brilliantly commanded, had been sent as a gift.

WAYS TO RAISE CASH IN A PINCH

The vocabulary here may seem a shade under-elegant (pawn, consign, resell, etc.). But the takeaway is gorgeous nonetheless: You should never be too sentimental about things. Jackie certainly wasn't. As proof, think back to 1996, when John and Caroline, acting within the spirit of their mother's will, orchestrated what was perhaps the auction of the century. Many people were aghast at the Sotheby's liquidation of her personal effects, thinking that it was very un-Jackie-like. In fact, it was classic Jackie, as was the second auction, in February 2005, of an additional six hundred odds and ends.

The first Sotheby's bidding frenzy brought in $34.5 million. Since then, more of her belongings have turned up on eBay, the on-line auction site that surely would have fascinated Jackie, considering its anonymity. If you're thinking of unloading your excess valuables, keep in mind that eBay says its most popular categories include fashion items and electronics.

Another Jackie fave: consignment shops. Boutiques like Ina and Michael's in New York and Decades Two in Los Angeles aren't just recently hip. These types of shops, which match gently used clothing with new owners, were a secret depository for many of Jackie's finest frocks. Before you haul your duds off to the thrift shop, think about the cash you can raise by going this route. Typically, stores give you about half of what they earn from a sale (which, alas, can be as little as one-tenth of an item's original value). At the famous shop Encore in New York, Jackie sold everything from suits to coats—under another donor's name, of course. The best part: You can plow the funds back into your wardrobe to buy updated pieces.

An avid recycler, Jackie employed another clever method to restock her jewelry box. In 1962, having swooned over a $6,000 diamond star-burst clip (about $37,000 in today's money) at the London boutique Wartski, she mined her own collection (including a diamond gem pin that had been a wedding gift) for possible trades. After securing appraisals for her loot, she swapped some of the best stuff, paying a difference of about $2,000 ($12,500 now) to win the pin.

◆ ◆ ◆

"I think Jackie was very smart about people, and she didn't take money for granted. One thing we hear over and over, particularly with some celebrities and athletes, is that they end up loaning money and giving it away as soon as they strike it rich. Unless you're smart enough to surround yourself with good advisors to say 'no' on your behalf, it's difficult to do on your own." —JEAN CHATZKY, EDITOR-AT-LARGE, MONEY; FINANCIAL EDITOR, NBC'S TODAY SHOW

◆ ◆ ◆

IDENTIFY POTENTIAL INVESTMENT ADVISORS EARLY

Forget the idea that friends and money don't mix. In certain circumstances they do. The trick isn't to rely on your current coterie for financial advice, but to foster relationships with those who have managed to smartly grow their own wealth.

Cozy up to such persons well before you need them. So what if you're not exactly dripping with dough yet? That shouldn't preclude you from getting to know a few brilliant, dashing financier types.

Jackie first met Maurice Tempelsman in 1958. His flawless business and political connections made him the perfect partner for Jackie later in life. And it's no surprise that Mrs. O chose old acquaintance André Meyer—known as the "Picasso of Banking"—as another financial confidante.

Resist any urge or pressure to hire family members, or folks without a proven track record for multiplying fortunes. Also steer clear of financial "advisors" who try to sell you stocks, insurance, annuities, etc. They may be biased in favor of investments that line their coffers with commissions.

To protect your fortune from pillagers (likely suspect: you), enlist someone who will question any large purchases or account withdrawals. Before buying her 15-room apartment on Fifth Avenue, Jackie sought the blessing of Meyer, who okayed the $200,000 deal.

DIVERSIFY YOUR PURSE

Just as it's never good to stick with one beau, one job, one bag, it's not a good idea to cling too fiercely to the investment vehicles that are most familiar. Jackie's holdings, for sure, consisted of the stocks and real estate of a pragmatic investor. But she also believed in taking a few risks—and so should you. Assuming, that is, that you have sage advice or professional know-how yourself.

Tucked into Jackie's portfolio was a real estate limited partnership (its main holding: shopping centers, of course!) whose partners included none other than Barbra Streisand's brother. The point of the investment was to realize a loss—and in the process provide a much-needed tax shelter. Over the years, Jackie also invested in risky gold futures, and poured millions into more conservative, tax-exempt New York City municipal bonds.

Would she do things a bit differently today? Most certainly. And not because we're in a do-it-yourself investment age. Jackie would likely be much more aggressive with her portfolio, especially as a younger woman, for the simple reason that "diversify" is now a mantra practically glued to the lining of any smart woman's purse.

Until the late 1970s, when she received her settlement from the Onassis estate, Jackie, with annual expenses in the six figures, was considered to be asset rich and cash poor. Her paper wealth was jeopardized in 1975 when her stash of sure-thing New York City muni bonds came close to hitting the skids. After seeing the possible dangers of cramming too many Fabergé eggs together, Jackie would surely want to open up her fiscal horizons. (Cue Mr. Tempelsman.)

For investors with moderate risk tolerance, financial planners typically suggest an asset allocation of 60 percent stocks, 35 percent fixed income securities (such as bonds), and 5 percent cash. More aggressive types — those who are younger and have a longer investment horizon — can ratchet up their stock portfolio to 70 percent or more of total assets.

GRACE AND WILLS

In death, just as in life, you'll want to ensure, to the best of your ability, that your affairs be properly tended. This means choosing executors who will carry out your wishes with savvy, respect, and a minimum of backbiting or sentimentality. For this reason, you'd be wise to select an executor who is not related by blood. Though many folks ask kin to do their postmortem bidding, such a designation can lead to "I should have that!" spats. Depending on your bequests, it can also avoid relative-on-relative confrontations upon the reading of the will.

In hers, for example, Jackie effectively disinherited her younger sister Lee: "I have made no provision in this my Will for my sister, Lee B. Radziwell, for whom I have great affection because I have already done so during my lifetime."

Ouch.

When casting about for an executor, many folks turn to family in hopes of avoiding executor fees, which can range from 2 to 5 percent of an estate's value. But bickering relatives can shrink an estate by much more in the event that attorneys need to be called in. So when naming your executor, consider persons who don't have designs on your assets, and who have been loyal to a fault. Should you feel it necessary to name more than one executor — a decision that may depend on the size and complexity of your estate — it also helps if they don't have strong emotional ties to each other, as do siblings. If they're financially astute enough to preserve and grow your after-life nest egg, all the better.

Jackie covered all these bases. She chose as co-executors Maurice Tempelsman and friend Alexander Forger, a trusts and estates attorney at New York law firm Milbank, Tweed, Hadley & McCloy.

She also made sure to update her will—a task you should take up every several years. Jackie last revised her will on March 22, 1994, about two months before her death.

▪ **PEARL** ▪

One way for wealthy types to avoid stinging federal estate taxes—which may or may not eventually be completely repealed—is to give away worldly goods early, to friends, family, or anybody else. The idea is that tax-free gifts can reduce the value of your estate, and hence its exposure to those nasty tariffs. All gifts up to $11,000 per person, per year, have the ability to shrink your estate.

A generous Jackie, tax laws permitting, might have given away more of her wealth and possessions during her lifetime had she foreseen the staggering values her personal property would fetch at auction. In 1996 after distributions, Jackie's estate had $18 million, but owed taxes of $23 million—an amount her children were liable for.

Would Jackie . . .

Refuse cold hard cash, ever? Yes, there are limits to accepting the generosity of others—especially when the funds are substantial, and can be diverted elsewhere for better cause. In 1966, Jackie petitioned Congress to decrease her widow's

TO PRENUP OR NOT?

By many accounts, she did, with Ari Onassis in 1968. And if confronting the issue again today—being on the richer or poorer end of the marriage aisle—she most surely would. Why? Because rather than view it as a tool to limit wealth, many women increasingly value prenups for what money can't buy: certainty. You know what you stand to get or give at every point before, during, and after the marriage.

A stickler for detail, Jackie would also appreciate the clarity afforded by prenups, as they compel the parties to discuss serious financial matters and accurately disclose their assets.

Take into account annual expenses, which can ratchet up fast if your tastes call for a private masseuse and daily visits from the florist. Jackie got Ari to agree to finance her high-maintenance lifestyle, which, given her consumption rate, was half the battle won.

What about the idea that a prenup is a love-killer? Well, include it on the long list of unromantic drudgery you'll have to face (e.g., blood tests, marriage certificates, dinners with in-laws, etc.).

In the end, of course, Jackie wound up with more than she initially bargained for—about $26 million from Onassis's estate.

Suppose you're the one with the big cache, and find it awkward to ask your intended to sign? Try passing the prenup buck with some gentle subterfuge.

Have your attorney draft for you what celebrity divorce lawyer Raoul Felder calls a "wink wink" note. The letter should be matter-of-fact in tone and appear to follow up on financial matters discussed in a previous meeting. "Dear So and So, You came to speak to me about your estate recently, and I'd be remiss if I didn't mention the advantages of a prenuptial contract." You can bring up the letter in calm conversation, over a nice bottle of Vouvray. Or leave it discreetly on your desk for—who knows?—to see. If your money comes from inheritance, you might tell your mate that your parents are the ones who insist you finalize the deed. "Honey, they just won't leave *us* any money if they think it could ever be in jeopardy. . . ."

office allowance, to $30,000 down from $50,000. The funds, she argued, were excessive given her diminishing public role, and she felt no need for the government to overspend on postage and office equipment.

Similarly, it would be unbecoming for you to accept a church scholarship for your kids if you have already socked away enough for their educations. Why not let someone else benefit?

Extend loans to friends and relatives? Only if they are in dire need (e.g., termites are ravaging their roof), and only then if you are prepared to a) make it a "gift" and be liable for any taxes or b) sustain a loss. Otherwise, a firm "no." Doling out funds within your immediate family (husband, kids) is tricky enough. Go extending the loop, and the emotional/financial bonds may quickly tangle.

Jackie, of course, was more likely to offer a (small) loan

than consider financial aid applications from hangers-on. One example: When a young publishing colleague fell ill, Jackie approached him and said he was welcome to "a few bucks" if he got strapped.

Remember that there are many other ways to be generous. Open up your world of connections to folks in need, as Jackie did with an aspiring Spanish writer—she steered him to an agent after Doubleday rejected his manuscript.

Live on a "budget"? Yes, and she doubtless learned a lot by keeping one, even if hers wasn't the average Quicken sort. Both of Jackie's husbands wanted full accountings of her personal expenditures, which required her to keep detailed records of all bills—from hair sessions with Kenneth to booze for private parties (she got at least some of her tipple wholesale). The embedded lesson for her—and for you? To know, down to the last drachma, which way the money flows from month to month, and to prioritize expenditures accordingly.

Jackie's White House–era budget confirmed that she was simply unwilling and unable to curb her clothing purchases. Rather, she cut other areas, such as entertaining and pet supplies, to pick up the slack. By zealously accounting for every expense over just one week, we promise you'll find ways to reappropriate your hard-earned cash: Part of a $300 a month taxi habit, for instance, could easily be diverted to opera tickets. Or one-third of a designer handbag.

Pick up the tab on a date? Certainly not. After all, didn't you already pay in kind by springing for that manicure, blow-out, and other bodily mechanics for the big night out? You might, however, consider a Jackie-like exception to the rule. Once you've established that your escort is a serious marriage prospect, not just a four-date wonder, you may pay for a few drinks and meals. Jackie did as much with the dreamy (and aloof) bachelor JFK, who was prone to forget his wallet at times.

Fib about money? What money? Well, let's just say that, like many women, Jackie felt the need to artfully conceal certain expenses from the men in her life. To escape the President's fiscal wrath, Jackie had a few tricks: She'd quietly submit invoices to her husband's secretary for payment, or make certain indulgences—often decorative ones—practically vanish by chipping away at the debt on an installment plan. (While married to Onassis, she sometimes had her husband's sympathetic associates sign for certain bills, even seemingly benign ones, like an order for ten pillows.)

You can simulate such wily moves yourself by buying items on layaway or no-interest installment plans. If at all possible, make purchases at places that are apt to escape your spouse's notice. Find an antique dealer called "Lowe's," for instance, and you'll get a kiss for your sudden interest in home improvement items.

Carry a flashy American Express black Centurion card, or stick to simple gold plastic? We think she'd straddle the middle, since Jackie didn't mind a little exclusivity, but she also didn't like to throw her wealth in people's faces—waiters and store clerks included. Leaving the black card for celebs and rap stars, she'd probably go for a subtly precious alloy instead. Seconds Maria Bartiromo: "She'd carry platinum for sure. It has its benefits, but it's not too over-the-top."

Tip generously? Yes, assuming the service warranted it. She was known to be especially lavish with New York City cabbies, giving as much as a five-dollar dollop on top of an itty-bitty two-dollar fare. Feel free to be equally discretionary with gratuities—the 15 percent rule is so 1990s.

Chapter 9

Heirs and Force:

The Tenets of Passing the Torch

"People have too many theories about rearing children. I believe simply in love, security, and discipline."
—JBKO

I f you've chosen to have children, you're probably hip to Jackie's number-one goal when it came to raising Caroline and John Jr.: She wanted them to be little APs—Admirable People. And from a young age, they were—despite a tragedy bigger than any youngster should have to bear and the world's endless scrutiny. The classic images of Jackie and her young offspring capture their commendable spirit. There was John Jr. crawling under his father's desk in the Oval Office, and Caroline, grinning ear to ear, astride her pony Macaroni. And, decades later, Jackie standing proudly at the Kennedy Library opening, with her heartthrob son and reserved daughter by her side—proof positive of her fait accompli.

Jackie was less than lucky when it came to bearing children; she lost three babies in eight years. But as a child rearer, she was nothing less than formidable. Not to mention nontraditional: She brought a pregnant bunny to the White House so that Caroline and John Jr. could witness, rather than just read about, the birthing process. Still, she was as human as the next mother, and was alternately doting, strict, inspirational, playful, educational, demanding, and emotional. Above all, she had ironclad ideas about how to raise kids who didn't raise hell.

◆ ◆ ◆

"In terms of child-rearing, Jackie always had her eye on the ball: the importance of character. She did what many affluent parents don't—she focused on what her kids would eventually be in life, and she knew that what is important is that your child turns out to be loving, independent, productive, and moral." —MICHAEL THOMPSON, PhD, CHILD PSYCHOLOGIST; AUTHOR OF *THE PRESSURED CHILD: HELPING YOUR CHILD FIND SUCCESS IN SCHOOL AND LIFE*

◆ ◆ ◆

O–BEHAVE!

What are the rules of social engagement? For children, figuring them out is a daily adventure. And so it's essential to give kids clear guidance about how to conduct themselves—with or without you. Jackie and the nannies she employed over the years always made etiquette a top priority. She knew, like it or not, that a child's manners are a direct reflection on the parents—not on the kid.

By the time her children were school-aged, they had already adopted some of their mom's Emily Post–like manners. According to Jackie's half brother, Jamie Auchincloss, if there was one piece of cake left, Caroline and John Jr. would never take it. If offered it, they would say, "No, thanks. You have it."

Anti-Brat Strategy No. 1:
❖ Nail the Basics Early ❖

Even two-year-olds can find themselves in meet-and-greet situations, so instilling some early hosting skills is in order. Let them have some fun with it: They can pretend to be ambassadors from their favorite foreign land—a Japanese dignitary who bows or an Eskimo who rubs noses with guests. When her classmates arrived at the White House each morning (Jackie had set up a nursery school on the third floor), four-year-old Caroline greeted them at the door. When they left in the afternoons, she waved the students off.

The same goes for "please" and "thank you": The repetition of those precious pearls can't start soon enough. Caroline and John Jr. went to the White House kitchen to express gratitude to chef René Verdon for his cooking (with a little encouragement from Mom). The kitchen staff thought their *mercis* were charming—and the children earned the all-important moniker of well behaved.

Anti-Brat Strategy No. 2:
❖ Help Your Child Deconstruct Adults ❖

Your Hasidic boss's yarmulka or his wife's wig are the last things you want your child to comment on when the couple shows up for dinner. So prepare your little ones in advance by educating them a bit—and make it fun. Jackie prepped Caroline and John Jr. before greeting visiting dignitaries by throwing in a few colorful details. Before meeting a head of state, says Baldrige, she would take them aside in the family quarters and explain the drill with storybook precision: "This lady is a queen. She's very beautiful and has many jewels and has two children just your ages. And I know you'll make a good impression on her so she can tell her children what good children you are." They were immediately interested—and eager to please for all the right reasons.

Just be judicious with your explanations: You don't want "Mommy's boss pays her the money for the toys you love, so please be nice" to come out as "Will you get me the new Bug Blast Adventure Hero Tarantula Attack Spider-Man? Mommy says you pay for all my toys."

Anti-Brat Strategy No. 3:
Expose Them to Folks Who Aren't Like You

Nothing in life is equal, a reality that hits kids hard in a society increasingly measured by material possessions. Let them drool over their wealthy friend's Olympic-sized pool—and then have them experience a less-fortunate friend exclaiming over their stuffed-animal collection.

Despite Secret Service escorts and the relentless paparazzi, Jackie made sure to immerse Caroline and John Jr. in the real world. One frequent destination during the White House years was the home of Mary Gallagher, who had two young sons. According to Gallagher, the first time they visited, Caroline walked into the kitchen and asked with surprise, "Where is your cook?" Gallagher's reply: "You're looking at her."

Jacqueline Hirsh, who was the French teacher for the White House school, used to take Caroline for an outing every Monday afternoon. At Jackie's request, they did ordinary things, such as take the public bus, go shopping, and watch Hirsh's son's football games. The teacher would playfully insert French phrases while chatting about their adventures, and Caroline would later proudly repeat her newly learned bon mots to her parents. And during a two-week trek to Ravello, Italy, in 1962, Caroline had as playmates children of local trades-men—youngsters from an entirely different world. Despite the lan-guage barrier, "they communicated perfectly," noted *Time*.

The benefits of exposure to other lifestyles apparently rubbed off on John Jr., too. At Brown in the early 1980s, he organized so-called "punk-funk" parties—shindigs that brought together different music fans, and races, who grooved to both white and black music. This was newly hip at the time; MTV had only just started airing Mi-chael Jackson videos—the first black artist to find stardom on the network.

Anti-Brat Strategy No. 4:
Release Your Inner Hipness

You get to be the disciplinarian most days of the year, so why not sur-prise your brood—and make them appreciate yet another facet of you—by showing them your cool side once in a while? There's noth-ing wrong with blaring their iPod tunes in the car, or wearing Manolos to the school play. In 1970, Jackie donned a sassy outfit—jeans and mink—to accompany John Jr. ice-skating at Rockefeller Center. As an adolescent, Caroline and her mother often seemed thick as thieves, carrying on like schoolgirls and chattering in French to throw off those around them.

Anti-Brat Strategy No. 5:
Embrace Their Inner Brat

Children will gladly adopt good manners and appropriate behavior—if you also allow them plenty of time to be their loud, silly, messy selves. Jackie occasionally let her children run up and down the White House corridors, making noise and spewing toys in every direction. And after she moved to New York, she'd take them to one of her favorite home-furnishing stores—a duplex boutique on East 60th Street called Scarabaeus—and let them have pillow fights upstairs while she shopped for fish-themed *objets.*

Remember that children don't always need to be held to adult standards. Young ones probably won't make it through a long Greek wedding ceremony, so don't expect them to; sit near the back. Even teens have their limits, as Jackie discovered, when she took Caroline to the Royal Geographical Society, hoping to inspire some interest in far-flung adventure. The director of the RGS, however, noted that Jackie asked all the questions while Caroline stood by looking terribly bored.

Anti-Brat Strategy No. 6:
Expand Their Palates—So You Can Eat Well, Too

Your kids' inevitable picky eating shouldn't preclude your supping on coq au vin at home, not to mention delectables at restaurants and friends' houses. To avoid embarrassing screams of "Yuck!" and "I hate that!," practice sampling novel flavors at home, one bite at a time. The Kennedy children were taught to try new foods using the "one-spoonful, two-spoonful" rule. On first sampling, they were required to eat only one bite. The next time the dish was served, however, they were encouraged to try two bites. "Sure enough, the day would come when they would eat up their spinach or whatever it was without a murmur," wrote White House nanny Maud Shaw.

Anti-Brat Strategy No. 7:
More Chores!

There's nothing like some good old-fashioned hard labor to keep your little charges in line—making their beds, clearing the table, and emp-tying the trash are all excellent responsibilities for them to have. Be-fore the White House, for instance, Caroline washed the lunch dishes daily. Even with the swarm of servants that came with the Executive

Mansion, Jackie made sure her two children towed the line on the basics, like tidying their rooms.

If this sounds tough-minded, readjust your settings: Kids enjoy being trusted to handle tasks, so don't over-serve them. On that note, Jackie asked the Secret Service agents never to do favors for the children—like picking up their things or carrying belongings for them. "If John would forget his bike in Central Park, she'd make him go back for it," recalls longtime Kennedy family aide Melody Miller.

FROM BASSINET TO OVAL OFFICE:
Choosing Normal over Formal

Jackie insisted that her children be shielded from the maelstrom of politics and the social swirl of the White House; she wished them to lead as normal a life as possible. They had their friends over to play, romped on the grass, ate hot dogs, watched Disney movies. Of course, their house was the White House, their grass was the East Lawn, a French chef roasted their wieners, and they viewed movies in a huge screening room—but it was precisely these facts that Jackie tried to make matter-of-fact to her children. She shared her approach years later with Hillary Clinton. "Surround [Chelsea] with friends and family, but don't spoil her," Jackie admonished. "Don't let her think she's someone special or entitled."

Still, Jackie wasn't always able to protect her kids from their celebrity status. "Caroline was knocked down by a charge of photographers when I took her out to try to teach her how to ski. How do you explain that to a child?" Jackie told a newspaper reporter in 1967.

Most of us are actually luckier than that: We don't have to work quite as hard to make life "normal" for our children. What is normal, anyway? It's a series of routines that imply boundaries and security to children—exactly what Jackie was after.

Conjure a Magic Kingdom

A child's most enchanted, comforting place ought to be his or her own bedroom (even for adult Jackie it was her sanctuary; she loved taking breakfast in bed, held staff meetings sheetside, and snuck frequent naps). For little ones, spending night after night in their own rooms does not breed boredom—it promotes security through familiarity. The night of JFK's assassination, for example, Jackie demanded that Caroline and John Jr. sleep at the White House in the comfort of their own beds, rather than spend the night at a relative's.

None of us, especially children, relish change. If, for instance, your mate's fab new job forces you to relocate, hand-carry your child's favorite possessions so that she is immediately surrounded by them at the new home. When Jackie moved the family from Washington to New York in 1964, she instructed decorators to make the children's rooms as close to their former quarters as possible. Caroline's was to be the same shade of pale pink, and there was plenty of room for all her toys, including a favorite, a huge dollhouse—a gift from Madame de Gaulle. John Jr.'s room remained blue and white, and lacked only the two-ring gas stove used for heating formula at the White House.

Save Them from the Mind Hole

Your children will sponge up all sorts of hideous pop-culture references by the time they begin school; just watch an episode or two of teen dramas like *The O.C.* to understand—and perhaps curdle your blood at the same time. The more you can teach them while they are still under your roof full-time, the better.

Jackie went so far as to homeschool Caroline during the White House years—"I want to have her home with me as long as I can," she said. Although there were full-time teachers, she and other parents often dropped by to help with a craft project or read aloud.

Instilling a love of words is another way Jackie left her imprint on her children early. On Election Day 1960, Caroline, just shy of three years old, recited for JFK two Edna St. Vincent Millay poems Jackie had taught her, "First Fig" and "Second Fig."

Often, the best way to get the message across is to let your kids hear it elsewhere. If the family minister raves about their grandmother who put twelve children through college singlehandedly, the message will crystallize. Much later, Caroline spent ten months taking a Sotheby's "Works of Art" course in London in 1975. Why? "[Caroline] will have money, and she will be better off for having the taste not to waste it," explained Jackie.

Act as Social Secretary for Your Children

Not every child is a natural social wunderkind. And yet, as a parent you know that whether they attend public or private school (see "Private vs. Public," p. 239), their circle of friends can have a profound effect on how they behave. And down the road, the parents of those good eggs can also be important references when they're trying to get into a prep school or college.

When Jackie and the children moved to New York City, she quickly realized that Caroline wasn't being invited to any of the birthday parties for her classmates at Convent of the Sacred Heart. She finally did what a mother should do—go on the offensive—and called another mom, explaining that Caroline would love to be included in the next shindig, as well as have friends come over. Suddenly, the mailbox was flooded with invites.

LIMITING PRIVILEGE

No child should receive too much; he or she will develop a sense of entitlement to carry through life. On the other hand, our consumer-driven world has upped the ante on what kids expect: Game Boys and PlayStation 2s abound. It's a treacherous balance to strike. Some Jackie-based strategies:

Pick your battles. When your child wants you to buy the latest Rolls-Royce to drive him around in, the answer is easy. But before you give an automatic "no" to electronic indulgences, think each one through. A cell phone can be a good safety device — just limit the minutes. Video games — sensible math- and science-based ones — can be as good a learning tool as any.

◆ ◆ ◆

"Jackie would have bought her children the most expensive and the latest electronic gadgets. She knew what helps people get ahead in the world, and computer literacy definitely helps children get ahead." —LETITIA BALDRIGE

◆ ◆ ◆

Be a consistent disciplinarian. But don't be afraid to lighten up every once in a while. If all your offspring hear is "no," they'll tune you right out — no matter how old they are. Jackie was forever strict with John Jr. But when, as an adult, he had one too many wild shindigs at Red Gate Farm — her beloved home on Martha's Vineyard — and left the place littered with partying refuse, instead of forbidding further socializing chez elle, Jackie simply banished him to the property's guesthouse.

COME YE:
Fostering Intellectual Curiosity

Bring history to life (with a few gory details). According to Letitia Baldrige, Jackie was a master at inspiring inquisitiveness in her children. If she was teaching them about a historical figure, Jackie would become quite engaged in the description. "She didn't just say 'the Prime Minister.' She'd give the whole history of Winston Churchill and the war so that these figures came alive." And when Jackie read to her children from a history book—on Henry VIII, for instance—she made sure to embellish the story with details that would be fascinating to a child (his extraordinary girth, his eating habits, his wife troubles, etc.) The children, of course, adored it.

Feed them some highbrow broccoli. You don't have to dwell on one Renoir for hours, but make the effort to show your children the great works—and help instill a love of the arts in them. Jackie would take her two to noteworthy exhibits when they were very young—such as seeing the *Mona Lisa* at the Louvre in Paris—but she'd stay only a very short time (both because of security issues and the kids' attention span). These days, art outings come with extra carrots: Museums like MOMA now have cool merchandise to cruise—and celebrity sightings are common at the Getty in L.A.

continues . . .

Venture forth. Flick your overprotective switch to "off." Kids need thrills as much as you do. Jackie had a world-class curiosity about other countries and cultures, which she shared eagerly with her children; photographer Peter Beard remembers her as a "very gutsy mother." In the first few months of 1966 alone, they journeyed to Sun Valley, Gstaad, Rome, Argentina, Spain, and Hawaii—with a few stops through New York in between. She loved to get them to take risks, like the time she dared John Jr. to dive off the highest point of Ari's yacht.

Later, she would also prompt them to travel on their own; John Jr. was particularly infected with the adventure bug. When he was fifteen, he and his cousin Timothy Shriver journeyed to Guatemala to help earthquake survivors. In 1979 Jackie sent him on a ten-week National Outdoor Leadership School program in Kenya. Jackie felt such experiences were character-building—and also an excellent way to channel all his youthful energy while giving him a few real-world skills.

Become a human Discovery Channel. Subscribe to *National Geographic* and *The New Yorker* (for which Jackie once wrote an article). Make the Discovery and Learning channels and PBS defaults on your remote control. Take regular trips to the local library so that your kids know that Barnes & Noble isn't one. Play "geography" while traveling in the car—a favorite of Jackie's and her children—and get clues from your vehicle's navigation system. "The kids are great. They know the names of the capitals of all the states—I never did—and now they throw in words like Morocco and Ethiopia like old friends," she once told an interviewer.

Let them glimpse what they are missing. Allow treats only sporadically, and make them the kind your kids will really savor. For example, the Kennedy children most often ate at home. But when Caroline was ten, Jackie let her hold court at chichi French eatery La Caravelle, where she hosted six friends for a very grown-up—and expensive— Christmas lunch.

Troubleshoot as needed. It's one thing to let your child rebel against your authority occasionally, quite another to be aware of more serious problems. And if the latter do surface, it's better to err on the safe side and seek help. As an adolescent, John Jr.'s budding taste for partying and other bad-boy behaviors steadily grew. Jackie, rather than dismiss the behavior as teen folly as many parents would, felt compelled to send him for counseling.

PRIVATE VS. PUBLIC:
The Schooling Debate

Go figure: You attended a highfalutin boarding school and struggled to get into a (low) top-twenty college, yet your mate made it into the Ivy League from a large public high school. The educational debate is an endless one—and a relationship-tester. Depending on your values, your bank account, and where you live, the choices you make for your children will vary. Jackie (a product of one of the top boarding schools of her day) chose to send her own children to private institutions—in part because she was a fan of the education they provide. But equally important to her was the added security they could offer her constantly hounded children: Public schools are public property and private schools are not. And yet Jackie and the Kennedy clan were staunch supporters of public education—a good lesson for all.

Be a Rabble-Rouser

If you send your children to public school, it is your duty to fight for excellent programs. Don't let private-schoolers be the only ones to brag about hearing Itzhak Perlman in concert the night before. You must support—if not spearhead—parent- or community-run programs, from art leagues to music associations. A few potlucks can raise more money than you think. It is most certainly what Jackie—a front-fighter extraordinaire—would do. At the very least, pony up the funds for your children to experience some extracurricular enrichment so they can be bratty braggers, too.

Pitch for the Other Team

Should you decide that private schools are the way to go, don't think your work is done. Au contraire: Public-school causes need your time and money even more, and your involvement may be a good enough example to prevent your little ones from being like their overindulged classmates. Jackie was very active in several public-school initiatives over the years, including the Bedford Stuyvesant Restoration Corporation's art program in New York, which exposed inner-city kids to art and how to make it; Jackie was so pleased with the results that she hung several of the kids' works in her apartment. During his time at Brown, John Jr. furthered his mother's commitment to improving public education by volunteering for Upward Bound, a program that helps underprivileged kids bone up enough to get into college. Most recently, Caroline served as vice chair of New York City's Fund for Public Schools.

Share the Wealth

Private schools, with their top-dollar endowments, can afford to fund some interesting educational experiments. Why not see if any can be imported to the public sector? In the White House years, JFK and Jackie talked at length with Caroline's French tutor, Jacqueline Hirsch, about televising her forward-thinking methods of language instruction so that the entire country could benefit (sadly, a plan cut short by JFK's death).

YOUR NANNY DIARY

Whether you go back to work after having children, or—like Jackie—simply want some extra assistance, finding a person you trust with your kids is one of the toughest jobs you'll have. Some considerations:

Find a like mind. Beware the scantily clad au pair (cell phone attached to head): The only boobs hanging out around the house should be yours (nursing, of course). Jackie chose Maud Shaw because of her strict English sensibilities: Shaw believed that American children in general were spoiled. She worked hard to make sure the Kennedy kids weren't overindulged—Jackie's deep fear—but rather brought up in a manner "that makes them likeable, unspoiled, and nice to know."

Be sure they can let go. Possessiveness—a common byproduct of child care—has no place in a nanny's heart. She must be able to turn her charges back over to you without hesitation. Even more, she must share the details of the day with you in a way that allows you to feel you haven't missed any "special" moments—naughty or nice. According to staffers, when the President and First Lady came in, Maud Shaw would remove herself quietly.

Don't get burned by churn. Unfortunately, good nannies rarely stick around. And so you'll have to work to incentivize them. Overtime pay? Use of a car? Travel? Pick your perks to fit your situation.

Between Maud Shaw's departure in 1965 and Marta Sgubin's arrival in 1969, Caroline and John Jr. had a spate of babysitters; Jackie was so adamant about protecting the children's privacy that she fired workers with no notice if she discovered they had leaked one detail to outsiders. (To this day, none of those intermediary nannies have talked publicly, so the specter of Jackie's wrath appears to be as potent as ever.)

How to find a good one? Agencies abound—and in today's security-conscious world they are the best, if most expensive, route. And then there's the time-honored classified—be it in print form or on the ever-burgeoning Craig's List. In 1965, when Maud Shaw was retiring, Jackie—still favoring a European-born caregiver—ran this ad in *The Times* (*London*): "Extremely reliable and competent young woman, 25–35, needed to look after girl of seven and boy of four in New York City: English or French native language."

◆ ◆ ◆

"Jackie's ad for a nanny is so innocent. Today it would be filled with musts, like 'must drive,' 'must submit to a blood test,' 'must sign a confidentiality agreement.' As for posting it online, I don't think Jackie would ever do that." —BARBARA KLINE, AUTHOR OF *WHITE HOUSE NANNIES: TRUE TALES FROM THE OTHER DEPARTMENT OF HOMELAND SECURITY*

◆ ◆ ◆

Go foreign to save on language lessons. What better way to expose your child to other languages, mores, traditions? Jackie insisted that her nannies speak French, and fibbed to her children that the new helper didn't understand English. As John Jr. remembered, "It was part of my mother's tireless effort to get my sister and me to learn French. But after a few weeks they'd break down and . . . we'd say a tearful good-bye (in English) and wait for the next one to appear."

Whose child is this? It's as easy to plop kids in front of a video as it is to hand them to a nanny. Jackie once said, "Children grow away from busy parents because busy parents grow away from the children."

It was a struggle for Jackie, despite her brave words. During her first year of marriage to Onassis, Jackie was gone more often than she was home. So she entrusted Caroline and John Jr. in large part to her mother, Janet, and Sgubin, who took John Jr. to his first day at Collegiate, a prestigious private boys' school in Manhattan. In the end, only you can know the right balance between time spent with you and time spent on someone else's lap (and meter).

DISCIPLINE:
How Much Is Enough?

The short answer? Plenty. Especially if you are in a position to hand your children a weighty legacy, they need to be fed a strict diet of control served up with lots of love. That's certainly what Jackie believed. In Molly Van Renssalaer Thayer's biography *Jacqueline Bouvier Kennedy*, there's an adorable photo of mother and daughter. The caption, though, quickly gets to the tougher heart of Jackie's child-rearing psychology: "When Caroline hurts herself, her mother says sternly, 'Kennedys don't cry.' "

❖ Try an Indirect Approach ❖

So five-year-old Junior thinks he knows best and wants to override your no-pigging-out-on-Halloween-candy decision? Let him do it, and don't rub it in when he gets sick. The experience allows him to test his independence—and learn that Mom does know a thing or two.

Jackie would beseech you to remember the old adage about "give them enough rope . . ." When John Jr. was eleven, he and she locked horns over his disappointing report card. Jackie pushed hard to get him to buck up at school—too hard. John Jr. angrily announced that he was running away to Hickory Hill, his aunt Ethel's home in Virginia, where he figured he'd be treated better. Rather than quash his plan, Jackie encouraged him to go, and then quietly called Ethel. Jackie asked her if she'd administer a heavy dose of chores, which Ethel agreed to do. After four long days, John Jr. begged to come back home—and promised to focus on his studies.

Reinforce Rest and Ritual

Kids need downtime and familiar routine, so combine both at bedtime. In the White House, Jackie made sure that Caroline and John Jr. were tucked in promptly each evening at seven without any fuss. They got one ten-minute warning while they were playing, and then they were off to change into pajamas, wash up, hear a story, say their prayers, and then get kissed good-night by their mother—and almost always by their father as well, no matter what diplomatic crisis he was handling. (Note to dads: If a president can pull this off, so can you.)

Be Prepared to Lose a Few

Jackie's will didn't always hold—nor will yours, so know when to let go. The idea of attending a debutante ball did not appeal at all to a bohemian teenage Caroline. Jackie, a former deb herself, had hoped her daughter would "come out" as well, but finally acquiesced.

Use the Trump Card: Balance

As long as you are levelheaded with kids, they will respond in kind; if you lose it, they'll play you for all you are worth. Jackie got the point while her kids were young: When they argued with her, she remained calm, repeating what she wanted them to do. But later on, she struggled harder for self-control, as evidenced by her sparring with John Jr. over his taste in women (see "Mommy Dearest," p. 246).

ENCOURAGE FREE EXPRESSION, BY GEORGE!

Treat children as the adults you want them to become. Kids are instinctively wary of people who baby-talk to them; every child appreciates being taken seriously. Jackie was artful in her ability to make children feel important. "She was the type of woman who talked to children on their level and with great enthusiasm," says Baldrige. "She was forever enticing them to do something creative."

Turn Your Child's Shortcomings into Creative Assets

If your daughter is vexingly shy around strangers, embrace the positive aspects of her timidity instead of forcing her into uncomfortable social situations. Chances are good, for example, that she's a keen observer, so encourage her to write or paint to express herself.

Jackie saw early on that John Jr.'s strengths did not include scholastic performance. And so (after wrestling with him over it), she bypassed the most hard-nosed private schools in favor of Manhattan's Collegiate, which was known to have a more creative atmosphere. Years later (and after he did time at a strict boarding school), she supported his choice of Brown University for the same reason.

Instill a Dynasty Mindset

Implant in your children as early as possible a sense of family pride—even if they didn't come from a Kennedy-level background. You might begin by taking them to Ellis Island, for example, or wherever your family roots began. Jackie made sure that Pierre Salinger, Robert McNamara, and other members of JFK's inner circle spent time with Caroline and John Jr. when they became teens. She insisted that they learn from them who their father really was—not from history books or sugar-coated Camelot accounts, which could never capture the whole man.

MOMMY DEAREST

Whether your children want to hear it or not, there will be plenty of opportunities to continue to instruct—OK, manipulate—them as they become adults. Jackie felt no compunction about directing her children on how their lives should proceed. Here's the crazy part: They (usually) listened.

When Tough Love Is in Order

It's hard to squelch a dream, but if your daughter can't carry a tune and yet aspires to be the next Mariah Carey, you'll be doing her a favor. Caroline longed to become a professional photographer and was even offered an exhibit at a Manhattan gallery. Jackie knew that the images would fetch high sums—an estimated $10,000 each—but more so for her daughter's name than her talent. She put the brakes on the show and any possible reviews. But she did know enough to strike a compromise: Caroline did eventually have the exhibit, but Jackie insisted that it be without any press or fanfare.

Even though she herself had participated in the drama club at

Miss Porter's, Jackie was also opposed to John Jr.'s acting. She felt a stage life didn't befit the son of a president. To drive her point home, when John Jr. appeared in *Winners* at Manhattan's Irish Arts Center in 1985, Jackie (and Caroline) failed to attend the show, and Jackie did her best to suppress any reviews.

◆ Run Interference in Their Relationships ◆

It's always tricky to get involved in your children's affairs of the heart— and impossible to not have strong opinions about their choice of mates. When you like them, do what you can to support the match—it'll make everyone involved feel great. But when you disapprove, your instinct to prevent a disastrous union can get in the way of your relationship with your child. There's a fine line between dislike and branding a mate potentially harmful; cross it with care.

Jackie did. On the positive side: Caroline was dating writer Tom Carney during her junior and senior years at college. Carney, who had already published a novel, was in the process of working on a screenplay with a partner. Jackie tried to help him by pitching it to Swifty Lazar and Sue Mengers, two top Hollywood agents of the day. Her attempt failed, but both Caroline and Carney were deeply appreciative of her efforts.

When it came to love and "Mother," as he called her, John Jr. wasn't quite as lucky as his sister. Less trusting of her son's choices, Jackie was fond of screening his calls and saying he wasn't available if she didn't approve of the young lady on the line. Those unlucky dates included Madonna and Daryl Hannah, who was still involved with John Jr. when Jackie died. Many believe that Jackie's opinion carried enough weight with her son to possibly prevent a marriage.

SURVIVING STEPPARENTING:
The Dos and Don'ts

You love him, therefore you marry him—and his kids resent you for it. It's a story whose ending rarely changes: Children—whether wee or grown—don't see the need for another parent to "step" in. It was no different for Jackie—who grew up as a stepchild herself in the wealthy Auchincloss clan—when she married Onassis, who had two adult children. She learned the hard way how to navigate her new status.

✦ Do: ✦

✦ **Ignore their initial ambivalence; it will pass.** You must learn— quickly—to remain composed even in the face of open hostility from your husband's children. Jackie understood such pain. Ari's son, Alexander, was hell-bent on defying his father and snubbing Jackie. Tensions peaked at lunch one day when Alexander refused to sit with her. When Ari finally coerced him to take a seat, he stewed in sullen silence. Jackie, ignoring his pouting, carried on with the meal, chatting and looking generally fabulous.

✦ **Engage them through activities.** Sitting around a tense dinner table isn't the way to break the ice. Depending on the kids' ages, hit the zoo, catch an IMAX, rent go-karts, or shop— which is what Jackie chose to do with Christina.

✦ **Find an ally on your mate's side.** Sidle up to a sister, a friend, or—the best—the ex-wife if personal politics permit. Anyone who speaks well of you to the kids behind your back is worth her weight in rubies. For Jackie, it was Artemis, Ari's sister.

Don't:

Try to be their new mother. Instead, reassure them you're just an additional support person. Jackie refrained from stepping into the maternal role with Onassis's son and daughter; her frequent absences to be with her own children—who were still quite young—would drive that point home, she hoped.

Assume your child-rearing opinions will be welcome. Unless they are endangering themselves—or you!—it's often a good idea to keep mum. You may find Little Brian's PlayStation habit unhealthy, but his computer-savvy dad doesn't. Jackie learned this with Onassis early in their marriage. About to depart with Jackie on a trip, Ari tried to get an unruly Alexander to bid them farewell. As Onassis's secretary Kiki Moutsatsos overheard, Jackie finally lost her cool and said, "I do not know why your children are so rude to me." His retort: "Worry only about your own children, not mine, my dear."

Make him choose between them and you. Chances are you won't always like to hear his answer. Instead, avoid polarizing discussions and remember that you are a team. Jackie confronted this reality when Alexander died in a plane crash. Ari fell apart—and blamed Jackie for bringing the "Kennedy curse" into his house. It was the beginning of the end of their marriage, for Onassis was never quite able to see that she was an innocent—and supportive—bystander.

GRAND (PARENT) GESTURES

There you are, ruling your world and looking better and better as you do it. And then your child goes and has a baby—sticking you with the decidedly un-chic title of grandmother. You can mope—or you can siphon off some of the little one's youthful zeal. Jackie made the most of the role, and earned the moniker "Grand-jackie" from Caroline's three offspring. She'd see Rose, Tatiana, and Jack several times a week, taking them to a playground in Central Park or for ice cream, and lavishing them with toys from FAO Schwarz. A few of her Grand Rules:

Overindulge them—because you can. Hey, they're not your responsibility, so do what you couldn't do as a parent and spoil the grandkids a bit. Jackie let her three have full run of her home, and even when the occasional "disaster" occurred—Rose stained an expensive carpet—Jackie never let it take on any importance. "It doesn't matter—it's only an old rug!" she reassured.

Embrace the chance to be five again. How long has it been since you played dress-up, or marched around drumming on a pot? Exactly. Grandchildren give you the excuse to do all sorts of silly things. Jackie kept a giant chest at her apartment; the children would load up on necklaces, rings, and other baubles. Then, wrote Nancy Tuckerman, Jackie's long-term personal assistant, in a foreword to the 1996 Sotheby's auction catalog, "Jackie would take them on a so-called fantasy adventure. She'd weave a spell-binding tale while leading them through the darkened apartment, opening closet doors in search of ghosts and mysterious creatures. Once they were finished playing, they'd have their traditional afternoon tea party sitting on the living-room floor."

Heed the call of the wild. Little ones adore the great outdoors, so let it be your playground. Jackie loved hosting her grandchildren on the Vineyard. They spent whole days exploring, splashing in the waves, and discovering the wonders of nature, coming inside only when Sgubin called them for lunch. Even after she became sick, she took them sledding in Central Park.

Would Jackie...

- **Spank her children?** Yes, but only in private and only as a last resort. John Jr. once said, "My mother was very strict with me. Caroline could do just about anything, but if I stepped out of line, I got a swat." But given her penchant for following the latest philosophies, she'd surely be on board with today's wisdom—that violence teaches violence—and refrain.

- **Use teenage babysitters?** No. Jackie preferred more worldly folks to look after her precious ones. She could have had the pick of them, too: Hundreds of letters from young women offering their services flooded the White House. Today, Ivy League schools have babysitting services that cater to the well-to-do, but why have a term-paper-crazed student when you can have a professional caregiver—a Jackie must—instead?

Always lavish her children with the most expensive, up-to-date gifts? No, she'd be horrified by the idea of bestowing Jaguars and breast jobs upon sixteen-year-olds—both common presents these days among the nouveau elite. While attending Brown University, John Jr. hauled himself around Providence, Rhode Island, in a beat-up Honda Civic.

Let others discipline her kids? Yes, especially if they're at all in harm's way. It's almost impossible to keep an eye on offspring at all times, so be grateful when you're surrounded by like-minded, common-sense folks. When a ringmaster at one of Jackie's horse shows implored a few youngsters, including Caroline, to get their butts off a fence, the stubborn Kennedy didn't budge at first. After a second entreaty, she dismounted. Jackie glanced at the ringmaster in silent, smiling approval.

Force her children to take lessons if they didn't want to? No. It's a tough question for parents who want their little ones to excel, and it's even harder when the parent has dreams of passing down a heartfelt hobby. Jackie wouldn't force her kids to practice dance, painting, football, or any other extracurricular unless they loved it themselves. One example: While taking riding lessons in New York City, Caroline was more into giggling with her friends over boys than posting. "I think Jackie had the wisdom to realize that this was more her passion than Caroline's," recalls Claremont Riding Academy proprietor Paul Novograd. "So the lessons discontinued." The anti-pressure payoff? Caroline came to embrace riding—and now shares the sport with her own daughters.

Let her children party at home? Yes, to a point. Although Jackie would never have overtly supported breaking the law, she felt that her children were safer under her roof. For her, it was preferable to them being somewhere completely out of her control. Hence John Jr.'s wild house parties on Martha's Vineyard. It may be small consolation, but at least you'll know your precious ones aren't driving home drunk.

Condone living together before marriage? Although she was conservative at heart, Jackie would and did let a little living together slide. Besides, she was well aware of the example she and Maurice Tempelsman were setting. You can signal your approval (or disapproval) by how often you visit.

Chapter 10

Jackie Here and Now

"I do love to live in style."
— *JBKO*

If the preceding chapters have fulfilled their mission, you're prepared to sketch out your own, freehand rendition of Jackie's masterful living arts. You'll waft through your days with greater logic, style, and ease—even when Mercury is in retrograde. You'll reawaken any dormant cultural cells, finding new ways to boost your spirits, your charisma, your munificence. You'll even have some solid case law to justify putting certain family members on "pause."

Yet the urge to slip into the icon's shoes never really fades. It's why Sotheby's has held two enormous Jackie auctions. And why new books, exhibits, and programs find their Jackie fan base year after year. But only in these pages will you find something more tangible, accessible: a here-and-now roadmap to all things JBKO—Jackie Brands, Kicks, and Obsessions.

STYLE:
Clothing and Accessories

Jackie knew a classic when she saw one. Which helps to explain why so many of the labels, stores, and boutiques she favored have never really fallen out of fashion. Not all of them are expensive—a testament to Jackie's lifelong high/low aesthetic. But even the loftier names, which boast wear-it-into-the-ground longevity, can often justify their pedigree prices.

Giorgio Armani. Whether you go with more affordable Emporio Armani or the high-end black label, his understated, luxurious theme is consistent. Jackie appreciated his precision tailoring, especially for suits. In 1979, she also snagged one of his sheared mink jackets. For store locations, go to www.giorgioarmani.com.

Manolo Blahnik. When it comes to makings legs and toes look sexy, Manolo is the ne plus ultra—in our day as well as in Jackie's. Aside from a few peau de soie styles for formal attire, she favored his sleek flats, which she felt made her size-10 feet look daintier. www.neimanmarcus.com, www.bergdorfgoodman.com.

Carolina Herrera. Jackie was a major consumer of Herrera's sumptuous, patrician attire. She even passed down her love of the clothes to her daughter: Caroline's wedding dress was a special creation by the designer. Herrera's flagship store is located at 954 Madison Ave. (at 75th St.). Her clothes—lately on the flirty side—are also available at select Neiman Marcus and Saks Fifth Avenue stores. www.carolinaherrera.com.

Cartier. It's hard to beat the classic, clean lines of a Cartier time-piece. For much of her life, Jackie favored the French maker's original Tank watch in gold. When spending big bucks on a watch, Jackie would surely insist on a mechanical, not a quartz, movement. www.cartier.com.

Chanel. No matter how many reinterpretations have surfaced, there is still only one Chanel—particularly for a sophisticated skirt suit. Jackie had several, including an oft-photographed white-and-black bouclé. www.chanel.com.

E. Vogel. Purveyors of custom-made riding boots, they were a favored supplier to Jackie. The shop provides a measuring kit to those who can't stop by, and can make slightly shorter street versions for non-riders who want to merely affect the equestrian look. Jackie preferred her dress boots in French calfskin. Prices from $660. 19 Howard St., New York; 212-925-2460; www.vogelboots.com.

Fogal. Whether your legs are gams or gourds, a great pair of stockings will take them to the next level. Jackie, known for her muscular calves, was happy to share her sheer secret with those who asked: "Fogal," she'd purr. www.fogal.com.

Gucci. Though it is unclear whether Jackie ever carried Gucci's famous purse named for her, she did favor other accessories from the Italian luxury line. One splurge: In 1968, right before marrying Onassis, she ducked into the Manhattan flagship to pick up a $1,480 brown crocodile bag (cost in today's dollars: about $7,800). www.gucci.com.

Jack Rogers sandals. Go directly to www.caramiastores.com for the largest selection of the casual, whip-stitched two-tone flats. Jackie wore them everywhere, from Capri to Central Park. They'll accommodate custom color combos, too.

Keds. As Jackie regularly showcased, the simple white sneaker is right up there with the white T-shirt. Keds still does them as plain as possible. www.keds.com.

Lacoste. The little French alligator has enjoyed a recent renaissance; now you can get those short-sleeve pique shirts in Jackie-snug proportions—this time, with a hint of stretch. www.lacoste.com.

Kenneth Jay Lane. This famous costume jewelry line is chic—again. And who can resist baubles that have appealed to everyone from Jackie to the cast of *Dynasty*? Available in trendy boutiques as well as department stores and online sites, the newly mod collection includes "coral" cuffs and turquoise horn-shaped pendants. At www. bloomingdales.com, www.saks.com, www.vivre.com, and www.net-a-porter.com.

Pucci. Jackie lounged around the White House in a pair of Pucci Capris; she celebrated her fortieth in a psychedelic mini dress, long pearls swinging. The Italian house has boutiques in New York, Palm Beach, and Europe, including the tiny outpost near the Florentine villa Emilio once called home. If you're lucky, you can snare a few pieces on eBay or at New York's famous discount department store Century 21. More retailers, such as Bergdorf's, are also carving out Pucci boutiques. Available at www.neimanmarcus.com, www.bergdorfgoodman. com, and www.eluxury.com.

Lilly Pulitzer. The designer, a Miss Porter's classmate of Jackie's, put festive pinks and greens on the map—as did a young First Lady when she sported the Classic Shift in a *Life* feature. Today, Pulitzer's array of prints goes beyond clothing alone, covering everything from baby gear and home accessories to shoes. www.lillypulitzer.com.

Valentino. When only the most impeccable, photogenic lines would do, Jackie called upon Valentino; he designed the cream and lace wedding ensemble she wore to her nuptials with Onassis. Outfitting MTV starlets and ladies who lunch, today he's the maestro with the broadest, surest range. www.valentino.it.

Roger Vivier. Of course Jackie was enamored of this Manolo predecessor, the cobbler who is said to have invented the stiletto. His name has returned to a new shoe line that spans heels and suede Pilgrim-buckle flats. Check out his boutique at Saks in New York and Neiman Marcus in Los Angeles. For other locations, go to www.rogervivier.com.

Louis Vuitton. It's hard to argue the practical perfection of the Noe bag—after all, it was designed to haul bottles of champagne. In black Epi leather, it was a Jackie staple. She also owned Vuitton's chic-again logo luggage, called Monogram—perhaps easier to pull off when your bags are going into the hold of your own private jet. www.vuitton.com.

Zoran. Later in life, Jackie was a devotee—or Zoranian, as zealots are known—of the designer's comfortably chic shapes. Think buttonless, zipperless, snapless pants and skirts, and unlined, flowing jackets and coats. But this is no muumuu wear: Zoran uses only the costliest and yummiest alpacas and cashmeres, silks and velvets for his timeless pieces. Available at Saks Fifth Ave., or call the designer directly at 212-233-2025.

SHOPPING

Encore. This consignment shop was where Jackie's clothes found new life and new owners. 1132 Madison Ave. (between 84th and 85th Sts.), New York; 212-879-2850; www.encoreresale.com.

Gap. We'll never stop needing a simple white or black foundation to go under our finely honed jackets. Jackie preferred all-cotton and snug-fitting basics. www.gap.com.

Gem Palace. Jackie stocked her jewelry box with bling from the famous Gem Palace as early as 1962. Today, the family that runs this glittery empire continues to make special pieces for celebrities and other mogul types. The palace's designer, Munnu Kasliwal, also sells his wares at Barneys New York, among other U.S. stores. M I Road, Jaipur, 302001, Rajasthan, India.

Bergdorf Goodman. Still the top dog in boutique department stores, from service to selection. Jackie practically had the tailors and milliners here on call. Alas, there is only one—although Neiman Marcus, owned by the same parent company, comes close. 754 Fifth Ave., New York; 212-753-7300; www.bergdorfgoodman.com.

Hermès. While you're doing time on the waiting list for a Birkin, consider some alternatives. Jackie first carried Hermès's Constance shoulder bag (with the big H on the front) in the seventies. She also toted the Hermès Trim bag—a simple leather purse that tuck snugly under the arm. As for her magic-with-a-silk-scarf head wrap, attempt at your own risk. If you dare, try Hermès's "Horoscope" design, which suited Jackie fine. www.hermes.com.

Michael's. One of Manhattan's primo consignment shops, Michael's is said to have been a favorite secondhand repository for Jackie's frocks. The owner is mum on the subject, but don't let that keep you from the racks crammed with gently-worn couture. 1041 Madison Ave., New York; 212-737-7273; www.michaelconsignment.com.

Saks Fifth Avenue. She did live on the same thoroughfare, after all, so it's no surprise that Jackie liked the avenue's namesake store. In her younger days, she had the Saks staff order outfits from a French woman named Coco Chanel. For locations, www.saksfifthavenue.com.

Smythson of Bond Street. Want to add some British pomp to your prose? Smythson has a royal warrant and a queenly assortment of proper papers to prove it. Collections like "tangerine fashion" and quirky motif cards are all done up in classic English (and pricey) style. Jackie's fave hue? "Nile Blue." For orders and locations, www.smythson.com.

Mrs. John L. Strong Fine Stationery. If you didn't think paper could be bespoke, check out this collection, which spans the crispest custom-embossed pages and cards to "ready-to-write" sets. Jackie, Hillary Clinton, Bunny Mellon, and the Duchess of Windsor have all marked up the chic stuff. 699 Madison Ave., New York; 212-838-3775. For other locations, visit www.mrsstrong.com.

Tiffany. From brooches and silver tape measures to china, Jackie loved a little blue box as much as the rest of us. It's also the only place you'll find yummy Schlumberger jewelry—none under four-digit prices and many over five—another Jackie-preferred brand. For store locations, go to www.tiffany.com.

Van Cleef & Arpels. JFK purchased Jackie's emerald-and-diamond engagement ring here. Need we say more? If you can't afford the baubles out of the case, try auction houses and estate sales for more affordable, signed pieces. www.vca-jewelers.com.

Wartski. A high-end, family-run art and antiques dealership that specializes in fine jewelry, works by Fabergé—and the sort of starburst diamond brooch so striking that it inspired a young Mrs. Kennedy to trade in other treasures in order to acquire it. 14 Grafton St., London W1S 4DE; www.wartski.com.

STOCKING THE NEST

Where does a first impression begin? Often at your doorstep. Jackie had lots of house helpers, including interior designers, local shops, and offbeat purveyors of everything from fine antiquities to worry beads.

A La Vieille Russie. Jackie amassed a small treasure trove of items from this storied Manhattan art and antique dealership, which specializes in Fabergé eggs, estate jewelry, Russian art, and other assorted *objets*. 781 Fifth Ave., New York; 212-752-1727; www.alvr.com.

Flowers by Philip. Stem-happy Jackie required a constant supply of fresh blooms; this was a favorite Manhattan garden to pick from. 1141 Madison Ave., New York; 212-535-1388.

Grace Galleries Inc. To add a touch of worldliness to your walls, try the type of art-quality map that Jackie used as both a decorative and a functional object (geography lessons for the kids, don't you know). While genuine cartographer works can be prohibitive, this site also offers fine reproductions—the sort that would pass muster in Jackie's home. www.gracegalleries.com.

Irvine Fleming Interiors. Traditional but non-fussy living spaces are the hallmark at this firm. Partner Keith Irvine has hauled bolts of chintz for such famous clients as Diana Ross, Robert Shriver, Jr., and Jackie, too. 327 E. 58th St., New York; 212-888-6000.

Pier 1 Imports. Did she or didn't she? Jackie's gazillion baskets, mainly used for flowers, didn't bear labels. But at least one of her interior decorators liked to collect this retailer's modestly priced bamboo and wicker models. www.pier1.com.

Richard Keith Langham Inc. The courtly Mr. Langham remains at the top of the interior decorating pyramid. Known for bursts of color and

British country-house influences, he was one of the last decorators to touch up Jackie's New York interiors. 153 East 60th St., New York; 212-759-1212.

Schweitzer Linen. A sumptuous bed is a must in Jackie's cozy boudoir world. She preferred sheets and things from this family-run business in Manhattan. Fortuitously for out-of-towners, Schweitzer now sells a vast range of imported and domestic soft goods online. www.schweitzerlinen.com.

Slatkin & Co. The former home furnishings shop of this name was a favorite Jackie haunt. The business has been reinvented as a home fragrances empire now owned by Limited Brands Inc. A lover of candles and other sensory ditties, Jackie would surely adore their luscious scents. Available at Neiman Marcus, Bergdorf Goodman, and www.slatkin.com.

DING-DONG:
Visiting Places Jackie Called Home

Jackie often chose secluded estates and hard-to-find country houses that are now in private hands—and therefore impossible to tour. Her urban domiciles, however, make for interesting stops along your walking tours.

❖ Washington, D.C. ❖

3321 Dent Place, Georgetown. Three months after Jack and Jackie married in September 1953, they moved into this rental, but stayed only until June 1954.

2808 P Street, Georgetown. The Kennedys leased this home from January to May 1957.

3307 N Street, Georgetown. This, the most famous Kennedy George-town address, was purchased by the couple after Caroline's birth. From here they went to the White House on January 20, 1961.

The White House. Unfortunately, not much of Jackie's meticulous restoration remains—it was largely replaced by a Republican crew, start-ing with Nixon. Of all the spaces, the Blue Room, redecorated during the Clinton administration, is probably truest to the period stamps she left on the manse. For tour information, go to www.whitehouse.gov/history/tours/.

3017 N Street, Georgetown. After the assassination, and after borrow-ing the Harrimans' house—at 3038 N Street—Jackie bought this one. However, because she was hounded by the public and press, she stayed only ten months before selling it and moving to New York City. Al-though this house today bears no number, it is easy to find—it's the gargantuan one between 3019 and 3009.

◆ New York ◆

1040 Fifth Avenue, New York. Jackie's famous 15th floor-through looks out over Central Park and is on Museum Mile, steps away from the Guggenheim and the Metropolitan, among many others.

TRAVEL:
Jet-Setting Like Jackie

Want to get off like Jackie did? Check out these classic venues, which can fit the bill for travel both plain and swanky. And don't forget your Leica camera—Jackie's preferred brand for capturing memories.

Beverly Hills Hotel, Beverly Hills, Calif. The sprawling Sunset Boulevard landmark is a highfalutin 90210 institution—and has been since 1912. Its blush-pink walls and celebrity clientele attracted Jackie, who stayed there during her West Coast treks to work with Michael Jackson on his (and her) bestseller *Moonwalk*. Have a daiquiri (Jackie would approve) in the Polo Lounge—still a power-crowd hangout. 800-283-8885; www.beverlyhillshotel.com.

Red Fox Inn, Middleburg, Va. This eighteenth-century fieldstone bed-and-breakfast served as a favorite hunt-season haunt for Jackie. Trolling around in jodhpurs, she probably appreciated all the fresh flowers, and the inn's pedigree (it's on the National Register of Historic Places). When space was tight, the kindly owners put her up in their own personal quarters. 800-223-1728; www.redfox.com.

San Ysidro Ranch, Montecito, Calif. The newlywed Kennedys stopped at this luscious hilltop aerie on their honeymoon, no doubt choosing it for its tranquil low-key vibe. The rustic spa/ranch, long on the glamour-list circuit, recently underwent a major renovation and should be back to its former glory. 800-368-6788; www.sanysidro ranch.com.

The Waldorf=Astoria, New York. This is where Jackie and Jack cuddled up on their wedding night before heading off to Acapulco for their honeymoon. Though now part of the Hilton Hotel chain, its location and historical value make it worth a night—or an appointment at Kenneth's, the eponymous salon of Jackie's longtime stylist. 301 Park Ave., New York; 212-355-3000; www.waldorfastoria. com.

The *Christina O.* She's ba-a-ck! The 325-foot floating palace that was the setting for much of Jackie's time with Ari Onassis has been restored to 1960s perfection, to the tune of $50 million. You'll need to do a full-boat charter to gain access to this baby, which contains the same naughty bar and mosaic tile swimming pool that amused Jackie. *Christina* holds up to 36 guests, and sails in Mediterranean and Atlantic waters. Contact Titan Brokerage Corp., 011 30 1 428 0889; www.yachting-greece.com/Christina_O.htm.

Claridge's, London. This posh Londoner envelops guests in its Art Deco glory; Lalique vases, brass banisters, and old-world service seduce you in the lobby. Upstairs, choose rooms with decidedly English, or Art Deco, flair. Jackie and Ari used to alight here from time to time. Brook St., Mayfair, London W1K 4HR; www.claridges.co.uk.

Half Moon Hotel, Jamaica. A sprawling resort in Montego Bay that allows as little or as much privacy as you wish. Whether you dig hydrotherapy, golf, or horseback riding, prefer villa or hotel-style accommodations, it's all here. Jack and Jackie stayed at this perfectly moonlit perch for an extended spell in 1960 — long enough for Jackie to write up a storm on the hotel's sumptuous stationery. Rose Hall, Montego Bay; www.halfmoon-resort.com.

Hotel Raj Mahal Palace, Jaipur, India. Jackie's interludes in India sometimes found her staying at this eighteenth-century palace, in the heart of the Pink City, which was once home to Maharani Chandra Kunwar Ranawati. The palace was converted to a hotel in 1979. www.rajasthan.tajmahalindia.net.

La Perla Villas, Santorini Islands, Greece. Although Jackie never stayed here, she surely would today. The charming, whitewashed cavelike villas are owned and operated by Kiki Moutsatsos, Ari Onassis's faithful assistant, who was also close to Jackie. Check in, hang by the pool, and maybe, just maybe, she'll be kind enough to reminisce with you. www.laperlavillas.com.

Mont Tremblant Resort, Quebec, Canada. Jackie schussed there in 1968; since then, Quebec's largest and finest ski mountain has expanded and upgraded. www.tremblant.com.

Plaza Athénée, Paris. Well, Jackie didn't always have access to European palaces. This charming (and newly renovated) hotel was one of her standbys. A favorite with the fashion and celebrity crowds, the Athénée is at the top of any impeccable traveler's list—and home to one of chef Alain Ducasse's restaurants. Try a room with its own private terrace that allows you to dine al fresco in the shadow of the Eiffel Tower. Or one that has spectacular views overlooking one of the chicest city stretches. 25 Avenue Montaigne, Paris; www.plaza-athenee-paris.com.

Round Hill Resort, Jamaica. Never mind the tiny beach at this timeless oasis near Montego Bay. You can choose a hilltop bungalow (with pool and cook) once occupied by Clark Gable, Oscar Hammerstein, or Jackie herself. Ralph Lauren has his own place on the grounds, which still draw plenty of other celebrity types. Be sure to grab a few sheets of the hotel's classic pineapple embossed stationery for penning letters, as Jackie did. www.roundhilljamaica.com.

This and That Ritz. A ritzy traveler, of course, Jackie took to hotels thusly named at a very early age. There is simply no better a temporary address than the Hôtel Ritz in Paris, that indefatigable grande dame that she adored. Jackie also approved of some Ritz-Carlton establishments (unaffiliated with the Parisian hostelry). She stayed at the Ritz-Carlton Boston, and would most surely head for Milan's Bulgari Hotel & Resort, which is quietly operated by Ritz-Carlton. Just imagine: rubies *and* room service. www.ritz.com; www.ritzcarlton.com.

RESTAURANTS

❖ New York ❖

21 Club. Always and still a megaspot for megadeals to be cut—all over an unimpeachable tableside steak tartare and strong drinks. Jackie liked the fish Florentine, Cobb salads—and pistachio ice cream. 21 W. 52nd St., New York; 212-582-7200.

Café Carlyle. A favorite Jackie haunt for lunch. 35 E. 76th St., New York; 212-570-7189. www.thecarlyle.com.

Elaine's. Just as in Jackie's day, you'll still catch TV personalities, writers, and editors pontificating here on any given night—often under their own photographs that hang on the pub-like walls. 1703 Second Ave. (between 88th and 89th Sts.), New York; 212-534-8103.

The Four Seasons. Philip Johnson designed it to be the epitome of high-powered Manhattan restaurants—and it still is. 99 E. 52nd St., New York; 212-754-9494.

Serendipity 3. It's an ice-cream parlor in the best old-world sense; Jackie loved their frozen hot chocolate. Today, the treat is an Oprah fave. 225 East 60th St., New York; 212-838-3531. www.serendipity3.com.

❖ Paris ❖

Café Les Deux Magots. A perennial Left Bank hangout, Les Deux Magots drew Jackie through the decades—and still attracts crowds. According to Zagat's, the best meal these days is breakfast. 6, pl St-Germain-des-Prés, Paris; (33) 14 5485525.

Maxim's. She may be a centagenarian, but her over-the-top Art Nouveau beauty attracted Jackie, and is still alluring to le tout Paris. 3, rue Royale, Paris; www.maxims-de-paris.com.

PERFECTING THE JACKIE-O GLOW

Let's face it: A lot has to come from within. But for some extra help, Jackie relied on these time-honored potions:

Chanel No. 5. A classic scent that she adored. www.chanel.com.

Elizabeth Arden Flawless Finish foundation. Jackie adored the stuff—and many still concur, making this beauty staple particularly long-lived. www.elizabetharden.com.

Janet Sartin. There are namesake spas in New York (on Park Ave.) and Chicago; Sartin's high-end products are also available online at www.sartin.com.

Joy. Of course she wore what was, at the time, the most expensive fragrance in the world.

pHisoHex anti-acne facial wash. It's not expensive, but clearly it works—and has remained popular all these years, despite having to compete for shelf space with today's trendier concoctions.

Sardo bath oil for dry, itchy skin. Think medicinal—not frilly, sweet-smelling, or expensive.

❖ Favorite Workouts ❖

Claremont Riding Academy. Don't pass up a rare steed-and-skyline op-portunity. This is the only place in Manhattan where you can put a mount (yours or rented) through its paces in an indoor ring, and where horses are available to hire for a trot through Central Park. Jackie rode with Claremont, as did Caroline, who took lessons here. Horse hire: $50/hour; lessons start at $60. 175 West 89th St., New York; 212-724-5100.

Horseback Riding in Middleburg, Va. Jackie belonged to several hunt clubs, but this verdant region of Virginia is flush with inns, B&Bs, and horseback riding stables open to the public. www.middleburg online.com.

Jogging around the Reservoir at Central Park (now the Jacqueline Kennedy Onassis Reservoir). Still the hottest running route in Manhattan—and the best for celebrity sightings, too. 85th St. to 96th St., from east to west; www.centralparknyc.org.

Ocean Swimming, Martha's Vineyard, Mass. You don't need a beachfront estate to paddle the waters that Jackie loved (don't forget your leg-shaping fins). Her turf: Gay Head—although any of the island's myriad public beaches will do. www.mvol.com.

ON THE TABLE:
Food and Drink of Choice

Hers wasn't the average palate or grocery list. But Jackie certainly liked to consume everyday treats, from candy to fizzy water.

Tootsie Rolls and M&M's. Yes, even Jackie loved them. She was known to offer them to starstruck guests at her Doubleday office.

Duncan Hines. At one point, this classic cake mix in chocolate was the only acceptable brand for Jackie's pantry.

Lean Cuisine. One time Jackie returned from a trip to Middleburg, Va., spouting praise for the frozen dinners. "She couldn't get over that you just had to put one in the oven," said Marta Sgubin, Jackie's nanny/cook.

Champagne. De rigueur in the White House, and a beloved staple in Greece.

Baron Philip Rothschild
Dom Perignon
Krug
Moët et Chandon Imperial Brut

Wine and Spirits. Jackie favored these bottles—low to high—when entertaining at 1600 Pennsylvania Avenue.

Almaden Grenache Rosé
Bacardi rum
Chateâu Corton Grancey
Chateâu Haut-Brion
Chateâu de Puligny-Montrachet
Grands Echézeaux
Stolichnaya vodka

Bubbles.

Perrier

CULTURAL DIGS

She was here, she was there, she was most everywhere that housed any sort of cultural treasure—static or moving.

Grand Central Terminal. From the restaurant Métrazur on the east balcony, you can survey all that Jackie felt was important to preserve, from the vaulted ceilings to the famous clock. Or meet at the clubby Campbell Apartment for after-office cocktails. 110 E. 42nd St., New York; www.grandcentralterminal.com.

John F. Kennedy Library and Museum. There are more than 1,426 references to Jacqueline Kennedy on the library's Web site alone. In person, you can check out everything from her 1951 *Vogue* Prix de Paris essays to a dress that she wore during the televised tour of her newly natty White House. The library's gift shop has enough memorabilia to steep you in Jackie for decades. Columbia Point, Boston, Mass; www.jfklibrary.org.

The John F. Kennedy Center for the Performing Arts. A "living memorial" to President Kennedy, the facility is a national cultural center that is both publicly and privately funded. It hosts a wide array of world-class performing arts—the National Symphony Orchestra calls this home—as well as educational programs and workshops for adults and children. 2700 F St. NW, Washington, D.C.; www.kennedy-center.org.

Metropolitan Museum of Art. Go to admire the trove of treasures spanning Etruscan to modern, including the sublime Temple of Dendur that Jackie fought to bring to the U.S. (she could see the glass-encased Egyptian wonder from her Fifth Avenue apartment). Enjoy a glass of wine and free classical music on Friday evenings; in the summertime, head for the rooftop sculpture garden to sip daiquiris as you stroll amid the Joel Shapiro figures. 1000 Fifth Ave. (at 82nd St.), New York; 212-535-7710; www.metmuseum.org.

Metropolitan Opera House. Jackie fought to save the original Met structure at 39th Street. After it moved to Lincoln Center, she became a major benefactor, and was often seen at regular curtain drops for both the opera company and the American Ballet Theatre, where she long served on the board. Her preferred vantage point? The privacy-affording partiere boxes, bien sur. Lincoln Center, New York; 212-362-6000; www.metopera.org.

Versailles. "Humble" is the last word you'd ever use to describe the palatial chateau and grounds that Louis XIV built (and his successors added to); then again, its over-the-topness—both historically and decoratively—are what drew Jackie on so many visits. Gaze upon thyself in the Hall of Mirrors, where she once shone. And don't miss the spectacular Louis XV roll-top desk or Marie-Antoinette's Chinese vase collection—all items Mrs. O would have approved of. www.chateauversailles.fr.

PAGING JACKIE:
The Editor's Oeuvre

During her nineteen years as a book editor, Jackie explored lots of literary territory. As this partial list of her projects conveys, her tastes were eclectic, and her subject matter—from Michael Jackson to Russian history—was broad. Most of the titles below are still in print. For tough-to-find volumes, check out www.abebooks.com and www.alibris.com.

Beard, Peter. *Longing for Darkness: Kamante's Tales From Out of Africa*. Harcourt, 1975. (Jackie wrote an essay for this book.)

Beever, Antony, and Cooper, Artemis. *Paris After the Liberation, 1944 to 1949*. Doubleday, 1994.

Bernier, Olivier. *Louis XIV: A Royal Life*. Doubleday, 1987.

Brandon, Muffie. *Remember the Ladies: Women in America, 1750–1815*. Viking.

Campbell, Joseph, with Bill Moyers. *The Power of Myth*. Doubleday, 1989.

Cott, Jonathan. *Isis and Osiris: Exploring the Goddess Myth*. Doubleday, 1994.

Giles, Sarah. *Fred Astaire: His Friends Talk*. Doubleday, 1988.

Graham, Martha. *Blood Memory*. Doubleday, 1991.

Jackson, Michael. *Moonwalk*. Doubleday, 1988.

Jamison, Judith. *Dancing Spirit*. Doubleday, 1993.

Kirkland, Gelsey. *Dancing on My Grave*. Doubleday, 1987.

Lowe, David Garrard. *Stanford White's New York*. Doubleday, 1992.

Lyons, Robert. *Egyptian Time*. Doubleday, 1992.

Mason, Francis. *I Remember Balanchine*. Doubleday, 1991.

Onassis, Jacqueline, ed., and Zvorykin, Boris, illus. *The Firebird and Other Russian Fairy Tales*. Viking, 1978.

Onassis, Jacqueline, ed. *In the Russian Style*. (Metropolitan Museum of Art catalog.) Viking, 1976.

Patnaik, Naveen. *The Garden of Life: An Introduction to the Healing Plants of India*. Doubleday, 1993.

Plimpton, George. *Fireworks: A History and Celebration*. Doubleday, 1984.

Previn, Andre. *No Minor Chords: My Days in Hollywood*. Doubleday, 1991.

Radzinsky, Edvard. *The Last Tsar: The Life and Death of Nicholas II*. Doubleday, 1992.

Sis, Peter. *Three Golden Keys*. Doubleday, 1994.

Stenn, David. *Bombshell: The Life and Death of Jean Harlow*. Doubleday, 1993.

Turbeville, Deborah. *Unseen Versailles*. Doubleday, 1981.

Valenti, Jack. *Protect and Defend*. Doubleday, 1992.

Vreeland, Diana. *Allure*. Doubleday, 1980.

Wenner, Jann. *The Best of Rolling Stone: 25 Years of Journalism on the Edge*. Doubleday, 1993.

West, Dorothy. *The Wedding*. Doubleday, 1995.

SPIRITUAL JACKIE

Despite tragedies, doubts, and excommunication, Jackie found solace in places of worship over the course of her life.

Newport, R.I.

St. Mary's. Where JFK and Jackie walked down the aisle. Corner of Spring St. and Memorial Blvd., Newport, R.I.; 401-847-0475.

Washington, D.C.

Holy Trinity Roman Catholic Church. The Kennedys regularly attended mass here before and during their White House years. 3513 N Street, NW, Washington, D.C.; 202-337-2840.

Palm Beach

St. Edward's Church. The Kennedys' church of choice in Florida; Rose used to attend both Sunday masses—and Jackie was famously snapped exiting one Easter bare-legged in a sleeveless shift. 144 North County Rd., Palm Beach, Fla.; 561-832-0400.

New York

St. Ignatius Loyola. Jackie was christened, confirmed, and eulogized at this church. 980 Park Ave. (at 84th St.), New York; 212-288-3588.

St. Thomas More Catholic Church. Jackie's regular place of worship, where Rose Schlossberg was christened, and where JFK Jr.'s funeral was held. 65 East 89th St. (at Madison Ave.), New York; 212-876-7718.

Saint Patrick's Cathedral. Sen. Robert Kennedy was eulogized here. 14 East 51st St., New York; 212-753-2261.

St. Francis Xavier, Hyannis, Mass. This is where Jackie and Jack attended mass while visiting the family compound. 347 South St., Hyannis, Mass.; 508-775-5361.

◆ In Memoriam ◆

Arlington National Cemetery. In 1963, Jackie lit the eternal flame atop JFK's grave, which still burns today. Jackie, Patrick, and their stillborn daughter are buried alongside him. Arlington, Va.; www.arlington cemetery.org.

Acknowledgments

This book wouldn't have been possible without the wonderful support, guidance, and occasional kick in the pants we received from our beloved family, friends, and colleagues. Thanks to Barbara, Clarence, and Deborah Branch for their unfailing devotion—as well as all the emergency food deliveries and late-night cheerleading sessions; to Reeves Callaway for his cool head and kind heart; to Linda Buhler for her love and tireless bicoastal help; to Nicholas Callaway for his sage advice; and to Liliora Callaway for being adorable enough to cheer up even cranky, jet-lagged authors.

Also crucial were our generous sources, whom we'd like to thank for their thoughts, musings, recollections, and insights that are the backbone of this book. This rich cast includes people who knew Jacqueline Kennedy Onassis and those who admired her unforgettable living arts. Many were helpful by giving on-the-record interviews, and are attributed below and throughout the book. Some requested anonymity, which we have respected. Others led us to unlikely or hard-to-reach sources, and we are indebted to them as well.

First, a deep bow to Letitia Baldrige, who was as giving of her time as she was of her wisdom and recollections from the White House years and beyond.

Among the others who granted interviews or helped supply key information are, alphabetically: Hugh D. Auchincloss III, James Lee Auchincloss, Maria Bartiromo, George Beylerian, Stanley Bing, Manolo Blahnik, Mario Buatta, Joan Juliet Buck, Oleg Cassini, Jean Chatzky, Dr. Deepak Chopra, Joannie Danielides, Simon Doonan, Eve Ensler, Ed Epstein, Susan Fales-Hill, Frederic Fekkai, Raoul Felder, Thom Filicia, Pamela Fiori, Albert Hadley, Solange Herter, Thomas Hoving, Keith Irvine, Elaine Kaufman, Joan B. Kennedy, Barbara Kline, Ed Koch, Michael Kors, Richard Koshalek, Richard Keith Langham, Francesca Leoni, Robert Love, George Malkemus, Melody Miller, Thomas Morrissey, Kiki Feroudi Moutsatsos, Julian Niccolini, Paul Novograd, Patrick O'Connell, Dana Reuter, Ron Roge, Harry Slatkin, Joan Rivers, Ian Schrager, Aaron Shikler, Carly Simon, Nacole Snoep, Omarosa Manigault Stallworth, Radu Teodorescu, Dr. Michael Thompson, Blaine Trump, and Faye Wattleton.

There were also many folks who helped us chase down research materials for this book, and we owe them a special debt of gratitude. At the top of the list: Evelyn Cunningham—our indefatigable savior who served so ably as research coordinator. Thanks also to Stephen Plotkin, research archivist at the John Fitzgerald Kennedy Library; Sharon Kelly, research assistant at the JFK Library; Mary Rose, audiovisual archivist at the JFK Library; and John Shattuck, president of the John Fitzgerald Kennedy Library Foundation; Bernard Crystal at the Columbia University Rare Book and Manuscript Library; Jean Ashton at Columbia University; Tom Tierney at the *Women's Wear Daily* archives; Matthew Weigman at Sotheby's; Paula Hantman at Hantman's Auctioneers & Appraisers; Anne Anielewski at the New York Municipal Art Society; Lynn Swanson, Wilton Library Association; and Richard Reston of the *Vineyard Gazette*.

Other individuals played key strategic and motivational roles.

Thanks to Matthew Guma and Richard Pine at Inkwell Management—Matthew, your early and sustained enthusiasm means the world to us. We're also indebted to Ezra Doner for his savvy legal counsel; Jill Kneerim for her literary insights; Nicolette Wales and Regina Ranonis for their visual sensibilities; and Julie Moline, Deborah Weisgall, and Teri Agins for their thoughtful reading. At *The Wall Street Journal*, thanks to Paul Steiger, Melinda Beck, and Jeffrey Trachtenberg for encouraging this extracurricular gig. Finally, kudos to our champions at Gotham Books—publisher William Shinker and our editor, Lauren Marino. We are truly grateful that you and the amazing Penguin team have supported us beyond our wildest expectations.

A footnote: Many folks placed bets on whether two such good friends could pen a book together—and come out the other side intact. Well, despite all the logistical and deadline challenges, we survived the bumps and scrapes. The reward: We're as tight a pair as ever.

Sources

Many biographers, historians, and writers have studied Jacqueline Kennedy Onassis, the Kennedy administration, and the Kennedy and Onassis families. In addition to original interviews and other sources (including unpublished correspondence, oral history transcripts, memos, essays, invoices, itineraries, sketches, private photo collections, exhibitions, documentaries, etc.), the authors consulted more than 100 previously published books and articles.

The following is a list of works that provided the authors with substantial information about events in Jacqueline Kennedy Onassis's life. A select bibliography follows.

KEY SOURCES

Andersen, Christopher. *Jackie After Jack: Portrait of the Lady.* William Morrow, 1998.

——. *Sweet Caroline: Last Child of Camelot.* HarperCollins, 2003.

Baldrige, Letitia. *A Lady, First: My Life in the Kennedy White House and the American Embassies of Paris and Rome.* Penguin Books, 2002.

Bradford, Sarah. *America's Queen.* Viking, 2000.

Gallagher, Mary Barelli. *My Life with Jacqueline Kennedy.* David McKay Company Inc, 1969.

Heymann, C. David. *A Woman Named Jackie: An Intimate Biography of Jacqueline Bouvier Kennedy Onassis.* Birch Lane Press, 1994.

Keogh, Pamela Clarke. *Jackie Style.* HarperCollins, 2001.

Klein, Edward. *Farewell, Jackie: A Portrait of Her Final Days.* Viking, 2004.

———. *Just Jackie: Her Private Years.* Ballantine, 1998.

Smith, Sally Bedell. *Grace and Power: The Private World of the Kennedy White House.* Random House, 2004.

Spoto, Donald. *Jacqueline Bouvier Kennedy Onassis: A Life.* St. Martin's Press, 2000.

Taraborrelli, J. Randy. *Jackie, Ethel, Joan: Women of Camelot.* Time Warner, 2000.

West, J. B. *Upstairs at the White House: My Life with the First Ladies.* Warner, 1974.

SELECT BIBLIOGRAPHY

Abbott, James A., and Rice, Elaine M. *Designing Camelot: The Kennedy White House Restoration.* John Wiley & Sons, 1998.

Adler, Bill, ed. *The Eloquent Jacqueline Kennedy Onassis: A Portrait in Her Own Words.* William Morrow, 2004.

Andersen, Christopher. *The Day John Died.* William Morrow, 2000.

———. *Jack and Jackie: Portrait of an American Marriage.* Avon Books, 1996.

——. *Sweet Caroline: Last Child of Camelot*. HarperCollins, 2003.

Anthony, Carl Sferrazza. *As We Remember Her: Jacqueline Kennedy Onassis in the Words of Her Family and Friends*. HarperCollins, 1997.

——. *The Kennedy White House*. Touchstone, 2001.

Baldrige, Letitia, and Verdon, René. *In the Kennedy Style: Magical Evenings in the Kennedy White House*. Doubleday, 1998.

——. *Of Diamonds & Diplomats*. Ballantine Books, 1969.

Bartlett, Apple Parish, et al. *Sister: The Life of Legendary American Interior Decorator Mrs. Henry Parish II*. St. Martin's Press, 2000.

Blow, Richard. *American Son: A Portrait of John F. Kennedy, Jr*. Henry Holt & Co, 2002.

Bouvier, Jacqueline, and Bouvier, Lee. *One Special Summer*. Delacorte Press, 1974.

Bowles, Hamish. *Jacqueline Kennedy: The White House Years. Selections from the John F. Kennedy Library and Museum*. The Metropolitan Museum of Art, 2001.

Bradlee, Benjamin C. *Conversations with Kennedy*. Konecky & Konecky, 2000.

Cafarakis, Christian. *The Fabulous Onassis: His Life and Loves*. William Morrow, 1972.

Cassini, Oleg. *In My Own Fashion*. Pocket Books, 1990.

——. *A Thousand Days of Magic*. Rizzoli, 1995.

Clinton, Hillary Rodham. *Living History*. Scribner, 2003.

Connally, Nellie. *From Love Field: Our Final Hours with President John F. Kennedy*. Rugged Land, 2003.

David, Lester. *Jacqueline Kennedy Onassis: A Portrait of Her Private Years*. St. Martin's, 1994.

Davis, John H. *Jacqueline Bouvier: An Intimate Memoir.* John Wiley & Sons, 1996.

Dherbier, Yann-Brice, and Verlhac, Pierre-Henri: *Jackie: A Life in Pictures.* PowerHouse Books, 2004.

DuBois, Diana. *In Her Sister's Shadow: An Intimate Biography of Lee Radziwill.* Little, Brown and Company, 1995.

Duhême, Jacqueline. *Mrs. Kennedy Goes Abroad.* Artisan, 1998.

Evans, Peter. *Ari: The Life and Times of Aristotle Socrates Onassis.* Charter Books, 1986.

———. *Nemesis.* HarperCollins, 2004.

Flaherty, Tina Santi. *What Jackie Taught Us: Lessons from the Remarkable Life of Jacqueline Kennedy Onassis.* Perigee, 2004.

Fraser, Nicholas, et al. *Aristotle Onassis.* Lippincott, 1977.

Goodwin, Doris Kearns. *The Fitzgeralds and the Kennedys.* Simon and Schuster, 1987.

Hackett, Pat, ed. *The Andy Warhol Diaries.* Warner Books, 1989.

Heilman, Joan Rattner, ed. *Kenneth's Complete Book on Hair.* Doubleday, 1972.

Kelleher, K. L. *Jackie: Beyond the Myth of Camelot.* K. L. Kelleher, 2000.

Kennedy, Caroline. *The Best Loved Poems of Jacqueline Kennedy Onassis.* Hyperion, 2001.

Klein, Edward. *All Too Human: The Love Story of Jack and Jackie Kennedy.* Simon and Schuster, 1997.

———. *The Kennedy Curse.* St. Martin's, 2003.

Ladowsky, Ellen. *Jacqueline Kennedy Onassis.* Random House, 1997.

Leamer, Laurence. *The Kennedy Women: The Saga of an American Family.* Ballantine Books, 1995.

———. *Sons of Camelot: The Fate of an American Dynasty*. William Morrow, 2004.

Leaming, Barbara. *Mrs. Kennedy: The Missing History of the Kennedy Years*. Simon & Schuster, 2001.

Lincoln, Anne H. *The Kennedy White House Parties*. The Viking Press, 1967.

Marton, Kati. *Hidden Power: Presidential Marriages That Shaped Our Recent History*. Pantheon Books, 2001.

Moon, Vicky. *The Private Passion of Jackie Kennedy Onassis: Portrait of a Rider*. Regan Books, 2005.

Moutsatsos, Kiki Feroudi. *The Onassis Women*. Putnam, 1988.

Pottker, Jan. *Janet & Jackie: The Story of a Mother and Her Daughter, Jacqueline Kennedy Onassis*. St. Martin's Griffin, 2001.

Radziwill, Lee. *Happy Times*. Assouline, 2000.

Rhea, Mini. *I Was Jacqueline Kennedy's Dressmaker*. Fleet Publishing, 1962.

Sgubin, Marta. *Cooking for Madam: Recipes and Reminiscences from the Home of Jacqueline Kennedy Onassis*. Scribner, 1998.

Shaw, Maud. *White House Nannie: My Years with Caroline and John Kennedy, Jr.* New American Library, 1966.

Sotheby's. *The Estate of Jacqueline Kennedy Onassis*. Sotheby's, 1996.

———. *Property from Kennedy Family Homes*. Sotheby's, 2004.

Spada, James. *Jackie: Her Life in Pictures*. St. Martin's Press, 2000.

Thayer, Mary Van Rensselaer. *Jacqueline Bouvier Kennedy*. Doubleday, 1961.

———. *Jacqueline Kennedy: The White House Years*. Little, Brown and Co., 1967.

Verdon, René. *The White House Chef Cookbook*. Doubleday, 1968.

Vreeland, Diana. *D.V.* Alfred A. Knopf, 1984.

White, Theodore H. *In Search of History.* Harper & Row, 1978. pp. 517-525.

Zilkha, Bettina. *Ultimate Style: The Best of the Best Dressed List.* Assouline, 2004.

PERIODICALS

A.M. Globe, September 20, 1960: "Jackie Asks Press Treat Her As Person, Not Fashion Plate." (UPI)

A.M. Globe, June 14, 1961: "Mrs. Kennedy Gets Speed Ride in Crown Prince's Sports Car." (UPI)

A.M. Globe, February 12, 1970: "Jacqueline Upset for Glipatric." (UPI)

Departures, January/February 2001: "White House Confidential," by Martin Filler.

Harper's Bazaar, August 1994: "JBKO," by Amy Fine Collins.

McCall's, March 1972: "The Fabulous Onassis," by Christian Cafarakis with Jacques Harvey and Helen Eustis.

Money, October 1975: "The Pleasant Problems of Jacqueline Onassis," by Peter Bird Martin.

Money, August 1994: "Jackie's Will Offers Smart Tips," by Gary Belsky.

Ms., March 1979: "Jacqueline Kennedy Onassis Talks About Working," by Jacqueline Kennedy Onassis.

Ms., March 1979: "Why Do Women Work, Dear God, Why Do They Work?" by Gloria Steinem.

New York Daily News, November 17, 1998: "Kenney vs. Kin of Barbra in Mall Deal," by Salvator Arena.

The New York Times, April 20, 1966: "Mrs. Kennedy Asks $20,000 Cut in Her $50,000 Office Allowance," by Margorie Hunter.

The New York Times, July 30, 1964: "Baldwin May Design Kennedy Co-op," by George O'Brien.

The New York Times, July 29, 1964: "Apartment Taken by Mrs. Kennedy."

The New York Times, May 20, 1994: "Death of a First Lady: Jacqueline Kennedy Onassis Dies of Cancer at 64," by Robert D. McFadden.

The New York Times, December 22, 1996: "Value of Jackie Onassis' Estate Lowered," by David Kay Johnston.

The New York Times Magazine, May 31, 1970: "The Happy Jackie, The Sad Jackie, The Bad Jackie, The Good Jackie," by Susan Sheehan.

The New York Times Magazine, November 2, 1980: "A Clash of Taste at the White House," by Martin Filler.

The New Yorker, January 13, 1975: "Being Present" (by Jacqueline Kennedy Onassis; unsigned).

Newsweek, October 28, 1968: "The New First Lady of Skorpios."

Publisher's Weekly, April 19, 1993: "Editors at Work: Star Behind the Scenes," an interview with Jacqueline Kennedy Onassis by John F. Baker.

Publisher's Weekly, May 30, 1994: "Doubleday Colleagues Remember Jacqueline Kennedy Onassis," by Maureen O'Brien.

San Francisco Chronicle, January 21, 1985: "Jacqueline Onassis Gets Richer," by Leah Garchik.

Time, January 20, 1961: "Jackie."

Time, March 31, 1961: "People."

Time, October 25, 1968: "From Camelot to Elysium (via Olympic Airways)." (cover story—no byline)

Time, July 25, 1969: "Gucci on the Go."

Town & Country, July 1994: "In Loving Memory—Jacqueline Kennedy Onassis, 1929-1994," by Pamela Fiori.

Town & Country, April 2001: "First Among First Ladies," by Pamela Clarke Keogh.

Town & Country, September 2001: "Oh, Jackie," by Pamela Fiori.

Vogue, February 2005: "The First Lady of Letters," by Darcey Steinke.

ARCHIVE COLLECTIONS

John Fitzgerald Kennedy Library

Oral History Transcripts: Lawrence J. Arata, Janet Auchincloss, Charles Bartlett, Barbara Coleman, Roswell Gilpatric, Princess Grace of Monaco, August Heckscher, Dr. Roy Heffernan, Jacqueline Hirsh, John Hay Hooker, Jr., Joseph Karitas, Peter Lisagor, Nelson Pierce, Hugh Sidey, Cordenia Thaxton, Nancy Tuckerman and Pamela Turnure, J. B. West, Irvin Williams.

White House Social Files

Vogue Clippings

Vertical Files

Theodore White Camelot Documents

Audiovisual Collections

Personal Papers of Hugh D. Auchincloss III

❖ Other Collections ❖

Lyndon Baines Johnson Library
Oral History of Jacqueline Kennedy Onassis, 1974.

Columbia University
Rare Book & Manuscript Library
Mary B. Lasker papers, James Oliver Brown collection, Lionel Trilling
collection

Oral History Collection of Columbia University
Reminiscences of: Thomas H. Guinzburg, Aaron Shikler, Beatrice
and Bruce Gould

University of Kentucky
The John Sherman Cooper Oral History Project, interview with Jacqueline Kennedy Onassis, 1981.

Sercret Service Files

OTHER SOURCES

Last Will and Testament of Jacqueline Kennedy Onassis, March 22,
1994.

Hantman's Auctioneers & Appraisers: John F. Kennedy and Jacqueline
Kennedy Onassis Memorabilia Collection catalog, July 2003.

Hantman's Auctioneers & Appraisers: Political Memorabilia Auction
catalog, October 2004.

Jackie: Behind the Myth. PBS Home Video, Educational Broadcasting Corp., 1999.

Jackie: Power and Style. CineNova Productions Inc., 1999.

The Kennedy Mystique: Creating Camelot. Partisan/Blackstrap Productions, 2004; Wellspring Media, Inc., 2004.

ABOUT THE AUTHORS

Shelly Branch is an editor at *The Wall Street Journal*, where she also writes on retail, fashion, and pop culture. She was a staff writer at *Fortune* and *Money*, and has contributed to numerous other national publications. She lives in New York City.

Sue Callaway has been an editor at *Fortune, Esquire*, and *Men's Journal*. She has also served as general manager of Jaguar Cars U.S. and as director of marketing for Ford's luxury brands. She lives in Laguna Beach, California, with her husband and two children.